The Scarecrow Author Bibliographies

ALGERNON CHARLES
SWINBURNE

A Bibliography
of Secondary Works, 1861-1980

by KIRK H. BEETZ

The Scarecrow Author Bibliographies, No. 61

THE SCARECROW PRESS, INC.
Metuchen, N.J., & London • 1982

Z 8857
B 43
1982

Library of Congress Cataloging in Publication Data

Beetz, Kirk H., 1952-
   Algernon Charles Swinburne : bibliography of
secondary works, 1861-1980.

   (The Scarecrow author bibliographies ; no. 61)
   Includes indexes.
   1. Swinburne, Algernon Charles, 1837-1909--
Bibliography. I. Title. II. Series.
Z8857.B43 [PR5513]   016.821'8   82-3359
ISBN 0-8108-1541-9   AACR2

+ CONTENTS +

Swinburne and his work have evoked wildly varying responses from critics for over a hundred and twenty years. Early in his career, critics had already identified the issues that remain central to the study of Swinburne's writings. The issues typically are ambiguities: Is Swinburne's poetry great melody without intellectual substance? Is his criticism vague appreciation without methodology? These questions are answered yes, no, or maybe, depending on the critic one consults. Many of the issues seem peripheral to serious understanding of the poet's work: Swinburne is immoral. No, he is moralistic. No, he is amoral. He is a perverse sadist; he is a gentle love poet. His poetry is disgusting; his poetry is beautiful. Often, a critic ties Swinburne's personal life to his writings: Swinburne was a sadist, therefore his poetry promotes sexual perversion. He was childishly incapable of caring for himself, therefore his criticism--however accurately he may present the facts--conveys only childish understanding of its subjects. Swinburne attracts controversy. In over a century of study, critics have yet to reach a consensus about his work.

This broad range of opinion is not necessarily bad. Other Victorian authors have suffered because of dogmatic consensuses about their works. General agreement can discourage free inquiry; it can lead a scholar to believe a crucial issue to be settled when in fact the issue is generally misunderstood. In Swinburne's case, a lack of consensus has encouraged both lively, provocative criticism and crude exploitation. Such exploitation, most apparent in studies of his life, seems to originate in the poet's personal failings. Swinburne was easily exploited by those who sought to capitalize on his reputation for eccentricity. In his later years, his memory weakened so badly that T. J. Wise was able to convince him that a forgery of his work was genuine (see entry 1940), and he was unable to clarify the facts of his life and career.

Thus, such authors as Frank Harris (entry 1404) and Arthur Compton-Rickett (entry 1758) were able to repeat anecdotes that not only implied an intimacy with Swinburne that they probably did not

iv

have, but also bore odd resemblances to tales told by other people, although other sources were not cited. Edmund Gosse relied heavily on unreliable sources and possibly apocryphal anecdotes for his biography of Swinburne (entry 1240). Gosse's book is interesting for what it reveals about his relationship to Swinburne and for what it shows of the state of Swinburnean scholarship in the first two decades of the twentieth century. It is otherwise unreliable. The first good biography was La Jeunesse de Swinburne, by Georges Lafourcade (entry 1617), which was published in 1928. This he followed with Swinburne: A Literary Biography (entry 1728), which was published in 1932. Although several biographies have been published since Lafourcade's time, most followed Gosse's format, and only three are significant: those by Jean Overton Fuller (entry 2053), Donald Thomas (entry 2261), and Philip Henderson (entry 2166).

Fuller's book is eccentric, focusing on Swinburne's relationship with his cousin, Mary Leith. Controversial when published, the biography remains a potential source of confusion for the unwary reader because it is devoted to proving a thesis--that Leith was at the center of Swinburne's creative impulse. Thomas's book, on the other hand, is the sort on which scholars dote. Workmanlike but not stuffy, it presents the facts of Swinburne's life intelligently. Robert Greenberg (entry 2178) criticizes it for following Gosse's format, but Thomas seems to have been aware of the dangers in Gosse's study and to have successfully evaded most of them. Henderson's biography differs from both Fuller's and Thomas's-- from the first by presenting a full portrait of Swinburne and from the second by taking a wholly original approach to Swinburne's life. Henderson is a skilled biographer whose experience and understanding of the Victorian era are evident in his biography. He makes full use of previously unavailable materials; his Swinburne: Portrait of a Poet thus supplants Lafourcade's as the standard reference for Swinburne's life.

Of the other biographical sources presently available, C. Y. Lang's The Swinburne Letters (published 1959-1962) is probably the most important. As the present bibliography shows, several of Swinburne's letters have been uncovered since 1962, when the final volume of Lang's collection was published. However, Lang's effort remains one of the outstanding examples of literary research to come out of the study of the Victorian era. His introduction and notes show an understanding of Swinburne's life and work second, perhaps, only to that of Clyde Kenneth Hyder.

If one is to make sense of the criticisms and studies of Swinburne that have been published since 1861, one almost certainly must study the work of C. K. Hyder. He is the progenitor of a school of Swinburne study--the only cohesive group of critics in the great morass of scholarship on the poet. In my five years of research for the present book, I have come to call them the "rationalists." Hyder's common sense and efforts to move Swinburnean criticism out of visceral responses into logically rigorous investiga-

tions have spanned nearly five decades. Other "rationalists" include
such scholars as C. Y. Lang, Benjamin Franklin Fisher IV, and
Robert Greenberg. Hyder's Swinburne's Literary Career and Fame
(entry 1761), published in 1933, is the standard statement on Swinburne's reputation. Serious students will want to supplement the
book with Roger Leo Cayer's 1964 dissertation, Algernon Charles
Swinburne's Literary Reputation (entry 2024), which provides a useful outline of the history of critical attitudes toward Swinburne's
works.

Hyder has provided other basic research tools, including
Swinburne: The Critical Heritage (entry 2083), which presents
some early views of Swinburne and his work, and Swinburne as
Critic (published in 1972), which reprints the most important of
Swinburne's critical essays. Much of Swinburne's work has not
been so fortunate. The Bonchurch edition, The Complete Works
of Algernon Charles Swinburne (published 1925-1927), was pretty
much a lie from its inception: one of its editors, T. J. Wise,
had publicly (in his bibliography of Swinburne, entry 1412) declared
that some of the poet's works were unfit for publication; he objected
to their content. Errors and confusions in texts have annoyed
scholars using the Bonchurch texts. The 1904 edition, The Poems
of Algernon Charles Swinburne, and the 1905-1906 edition, The
Tragedies of Algernon Charles Swinburne (both published by Chatto
and Windus), are superior to the Bonchurch edition and have texts
that are preferable for use in serious criticism.

The texts of Swinburne's fiction have a stormy history, pri-
marily because of the work of Randolf Hughes, who published an
edition of the novel Lesbia Brandon in 1952. In his commentary on
the novel, Hughes expressed himself strongly, in terms that some
critics evidently found offensive. His edition evoked attacks notably
venomous even in a field of study that has a long history of disputes
between scholars. Hughes's commentary makes interesting reading,
but scholars have identified errors in facts in it, and thus students
should refer to his edition with caution. Edmund Wilson's The
Novels of A. C. Swinburne: Love's Cross-Currents: Lesbia Brandon provides useful texts for Swinburne's two novels (published in
1962). The 1905 edition of Love's Cross-Currents (also known as
A Year's Letters) has long been the standard reference for scholars,
but Francis Jacques Sypher's 1974 edition, A Year's Letters, seems
likely to supplant the earlier edition.

Not much about the state of Swinburne's bibliography can be
said except that it is a mess. The bibliographies of the late nineteenth and early twentieth centuries are woefully incomplete and
confusing. The T. J. Wise bibliography, the standard reference
for book collectors, is incomplete, inaccurate, sloppy, and deceit-
ful. I have spent years trying to produce a bibliography of Swinburne's works and have found that Wise did not make much effort
to list American editions, that when he lacked details he pretended
the details were unimportant, that he failed to differentiate between
titles of poems and first lines of poems, and--as Carter and Pollard

pointed out half a century ago--that Wise lists his forgeries of Swinburne's works as genuine first editions.

Major critical studies of Swinburne include John Drinkwater's
Swinburne: An Estimate (entry 1154), T. Earle Welby's A Study of
Swinburne (entry 1157), and Robert L. Peters's The Crowns of
Apollo (entry 2021). Other critics whose works are basic to the
study of Swinburne are Robert William Buchanan, Gilbert Keith
Chesterton, Samuel Claggett Chew, Thomas E. Connolly, Curtis
Dahl, Benjamin Franklin Fisher IV, Douglas C. Fricke, Frederick
James Furnivall, Robert A. Greenberg, Herbert John Clifford
Grierson, Antony H. Harrison, Clyde Kenneth Hyder, Coulson Kern-
ahan, Georges Lafourcade, Cecil Y. Lang, Kerry McSweeney, John
S. Mayfield, Terry L. Meyers, Alice Christina Meynell, Harold
George Nicolson, Alfred Noyes, Meredith Bragg Raymond, William
Michael Rossetti, Francis Jacques Sypher, Jr., and F. A. C. Wilson (entries for these scholars are listed in the Author-Editor In-
dex). Buchanan, Furnivall, Noyes, and Rossetti are interesting
because their views represent the early critical perspectives that
shaped the growth of Swinburnean studies. Furnivall's nasty attacks
on Swinburne's criticism almost equal Swinburne's own vicious
counterattacks. Chesterton and Meynell provide insights from their
own perspectives as poets. Much of what they have to say typifies
the ambiguous feelings of critics: Swinburne's work has much to
admire, but it is not wholly admirable; and how could such a pecul-
iar man write good literature? Chew, Connolly, Fisher, Hyder,
Lafourcade, Lang, Meyers, and Nicolson bring extensive knowledge
of Swinburne's life to their work, and their investigations of Swinburne's achievements often provide illumination and color. Of these
scholars, Chew and Hyder stand out as the most successful at dis-
tinguishing between their responses to Swinburne's personality and
to his writings, and Meyers as someone who possesses a special
affinity for Swinburne's work. The essays of R. L. Peters also
will reward the student of Swinburne.

The basic Swinburne library would comprise the following
works:

biography: Philip Henderson, Swinburne: The Portrait of a Poet
              (London: Routledge and Kegan Paul, 1974)

criticism: Clyde Kenneth Hyder, ed., Swinburne: The Critical
              Heritage (New York: Barnes and Noble, 1970)

              Robert L. Peters, The Crowns of Apollo: Swinburne's
              Principles of Literature and Art (Detroit: Wayne State
              University Press, 1965)

editions: The Poems of Algernon Charles Swinburne, 6 volumes
              (London: Chatto and Windus, 1904)

              The Tragedies of Algernon Charles Swinburne, 5
              volumes (London: Chatto and Windus, 1905-1906)

Cecil Y. Lang, ed., The Swinburne Letters, 6 volumes
(New Haven, Conn.: Yale University Press, 1959-1962

Edmund Wilson, ed., The Novels of A. C. Swinburne:
Love's Cross-Currents: Lesbia Brandon (New York:
Farrar, 1962)

Francis Jacques Sypher, ed., A Year's Letters (New
York: New York University Press, 1974)

C. K. Hyder, ed., Swinburne as Critic (London:
Routledge and Kegan Paul, 1972)

A complete scholarly edition of Swinburne's works is needed,
as is a good analytical bibliography of primary works. A gathering
of Swinburne's letters discovered since the publication of C. Y.
Lang's edition would also prove useful.

+   +   +

The organization of the present bibliography is chronological, with
works gathered together by year of publication from 1861 to 1981.
At the start of each year, I note any significant events, emphasizing
the publication of primary works that are reviewed in subsequent
entries. After my notes on the year, I list books, if any were
published, followed by dissertations and then periodical listings.
Within each section--books, dissertations, and periodicals--works
are listed alphabetically by author. I have provided short annotations in order to clarify a work's contents when a title is not suf-
ficiently descriptive, or to point out a work's significance. Books
are often followed by lists of reviews. Book reviews of secondary
works were included for their relevance to Swinburne. The bibliographic list is followed by two indexes, author-editor and subject.
The entries in each are organized alphabetically and are followed
by the relevant entry numbers for listed publications.

I would like here to acknowledge those who have gone before:
Theodore G. Ehrsam, Robert H. Deily, and Robert M. Smith,
whose "Algernon Charles Swinburne" in Bibliographies of Twelve
Victorian Authors (entry 1801) was an invaluable aid in my research.
The annual bibliography, edited by Richard C. Tobias, that appears
in Victorian Studies was helpful, as were C. K. Hyder's essays in
the two editions of The Victorian Poets: A Guide to Research (entries 1924 and 2054) and Robert A. Greenberg's bibliographic essays
in Victorian Poetry, discussing studies of Swinburne.

+ THE BIBLIOGRAPHY +

1861

In 1860, two hundred and fifty copies of Swinburne's verse dramas The Queen Mother and Rosamond were published. They attracted little notice besides the two short reviews listed below. The Spectator reviewer called the dramas' subjects "painful," while the Athenaeum reviewer called them "dull."

1 The Athenaeum, 37 (May 4, 1861), 595.
   Reprinted: C. K. Hyder, Swinburne: The Critical Heritage, page 2 (entry 2083).

2 The Spectator, 34 (Jan. 12, 1861), 42.
   Reprinted: C. K. Hyder, Swinburne: The Critical Heritage, page 1 (entry 2083).

1865

Swinburne's verse dramas Atalanta in Calydon and Chastelard were published separately in 1865. The reviews of Atalanta were generally favorable, but the reviews of Chastelard were more ambivalent, with some reviewers arguing that the play's portrait of Mary Queen of Scots and its depiction of events were inaccurate. These reviewers also found the play's sensibilities repellent.

3 The Athenaeum, 45 (April 1, 1865), 450-451.
   Review of Atalanta in Calydon.

1

4   The Athenaeum, 46 (Dec. 23, 1865), 880-881.
    Review of Chastelard.
    Reprinted: C. K. Hyder, Swinburne: The Critical Heritage,
    pages 17-21 (entry 2083).

5   Christian Examiner, 79 (Nov. 1865), 436.
    Review of Atalanta in Calydon.

6   The Examiner, July 15, 1865, pp. 440-441.
    Review of Atalanta in Calydon.

7   The London Review, 10 (April 8, 1865), 382-383.
    Review of Atalanta in Calydon.

8   The London Review, 11 (Dec. 9, 1865), 621-622.
    Review of Chastelard.

9   [Milnes, Richard Monckton]. "Swinburne's Atalanta in Calydon."
    The Edinburgh Review, 122 (July 1865), 202-216.
    Particularly sensitive review.

10 Norton, C. E. Nation (New York), 1 (Nov. 9, 1865), 590-591.
    Review of Atalanta in Calydon.

11 Notes and Queries, 3rd ser., 7 (April 1, 1865), 272.
    Review of Atalanta in Calydon.

12 "The Poetry of Praed and Lord Houghton." Quarterly Review,
    118 (Oct. 1865), 417.

13 The Reader, 5 (April 22, 1865), 447-448.
    Review of Atalanta in Calydon.

14 The Reader, 6 (Dec. 2, 1865), 621-622.
    Review of Chastelard.

15 Round Table, 1 (Nov. 4, 1865), 130-133.
    Review of Atalanta in Calydon.

16 The Saturday Review (London), 19 (May 6, 1865), 540-542.
    Review of Atalanta in Calydon.
    Reprinted: C. K. Hyder, Swinburne: The Critical Heritage,
    pages 9-16 (entry 2083).

17 [Skelton, John]. "Mr. Swinburne's Poems." Fraser's Magazine,
    71 (June 1865), 772-784.
    Discusses Atalanta in Calydon and The Queen-Mother and
    Rosamond.

18 The Spectator, 38 (April 15, 1865), 412-414.
    Review of Atalanta in Calydon.

19 The Spectator, 38 (Dec. 2, 1865), 1342-1344.
    Review of Chastelard.

20 Tablet, Aug. 12, 1865, p. 505
    Review of Atalanta in Calydon.

21 The Times, June 6, 1865, p. 6.

22 Warren, J. Leicester. The Fortnightly Review, 1 (May 15,
    1865), 75-80.

1866

The publication of Poems and Ballads in 1866 marked a major period in Swinburne's career. The volume won him recognition as an
important poet and began the critical controversies that comprise
much of the writings about him. Also published in 1866 were Notes
on Poems and Reviews, in which Swinburne replied to his critics,
and The Imaginative Literature of England (criticism).

Book

23 Rossetti, William Michael. Swinburne's Poems and Ballads:
    A Criticism. London: Hotten, 1866.
    Important defense of Swinburne's poetry.
    Reprinted: C. K. Hyder, Swinburne: The Critical Heritage,
    pages 57-91 (entry 2083).
    Excerpted: Kauver and Sorensen, eds., The Victorian Mind
    (entry 2068).
    Reviewed: London Review (entry 49); and The Spectator
    (entry 66).

Periodicals

24 The Athenaeum, 47 (March 17, 1866), 359.
    Review of A Selection from the Works of Lord Byron, edited
    by Swinburne (1866).

25 The Athenaeum, 48 (Aug. 18, 1866), 211.
    Note on Poems and Ballads.

26 The Athenaeum, 48 (Oct. 20, 1866), 501.
    Note on Poems and Ballads.

27 The Athenaeum, 48 (Nov. 3, 1866), 564-565.
    Review of Notes on Poems and Reviews.
    Reprinted: Living Age (entry 42).

28 [Buchanan, Robert William]. The Athenaeum, 48 (Aug. 4,
     1866), 137-138.
     Review of Poems and Ballads.
     Buchanan was particularly unsympathetic toward Swinburne's
     work.
     Reprinted: C. K. Hyder, Swinburne: The Critical Heritage,
     pages 30-34 (entry 2083).

29 _____. "Immorality in Authorship." The Fortnightly Re-
     view, 6 (Sept. 15, 1866), 33.

30 _____. "The Session of the Poets--August 1866." The
     Spectator, 39 (Sept. 15, 1866), 1028.
     Satirical poem that has Swinburne declaim--among other
     things--"All virtue is bosh!"
     Reprinted: C. K. Hyder, Swinburne: The Critical Heritage,
     pages 39-41 (entry 2083).

31 _____. "Mr. Buchanan on Immorality in Authorship." The
     Spectator, 39 (Sept. 22, 1866), 1049-1050.

32 "Calling a Thing by Its Right Name." Punch, 51 (Nov. 10,
     1866), 189.

33 "The Defence of Swinburne." The Saturday Review (London),
     22 (Nov. 17, 1866), 600-601.
     Review of Notes on Poems and Reviews.

34 Eclectic Magazine of Foreign Literature, n. s. 3 (June 1866),
     772.
     Discusses The Queen-Mother and Rosamond.

35 Eclectic Magazine of Foreign Literature, n. s. 4 (Dec. 1866),
     765.
     Review of Poems and Ballads.

36 Examiner, Oct. 27, 1866, p. 677.
     Review of Notes on Poems and Reviews.

37 Fun, Aug. 18, 1866, p. 236.
     Review of Poems and Ballads.

38 Fun, Nov. 17, 1866, p. 99.
     Review of Notes on Poems and Reviews.

39 Harper's Monthly Magazine, 32 (Jan. 1866), 258.
     Review of Atalanta in Calydon.

40 Illustrated London News, 49 (Aug. 25, 1866), 190.
     Note on Poems and Ballads.

41 [James, Henry]. "Swinburne's 'Chastelard.'" Nation (New
     York), 2 (Jan. 18, 1866), 83-84.

Review of Chastelard.
Reprinted: Notes and Reviews (entry 1443).

42 Living Age, 90 (Sept. 8, 1866), 633-636.
    Review of Poems and Ballads.

43 Living Age, 91 (Dec. 1, 1866), 564-568.
    Review of Notes on Poems and Reviews.
    Reprinted from The Athenaeum (entry 27).

44 [Lowell, James Russell]. "Swinburne's Tragedies." North
    American Review, 102 (April 1866), 544-555.
    Review of Atalanta in Calydon and Chastelard.
    Harsh evaluation of Swinburne's plays.
    Reprinted: My Study Windows (entry 387).

45 [Milnes, Richard Monckton]. Examiner, Oct. 6, 1866, p. 672.
    Review of Poems and Ballads.

46 _____. "Mr. Swinburne's Chastelard." The Fortnightly Re-
    view, 4 (April 15, 1866), 533-543.
    Review of Chastelard.

47 Morley, Henry. The Examiner, Sept. 22, 1866, pp. 597-599.
    Review of Chastelard and Poems and Ballads.
    Reprinted: C. K. Hyder, Swinburne: The Critical Heritage,
    pages 42-48 (entry 2083).

48 [Morley, John]. "Mr. Swinburne's New Poems." The Saturday
    Review (London), 22 (Aug. 4, 1866), 145-147.
    Review of Poems and Ballads.
    A stingingly negative evaluation of Poems and Ballads.
    Reprinted: Eclectic Magazine of Foreign Literature, 67 (Nov.
    1866), 556-560; C. K. Hyder, Swinburne: The Critical Heri-
    tage, pages 22-29 (entry 2083); A. Mordell, ed., Notorious
    Literary Attacks (entry 1554); and Kauver and Sorensen, eds.,
    The Victorian Mind (entry 2067).

49 "Mr. Rossetti's Criticism." The London Review, 13 (Dec. 1,
    1866), 610-611.
    Review of W. M. Rossetti's Swinburne's Poems and Ballads.
    (entry 23).

50 "Mr. Swinburne, His Crimes and His Critics." Eclectic Re-
    view, n. s. 11 (Dec. 1866), 493-508.

51 "Mr. Swinburne's Defense." London Review, 13 (Nov. 3, 1866),
    482-483.
    Review of Notes on Poems and Reviews.
    Reprinted: Living Age, 91 (Dec. 15, 1866), 661-664.

52 "Mr. Swinburne's Defense." Pall Mall Gazette, Nov. 2, 1866,
    pp. 9-10.
    Review of Notes on Poems and Reviews.

53   "Mr. Swinburne on His Critics." The Spectator, 39 (Nov. 3,
        1866), 1228-1229.
        Review of Notes on Poems and Reviews.

54   "Mr. Swinburne's Poems and Ballads." The London Review,
        13 (Aug. 4, 1866), 130-131.
        Review of Poems and Ballads.
        Reprinted: C. K. Hyder, Swinburne: The Critical Heritage,
        35-38 (entry 2083).

55   Nation (New York), 2 (May 1, 1866), 549.
        Review of The Queen-Mother and Rosamond.

56   National Quarterly Review, 13 (June 1866), 183-188.
        Review of The Queen-Mother and Rosamond.

57   National Quarterly Review, 14 (Dec. 1866), 150-158.
        Review of Poems and Ballads.

58   The New Englander, 25 (July 1866), 594.
        Review of The Queen-Mother and Rosamond.

59   Pall Mall Gazette, April 27, 1866, pp. 11-12.
        Review of Chastelard.

60   Reader, 7 (July 28, 1866), 675.
        Review of Poems and Ballads.

61   Round Table, 3 (Jan. 13, 1866), 18-19.
        Review of Chastelard.

62   Round Table, 4 (Dec. 8, 1866), 307-308.
        Review of Poems and Ballads.

63   The Saturday Review (London), 21 (May 26, 1866), 623-625.
        Review of Chastelard.

64   [Skelton, John]. "Mr. Swinburne and His Critics." Fraser's
        Magazine, 74 (Nov. 1866), 635-648.

65   The Spectator, 39 (March 31, 1866), 356-358.
        Review of A Selection from the Works of Lord Byron, edited
        by Swinburne (1866).

66   The Spectator, 39 (Nov. 24, 1866), 1311-1312.
        Review of W. M. Rossetti's Swinburne's Poems and Ballads
        (entry 23).

67   "Swinburne's Folly." The Pall Mall Gazette, Aug. 20, 1866,
        pp. 9-11.
        Review of Poems and Ballads.

68   "Swinburniana." The Pall Mall Gazette, Sept. 15, 1866, p. 13.

69 Sturgis, R., Jr. Nation (New York), 3 (Dec. 6, 1866), 446-447.
    Review of Poems and Ballads.

70 Tablet, Aug. 11, 1866, p. 506.
    Review of Poems and Ballads.

71 Thomson, James. "The Swinburne Controversy." National Re-
    former, Dec. 23, 1866, pp. 403-404.
    Reprinted: Satires and Profanities (entry 388).

72 Urban, Sylvanus. The Gentleman's Magazine, 220 (March
    1866), 398-401.
    Review of Chastelard.

73 Westminster Review, 86 (July 1866), 277.
    Review of Chastelard and A Selection from the Works of
    Lord Byron, edited by Swinburne (1866).

74 White, R. G. Galaxy, 2 (Dec. 1, 1866), 665-670.
    Review of Poems and Ballads.

1867

A Song of Italy, a poem hailing the Italian revolutionary Mazzini as
a "prophet," was published in 1867.

75 The Athenaeum, 49 (April 6, 1867), 446-448.
    Review of A Song of Italy.

76 Bayne, Peter. "Mr. Arnold and Mr. Swinburne." Contempo-
    rary Review, 6 (Nov. 1867), 337-356.
    Reprinted: Every Saturday, 4 (Dec. 14, 1867), 753-761; and
    New Eclectic, 1 (Feb. 1868), 144-164.

77 Carroll, Lewis [pseud. of Charles Lutwidge Dodgson]. "Atalan-
    ta in Camden-town." Punch, 53 (July 27, 1867), 38.
    Reprinted: The Collected Verse of Lewis Carroll (entry
    1723).

78 The Contemporary Review, 5 (July 1867), 385.
    Review of A Song of Italy.

79 Crescent Monthly, Feb. 1867.
    Listed in Twelve Victorian Authors (entry 1801), page 290.
    Not examined.

80 Etienne, Louis. "Le Paganisme Poétique en Angleterre."

Revue des Deux Mondes, 69 (May 15, 1867), 291-317.
Discusses Atalanta in Calydon and Poems and Ballads.

81 The Examiner, April 13, 1867, p. 230.
    Review of A Song of Italy.

82 Galaxy, 3 (Feb. 1, 1867), 340.
    Note about Swinburne.

83 Galaxy, 3 (April 1, 1867), 798-799.
    Comment on W. Winwood Reade's remarks about Swinburne
    in the March 15th issue of Galaxy (entry 93).

84 Gildersleeve, Basil L. "The Legend of Venus." Southern Re-
    view, 1 (April 1867), 352-382.
    Review of Poems and Ballads.
    Reprinted: Essays and Studies (entry 505).

85 "Literary Activity in England." The Saturday Review, 23 (Jan.
    12, 1867), 45-46.

86 "Mr. Swinburne as Critic." Spectator, 40 (Oct. 5, 1867),
    1109-1111.
    Reprinted: Living Age, 95 (Nov. 16, 1867), 397-400.

87 "Mr. Swinburne's Italy." The Spectator, 40 (April 13, 1867),
    415-416.
    Review of A Song of Italy.

88 "Mr. Swinburne's Poetry." Westminster Review, 87 (April 1,
    1867), 210-220.

89 Norton, C. E. North American Review, 105 (July 1867), 324-
    325.
    Review of A Song of Italy.

90 Page, H. A. [pseudonym of Alexander Hay Japp]. "The Moral-
    ity of Literary Art." The Contemporary Review, 5 (June
    1867), 161-189.

91 The Pall Mall Gazette, April 13, 1867, p. 11.
    Review of A Song of Italy.

92 Purnell, T. Every Saturday, 3 (May 4, 1867), 551-553.
    Review of A Song of Italy.

93 Reade, W. Winwood. "Mr. Swinburne: A Sketch." Galaxy, 3
    (March 15, 1867), 682-684.
    See Galaxy for April 1st (entry 83).

94 Round Table, 6 (July 6, 1867), 9-10.
    Review of A Song of Italy.

95   "Swinburne's Song of Italy." Saturday Review (London), 23
     (April 20, 1867), 503-504.
     Review of A Song of Italy.

96   Taylor, Bayard.   North American Review, 104 (Jan. 1867),
     287-292.
     Review of Poems and Ballads.

97   Tyrwhitt, R. St. John.   "Ancilla Domini: Thoughts on Chris-
     tian Art: VI--The Immoral Theory of Art." The Contem-
     porary Review, 5 (Aug. 1867), 418-436.

98   The Westminster Review, 88 (July 1867), 148-149.
     Review of A Song of Italy.

99   White, Richard Grant.   The Galaxy, 3 (Jan. 1, 1867), 114.
     Letter to the editor.

1868

Swinburne's critical study William Blake was published in 1868.

100 American Quarterly Church Review, 20 (Oct. 1868), 461-463.
     Discusses Swinburne's poem "Siena," later included in
     Songs Before Sunrise (1871).

101 The Athenaeum, 51 (Jan. 4, 1868), 12-13.
     Review of William Blake.

102 "Companions of the Bath." The Mask, 1 (Aug. 1868), 193-195.

103 Conway, Moncure D.   Fortnightly Review, n.s. 3 (Feb. 1,
     1868) 216-220.
     Review of William Blake.

104 "Criticisms on Contemporaries: No. 1. Mr. Algernon Charles
     Swinburne." Tinsley's Magazine, 3 (Aug. 1868), 26-36.

105 Davidson, Tom.   Radical, 3 (Jan. 1868), 316-323.
     Review of Poems and Ballads.

106 Examiner, Feb. 8, 1868, pp. 84-86.
     Review of William Blake.

107 "Fashion in Poetry." St. Pauls Magazine, 1 (March 1868),
     693-708.

108   London Quarterly Review, 29 (Jan. 1868), 323-324.
         Review of Chastelard.

109   "Mr. Swinburne's Essay on Blake." Broadway Annual, 1868,
         pp. 723-730.
         Review of William Blake.

110   "The Neo-Classical Drama." Christian Remembrancer, n. s.
         55 (Jan. 1868), 45-50.
         Review of Atalanta in Calydon.

111   "Poetry and Italian Politics." Tinsley's Magazine, 2 (Feb.
         1868), 95-100.

112   The Spectator, 41 (March 14, 1868), 320-322.
         Review of William Blake.

113   Westminster Review, 89 (April 1868), 587-588.
         Review of William Blake.

1869

---

114   "Algernon Charles Swinburne: Poet and Critic." London
         Quarterly Review, 31 (Jan. 1869), 370-401.
         Survey of the works of Swinburne.

115   The Athenaeum, 54 (Aug. 21, 1869), 237.
         Review of Swinburne's edition of Coleridge's Christabel.

116   [Austin, Alfred]. "The Poetry of the Period: Mr. Swin-
         burne." Temple Bar, 26 (July 1869), 457-474, and 28
         (Dec. 1869), 35-48.
         Reprinted: The Poetry of the Period (entry 121).

117   De Bow's Review, n. s. 6 (March 1869), 231-239.
         Review of Atalanta in Calydon.

118   Porter, Noah. "Books and Reading." Hours at Home, 9
         (May 1869), 47.
         Reprinted: Books and Reading (entry 123).

119   "Roman Catholic Poets." Temple Bar, 27 (Sept. 1869), 170-
         186, and 28 (Dec. 1869), 33-48.

120   The Times, Oct. 14, 1869.
         Mentioned in T. J. Wise's bibliography (entry 1412), page
         44.   Not examined.

1870

Swinburne's Ode on the Proclamation of the French Republic (hereafter referred to as French Republic) was published in 1870.

Books

121 Austin, Alfred.   "A. C. Swinburne."   Poetry of the Period.
         London: Bentley, 1870.
         Reprinted from the Temple Bar (entry 116).
         Reprinted: C. K. Hyder, Swinburne: The Critical Heritage,
         pages 92-111, using the slightly emended book version (en-
         try 2083).

122 Friswell, James Hain.   "Mr. Algernon C. Swinburne."   Mod-
         ern Men of Letters Honestly Criticized.   London: Hodder
         and Stoughton, 1870.   pp. 297-310.

123 Porter, Noah.   "Books and Reading."   Books and Reading.
         New York: Scribner, [1870].
         Reprinted from Hours at Home (entry 118).

Periodicals

124 The Academy, 2 (Oct. 22, 1870), 82-89.

125 The Athenaeum, 2 (Sept. 17, 1870), 364.
         Review of French Republic.

126 Examiner and London Review, Sept. 24, 1870, pp. 613-614.
         Review of French Republic.

127 [Forman, H. Buxton].   Contemporary Review, 13 (Feb. 1870),
         296-298.
         Review of Swinburne's edition of Coleridge's Christabel.

128 The Graphic, 2 (Sept. 24, 1870), 298-299.
         Review of French Republic.

129 [Stoddard, R. H.].   "Algernon Charles Swinburne."   Appleton's
         Journal, 3 (April 2, 1870), 378-381.

130 "Swinburne's Ode."   The Saturday Review (London), 30 (Sept.
         24, 1870), 403-404.

1871

Swinburne published a collection of verse, Songs Before Sunrise, in 1871.

Books

131   Forman, Harry Buxton. "A. C. Swinburne." Our Living
       Poets. London: Tinsley, 1871. pp. 333-373.

132   An Imitation of A. C. Swinburne's Ode on the Proclamation of
       the French Republic, September 4, 1870. London: Provost,
       1871.

Periodicals

133   Amos, Sheldon. The Fortnightly Review, 15 (Feb. 1, 1871),
       281-282.
       Review of Songs Before Sunrise.

134   The Athenaeum, 57 (Jan. 14, 1871), 41-42.
       Review of Songs Before Sunrise.

135   [Baynes, Thomas Spencer]. "Swinburne's Poems." Edinburgh
       Review, 134 (July 1871), 71-99.
       Excerpted: C. K. Hyder, Swinburne: The Critical Heri-
       tage, pages 133-138 (entry 2083).

136   [Buchanan, Robert William, writing as "Thomas Maitland"].
       "The Fleshly School of Poetry." Contemporary Review,
       18 (Oct. 1871), 334-350.
       Virulent attack on Swinburne and Dante Gabriel Rossetti.
       Although Buchanan later recanted much of what he says in
       the present essay, he is probably best remembered for it.
       Reprinted: The Fleshly School of Poetry (entry 146).

137   Examiner, Jan. 14, 1871, pp. 45-46.
       Review of Songs Before Sunrise.

138   Fountain, Lucy. "An Evening with Swinburne." Galaxy, 12
       (Aug. 1871), 231-234.

139   Graphic, 3 (Jan. 28, 1871), 87.
       Review of Songs Before Sunrise.

140   Hüffer, Franz. Academy, 2 (Jan. 15, 1871), 87-89.
       Review of Songs Before Sunrise.
       Reprinted: C. K. Hyder, Swinburne: The Critical Heritage,
       pages 139-145 (entry 2083).

141   Literary World (Boston), March 1, 1871, pp. 154-155.
       Review of Songs Before Sunrise.

142 The London Quarterly Review, 35 (Jan. 1871), 517-519.
       Review of French Republic.

143 The Saturday Review (London), 31 (Jan. 14, 1871), 54-55.
       Review of Songs Before Sunrise.
       Reprinted: C. K. Hyder, Swinburne: The Critical Heritage,
       pages 127-132 (entry 2083).

144 Tinsley's Magazine, 8 (June 1871), 561-568.
       Review of Songs Before Sunrise.

145 Westminster Review, n. s. 39 (April 1871), 579-580.
       Review of Songs Before Sunrise.

1872

In 1872, Swinburne again replied to his critics, this time with
Under the Microscope, a tough-minded analysis of the works of
those who derogated his own writings.

Book

146 [Buchanan, Robert William, writing as "Thomas Maitland"].
       The Fleshly School of Poetry and Other Phenomena of the
       Day. London: Strahan, 1872. See entry 136.

Periodicals

147 "Algernon Charles Swinburne." Once a Week, 26 (March 23,
       1872), 281.

148 Appleton's Journal, 7 (June 8, 1872), 637.

148a Bierce, Ambrose. "Letter from London." Daily Alta Cali-
        fornia, Oct. 26, 1872.
        Reprinted: Weekly Alta California, Nov. 2, 1872.
        See entry 2237.

149 [Buchanan, Robert William, writing as "Thomas Maitland"].
       "The Monkey and the Microscope." St. Pauls Magazine,
       11 (Aug. 1872), 240.
       Satirical poem about Under the Microscope.

150 "Coterie Glory." The Saturday Review (London), 33 (Feb. 24,
       1872), 239-240.

151 Courthorpe, W. J. "The Latest Development of Literary

Poetry: Swinburne, Rossetti, Morris." The Quarterly Review, 132 (Jan. 1872), 263.

152   Hayward, Abraham. The Quarterly Review, 132 (Jan. 1872), 59-69.
      Reprinted: Eclectic Magazine of Foreign Literature, 78 (April 1872), 385-390.
      Review of Songs Before Sunrise.

153   Hilton, A. C. "Octopus." Light Green, 1 (1872).
      Poetic parody of "Dolores."
      Reprinted: C. K. Hyder, Swinburne: The Critical Heritage, pages 156-157 (entry 2083).

154   Hutton, Richard H. "Tennyson." Macmillan's Magazine, 27 (Dec. 1872), 143-167.

155   "The Later English Poets." The Quarterly Review, 132 (Jan. 1872), 563-569.
      Reprinted: Eclectic Magazine of Foreign Literature, 78 (April 1872), 390-394.

156   "Mr. Buchanan and the Fleshly Poets." Saturday Review (London), 33 (June 1, 1872), 700-701.

157   "Mr. Swinburne Among the Fleas." Examiner, July 6, 1872, 673-674.
      Review of Under the Microscope.

158   "Novelties in Poetry and Criticism." Fraser's Magazine, n. s. 5 (May 1872), 588-596.

159   Simcox, G. A. "Art and Morality." Macmillan's Magazine, 26 (Oct. 1872), 487-492.

160   Taylor, Bayard. "Diversions of the Echo Club. Night the Second." Atlantic Monthly, 29 (Feb. 1872), 171-172.
      Reprinted: The Echo Club (entry 209).

1873

Book

161   Devey, Joseph. "Androtheist School:--Swinburne." A Comparative Estimate of Modern English Poets. London: Moxon, 1873. pp. 337-354.

Periodicals

162 Addis, John. "Horsel." Notes and Queries, 4th ser., 11
     (Feb. 8, 1873), 127.

163 "Pope Boniface VIII." Notes and Queries, 4th ser., 11 (May
     3, 1873), 361.

164 The Spectator, 46 (May 24, 1873), 655, and 46 (May 31,
     1873), 697.
     Discusses Swinburne's series of sonnets, Dirae.

1874

Swinburne published another drama in verse in 1874, Bothwell.

165 Belgravia, 23 (June 1874), 516-528.
     Review of Bothwell.

166 "Emerson: A Literary Interview." Frank Leslie's Illustrated
     Newspaper, 37 (Jan. 3, 1874), 275.
     See C. K. Hyder, "Emerson on Swinburne" (entry 1773).

167 Examiner, May 30, 1874, pp. 568-570.
     Review of Bothwell.

168 [Milnes, Richard Monckton]. Fortnightly Review, 22 (July 1,
     1874), 76-88.
     Review of Bothwell.
     Reprinted: Canadian Monthly and National Review, 6 (Aug.
     1874), 174-182; and Eclectic Magazine of Foreign Literature,
     83 (Sept. 1874), 302-309.

169 The London Quarterly Review, 42 (July 1874), 508-513.
     Review of Bothwell.

170 "Men of the Day. --No. XCI: Mr. Algernon Charles Swinburne."
     Vanity Fair, 12 (Nov. 21, 1874), 285.

171 Milner, George. "On a Recent Poem by Mr. Swinburne."
     Papers of the Manchester Literary Club, 1 (1874), 53-55.

172 Morley, John. "On Mr. Swinburne's 'Bothwell.'" Macmillan's
     Magazine, 30 (Oct. 1874), 521-529.
     Review of Bothwell.

173 "Mr. Swinburne's Bothwell." The Athenaeum, 63 (May 23,

1874), 689-690.
Review of Bothwell.

174   "Notes and News." Academy, 6 (Oct. 31, 1874), 480-481.

175   Saintsbury, George. Academy, 5 (June 13, 1874), 651-653.
        Review of Bothwell.

176   Saturday Review (London), 37 (June 6, 1874), 719-721.
        Review of Bothwell.

177   "Scepticism and Modern Poetry." Blackwood's Magazine, 115
        (Feb. 1874), 223-231.

178   "A Song After Sunset." Punch, 67 (Aug. 1, 1874), 45.

179   The Spectator, 47 (June 6, 1874), 724-726.
        Review of Bothwell.

180   "Swinburne and De Vere." Catholic World, 20 (Dec. 1874),
        346-353.
        Review of Bothwell.

181   Temple Bar, 41 (July 1874), 545-551.
        Review of Bothwell.

182   The Westminster Review, n. s. 46 (July 1874), 296-297.
        Review of Bothwell.

1875

Swinburne was active in 1875. He published two pieces of criticism,
George Chapman and Essays and Studies; poetry, Songs of Two Na-
tions; and a nasty attack on Robert Buchanan, "The Devil's Due"
(The Examiner, Dec. 11, 1875, p. 1388), which he signed "Thomas
Maitland, St. Kilda" ("Thomas Maitland" was Buchanan's customary
pseudonym).

Books

183   [Carnegie, Robert]. Jonas Fisher: A Poem in Brown and
        White. London: Kegan, Paul, Trench, Trübner, 1875.

184   Milner, George. "On a Recent Poem by Mr. Swinburne:
        'The Year of the Rose.'" Transactions of the Manchester
        Literary Club. London: Trübner, 1875. pp. 53-55.

185 Stedman, E. C. "Latter-Day Singers: Algernon Charles
     Swinburne." Victorian Poets. Boston: Houghton, Mifflin,
     1875.
     Excerpted: C. K. Hyder, Swinburne: The Critical Heri-
     tage, pages 158-162 (entry 2083).

Periodicals

186 Academy, 7 (April 10, 1875), 371.
     Review of Songs of Two Nations.

187 American Bibliopolist, 7 (June 1875), 128-129.
     Review of Essays and Studies.

188 "Art and Morality." The Cornhill Magazine, 32 (July 1875),
     91-101.

189 The Athenaeum, 65 (May 22, 1875), 681.
     Review of Essays and Studies.

190 Benton, Joel. "Mr. Swinburne's Prose." Appleton's Journal,
     14 (Nov. 13, 1875), 628-629.
     Review of Essays and Studies.

191 British Quarterly, 62 (Oct. 1875), 563-565.
     Review of Essays and Studies.

192 Collette, C. H. "The Suppression of Vice." The Athenaeum,
     65 (June 5, 1875), 750.
     In response to Thomas Purnell's "The Suppression of Vice"
     in the May 8th issue of The Athenaeum (entry 199).

193 Gosse, Edmund. "Mr. Swinburne on Chapman." The Examin-
     er, Feb. 20, 1875, pp. 214-216.
     Review of George Chapman.

194 _____. The Examiner, March 27, 1875, pp. 354-355.
     Review of Songs of Two Nations.

195 _____. The Examiner, June 12, 1875, pp. 665-666.
     Review of Essays and Studies.

196 Hewlett, Henry G. "Modern Ballads." Contemporary Review,
     26 (Nov. 1875), 973-980.

197 James, Henry. "Swinburne's Essays." Nation (New York),
     21 (July 29, 1875), 73-74.
     Review of Essays and Studies.
     Reprinted: Views and Reviews (entry 932).

198 Pall Mall Gazette, June 23, 1875, pp. 11-12.
     Review of Essays and Studies.

199   Purnell, Thomas.   "The Suppression of Vice." The Athenaeum,
         65 (May 8, 1875), 622.
         This letter was replied to by C. H. Collette (entry 192)
         and Swinburne (The Athenaeum, 65 [May 29, 1875], 720).

200   Saintsbury, George.   Academy, 8 (July 3, 1875), 4-6.
         Review of Essays and Studies.

201   Saturday Review (London), 40 (July 10, 1875), 54-55.
         Review of Essays and Studies.

202   Scribner's Monthly, 10 (Aug. 1875), 513-514.
         Review of Essays and Studies.

203   The Spectator, 48 (March 20, 1875), 377-378.
         Review of George Chapman.

204   The Spectator, 48 (July 3, 1875), 855-857.
         Review of Essays and Studies.

205   Stedman, Edmund Clarence.   "Algernon Charles Swinburne."
         Scribner's Monthly, 9 (March 1875), 585-596.

206   Symonds, John Addington.   Academy, 7 (May 1, 1875), 442-
         443.
         Review of George Chapman.

207   Westminster Review, n. s. 47 (April 1875), 546-547.
         Review of George Chapman.

208   Westminster Review, n. s. 48 (July 1875), 297-298.

1876

Erechtheus, a verse drama, was favorably criticized in most reviews; Notes of an English Republican on the Muscovite Crusade
featured an attack on Thomas Carlyle.   (Hereafter referred to as
Muscovite Crusade.)

Book

209   Taylor, Bayard.   The Echo Club: and Other Literary Diver-
         sions.   Boston: Osgood, 1876. pp. 37-43.
         Reprinted from Atlantic Monthly's Feb. 1872 issue (entry
         160).

Periodicals

210 Academy, 10 (Dec. 23, 1876), 604.
    Review of Muscovite Crusade.

211 The Athenaeum, 67 (Jan. 1, 1876), 13-14.
    Review of Erechtheus.

212 The Athenaeum, 67 (Feb. 5, 1876), 191-192.
    Review of Charles Wells's Joseph and His Brethren,
    edited by Swinburne.

213 The Athenaeum, 68 (Dec. 23, 1876), 827.
    Review of Muscovite Crusade.

214 British Quarterly Review, 63 (April 1876), 568-571.
    Review of Erechtheus.

215 "Erechtheus: A Tragedy." Edinburgh Review, 144 (July
    1876), 147-168.
    Review of Erechtheus.

216 Furnivall, Frederick James. "Mr. Swinburne and Mr.
    Spedding--Shakespeare's 'Henry VIII.'" Academy, 9 (Jan.
    8, 1876), 34-35, and 9 (Jan. 29, 1876), 98-99.

217 Gosse, Edmund. The Examiner, Jan. 8, 1876, pp. 41-43.
    Review of Erechtheus.

218 Gray, Russell. North American Review, 123 (April 1876),
    220-221.
    Review of Essays and Studies.

219 International Review, 3 (Aug. 1876), 552-553.
    Review of Erechtheus.

220 Jewell, Alfred. "'The Ancient Mariner.'" Notes and Que-
    ries, 5th ser., 5 (Jan. 29, 1876), 89.

221 The London Quarterly Review, 46 (April 1876), 249-254.
    Review of Erechtheus.

222 Pall Mall Gazette, Jan. 15, 1876, pp. 12-13.
    Review of Erechtheus.

223 "Portraits in Oil: LXXXVIII. 'The Bard.'" The World,
    March 29, 1876, pp. 4-5.

224 Quarterly Review, 141 (April 1876), 507-526.
    Review of Essays and Studies.

225 Saintsbury, George. "Modern English Prose." Fortnightly
    Review, n. s. 19 (Feb. 1876), 255-256.

226 The Saturday Review (London), 41 (Jan. 8, 1876), 50-51.
     Review of Erechtheus.

227 Scribner's Magazine, 12 (June 1876), 276-278.
     Review of Charles Wells's Joseph and His Brethren,
     edited by Swinburne.

228 Scribner's Monthly, 12 (May 1876), 130-133.
     Review of Erechtheus.

229 The Spectator, 49 (Jan. 1, 1876), 15-17.
     Review of Erechtheus.

230 "Swinburne Versus Carlyle." The Spectator, 49 (Dec. 23,
     1876), 1606-1607.
     Review of Muscovite Crusade.

231 Symonds, John Addington. Academy, 9 (Jan. 8, 1876), 23-24.
     Review of Erechtheus.
     Reprinted: C. K. Hyder, Swinburne: The Critical Heri-
     tage, pages 163-169 (entry 2083).

232 Westminster Review, n. s. 49 (April 1876), 580-581.
     Review of Charles Wells's Joseph and His Brethren,
     edited by Swinburne, and of Erechtheus.

233 The World, Jan. 5, 1876, p. 19.
     Review of Erechtheus.

1877

Swinburne published A Note on Charlotte Brontë (hereafter referred
to as Charlotte Brontë) in 1877.

234 Asher, David. "Miscellen." Archiv für das Studium der
     neueren Sprachen und Literaturen, 58 (1877), 108-122.

235 The Athenaeum, 70 (Sept. 1, 1877), 261-264.
     Review of Charlotte Brontë.

236 Bayne, Thomas. "Algernon Charles Swinburne." St. James
     Magazine, 40 (1877), 436-447.

237 British Quarterly Review, 66 (Oct. 1877), 253.
     Review of Charlotte Brontë.

238 Clifford, William Kingdon. "Cosmic Emotion." Nineteenth

Century, 2 (Oct. 1877), 411-429.
Reprinted: Lectures and Essays (entry 267); and Cosmic
Emotion (entry 472).
Excerpted: C. K. Hyder, Swinburne: The Critical Heri-
tage, pages 170-176.

239 Contemporary Review, 30 (Oct. 1877), 901-902.
Review of Charlotte Brontë.

240 Dowden, Edward. Academy, 12 (Sept. 8, 1877), 233-234.
Review of Charlotte Brontë.

241 Examiner, Sept. 1, 1877, pp. 1105-1107.
Review of Charlotte Brontë.

242 Furnivall, Frederick James. "Chaucer." The Athenaeum,
69 (March 31, 1877), 417-418.

243 Gray, George H. B. "The Poetry of Algernon Charles Swinburne." Canadian Monthly and National Review, 12 (Nov.
1877), 509-513.

244 Pall Mall Gazette, Feb. 2, 1877, pp. 2-3.
Review of Muscovite Crusade.

245 The Spectator, 50 (Sept. 1, 1877), 1095-1097.
Review of Charlotte Brontë.

246 The Times, Nov. 2, 1877, p. 4.
Review of Charlotte Brontë.

247 The World, Sept. 19, 1877, p. 21.
Review of Charlotte Brontë.

1878

Swinburne's Poems and Ballads: Second Series was published in
1878.

Book

248 Selkirk, J. B. [pseudonym of James Buchan Brown]. Ethics
and Aesthetics of Modern Poetry. London: Smith, Elder,
1878. p. 12.

Periodicals

249   Appleton's Journal, n. s. 5 (Oct. 1878), 381-382.
        Review of Poems and Ballads: Second Series.

250   British Quarterly Review, 68 (Oct. 1878), 287-288.
        Review of Poems and Ballads: Second Series.

251   [Brown, James Buchan]. "Ethics and Aesthetics of Modern
        Poetry. " The Cornhill Magazine, 37 (May 1878), 569-583.

252   The Examiner, July 6, 1878, pp. 847-848.
        Review of Poems and Ballads: Second Series.

253   Literary World (Boston), 9 (Aug. 1878), 37.

254   Mallock, William H. "A Familiar Colloquy. " Nineteenth
        Century, 4 (Aug. 1878), 289-302.

255   Moulton, Louise Chandler. "An Evening with Swinburne. "
        Lippincott's Monthly Magazine, 21 (Feb. 1878), 254-255.

256   Nation (New York), 27 (July 18, 1878), 45-46.
        Review of Poems and Ballads: Second Series.

257   North American Review, 127 (Sept. -Oct. 1878), 342-344.
        Review of Poems and Ballads: Second Series.

258   Notes and Queries, 5th ser., 10 (Oct. 26, 1878), 339.
        Review of Poems and Ballads: Second Series.

259   Pall Mall Gazette, July 5, 1878, pp. 11-12.
        Review of Poems and Ballads: Second Series.

260   Quesnel, Léo. "La Poésie au XIXe Siècle en Angleterre. "
        Le Correspondant, 110 (March 10, 1878), 808-809.

261   Saintsbury, George. Academy, 14 (July 13, 1878), 25-26.
        Review of Poems and Ballads: Second Series.

262   The Saturday Review (London), 46 (July 20, 1878), 85-86.
        Review of Poems and Ballads: Second Series.

263   Smith, George Barnett. The International Review, 5 (Oct.
        1878), 697-698.
        Review of Poems and Ballads: Second Series.

264   [Watts, Theodore]. The Athenaeum, 2 (July 6, 1878), 7-9.
        Review of Poems and Ballads: Second Series.

265   Westminster Review, n. s. 54 (Oct. 1878), 563-564.
        Review of Poems and Ballads: Second Series.

266   Woodberry, G. E.   Atlantic Monthly, 41 (June 1878), 805-806.
      Review of Charlotte Brontë.

1879

Toward the end of 1879, Swinburne moved in with Theodore Watts
(later Theodore Watts-Dunton), who reviewed Swinburne's works for
The Athenaeum until 1899.

Books

267   Clifford, William Kingdon. "Cosmic Emotion." Lectures and
      Essays. Vol. II. Ed. Leslie Stephen and Frederick Pol-
      lock. London: 1879. pp. 253-285.
      First printed: Nineteenth Century, Oct. 1877 (entry 238).
      See entry 238 for other reprinting.

268   Furnivall, F. J.   Mr. Swinburne's "Flat Burglary" on Shake-
      speare: Two Letters from the "Spectator" of September
      6th and 13th, 1879. London: Trübner, 1879.
      Furnivall, who had founded the New Shakespeare Society,
      was angered by Swinburne's iconoclastic studies of Shake-
      speare, which had first appeared in The Fortnightly Review
      in 1875. Furnivall's anger was vented in abusive language.
      Reprinted from "Mr. Swinburne and Shakespeare" (entry
      273).

269   Strodtmann, Adolf. "A. C. Swinburne nach einer Abhandlung
      von E. W. Gosse." Dichter Profile: Literaturbilder aus
      dem neunzehnten Jahrhundert. Vol. II. Berlin: Abenheim,
      1879. pp. 43-90.

Periodicals

270   Blackwood's Magazine, 126 (Oct. 1879), 419-420.
      Discusses Erechtheus.

271   Contemporary Review, 34 (Jan. 1879), 419.
      Review of Poems and Ballads: Second Series.

272   Furnivall, Frederick James. "Mr. Swinburne and the New
      Shakespeare Society." Birmingham Weekly Post, Sept. 6,
      1879, p. 4.

273   _____. "Mr. Swinburne and Shakespeare." The Spectator,
      52 (Sept. 6, 1879), 1130; and 52 (Sept. 13, 1879), 1159.

Reprinted: Mr. Swinburne's "Flat Burglary" on Shakespeare (entry 268).

274   Harrison, Frederic. "On the Choice of Books." The Fortnightly Review, 31 (April 1, 1879), 491-512.
Reprinted: The Choice of Books (entry 421).

275   Robinson, A. Mary F. "Zur geschichte der zeitgenössischen
poesie Englands: Algernon Charles Swinburne." Unsere
Zeit, 2 (Aug. 1, 1879), 181-199.

276   Rolfe, W. J. "Swinburne on Shakespeare." Literary World,
10 (Oct. 11, 1879), 329.

277   The Spectator, 52 (Aug. 9, 1879), 1019; and 52 (Aug. 16,
1879), 1043.

1880

In 1880, Swinburne published Songs of the Springtides, Studies in
Song, A Study of Shakespeare, and The Heptalogia, which parodies
seven poets, including himself, and which was published anonymous-
ly.

278   British Quarterly Review, 71 (April 1880), 262-263.
Review of A Study of Shakespeare.

279   British Quarterly Review, 72 (July 1880), 121-122.
Review of Songs of the Springtides.

280   Congdon, Charles. North American Review, 131 (Aug. 1880),
183-184.
Review of Songs of the Springtides.

281   Dial, 1 (July 1880), 59.
Review of Songs of the Springtides.

282   Dowden, Edward. Academy, 17 (Jan. 3, 1880), 1-2.
Review of A Study of Shakespeare.

283   _____. "Mr. Swinburne's 'Study of Shakespeare.'"
Academy, 17 (Jan. 17, 1880), 48-49.

284   The Examiner, Jan. 10, 1880, pp. 49-50.
Review of A Study of Shakespeare.

285   The Examiner, May 15, 1880, pp. 610-611.
Review of Songs of the Springtides.

286 Furnivall, Frederick James. "Mr. Swinburne's 'Study of
     Shakespeare.'" Academy, 17 (Jan. 10, 1880), 28.

287 _____. "Mr. Swinburne and Fletcher's Share in 'Henry
     VIII.'" Academy, 17 (June 26, 1880), 476.
     Letter.

288 _____. "Fletcher's and Shakespeare's Triple Endings."
     Academy, 18 (July 10, 1880), 27-28.

289 Gentleman's Magazine, 246 (June 1880), 752-753.
     Review of Songs of the Springtides.

290 Hayne, Paul Hamilton. "Sonnets to Algernon Charles Swin-
     burne." Literary World, 11 (Jan. 17, 1880), 24.
     Hayne was a fine American poet.
     Reprinted: Paul Hamilton Hayne (entry 334).

291 "A Love Agony." Punch, 78 (June 5, 1880), 254.
     Parody.

292 Lowell, Robert. Literary World, 11 (July 17, 1880), 239.
     Review of Songs of the Springtides.

293 McCarthy, Justin H. "How Jack Harris Became an Aesthet-
     ic." Belgravia, 41 (March 1880), 61-75.

294 Nation (New York), 30 (June 17, 1880), 458-459.
     Review of Songs of the Springtides.

295 Nineteenth Century, 8 (Aug. 1880), 332-333.
     Review of Songs of the Springtides.

296 Notes and Queries, 6th ser., 1 (May 1, 1880), 368.
     Review of A Study of Shakespeare.

297 Notes and Queries, 6th ser., 1 (May 22, 1880), 427.
     Review of Songs of the Springtides.

298 Saintsbury, George. Academy, 17 (May 22, 1880), 378-379.
     Review of Songs of the Springtides.

299 Saturday Review (London), 49 (Jan. 31, 1880), 159-160.
     Review of A Study of Shakespeare.

300 Saturday Review (London), 49 (May 29, 1880), 698-699.
     Review of Songs of the Springtides.

301 Scribner's Monthly, 20 (Oct. 1880), 943.
     Review of Songs of the Springtides.

302 Sharp, William. Modern Thought, Aug. 1, 1880, pp. 458-459.
     Review of Songs of the Springtides.

303 The Spectator, 53 (July 3, 1880), 850-852.
        Review of A Study of Shakespeare.
        Swinburne replied to this review in a letter to The Specta-
        tor, 53 (July 10, 1880), 877-878.

304 Usov, S. "Mozaika." Istorichevski Vestnik, no. 12 (1880),
        1051-1052.

305 [Watts, Theodore]. The Athenaeum, 75 (Jan. 31, 1880), 146-
        148.
        Review of A Study of Shakespeare.

306 _____. The Athenaeum, 75 (May 22, 1880), 655-657.
        Review of Songs of the Springtides.
        Reprinted: Appleton's Journal, n. s. 9 (Aug. 1880), 178-182.

307 Westminster Review, 113 (April 1880), 615-616.
        Review of A Study of Shakespeare.

308 Westminster Review, 114 (July 1880), 291-293.
        Review of Songs of the Springtides.

1881

Mary Stuart, a drama in verse, was Swinburne's most significant
publication in 1881.

Book

309/10 [Furnivall, Frederick James]. The "Co." of Pigsbrook &
        Co. London: privately published, [1881].
        "Pigsbrook" was a term Furnivall used for Swinburne.
        The "Co." refers to J. O. Halliwell-Phillips.

Periodicals

311 "Aesthetic." Punch, 81 (Dec. 24, 1881), 298.

312 American, 1 (Feb. 12, 1881), 288-289.
        Review of Studies in Song.

313 Austin, Alfred. "On a Recent Criticism of Mr. Swinburne's."
        Macmillan's Magazine, 43 (March 1881), 399-408.
        Reprinted: The Bridling of Pegasus (entry 1090).

314 British Quarterly Review, 73 (April 1881), 500-502.
        Review of Studies in Song.

315 The Congregationalist, 10 (Feb. 1881), 152-159.
     Review of Studies in Song.

316 Critic (New York), 1 (Dec. 17, 1881), 351.
     Review of Mary Stuart.

317 Dial, 1 (Jan. 1881), 192.
     Review of Studies in Song.

318 Dowden, Edward. Academy, 19 (Jan. 8, 1881), 20-21.
     Review of Studies in Song.

319 Literary World, 12 (Feb. 26, 1881), 72.
     Review of Studies in Song.

320 Morshead, E. D. A. Academy, 20 (Dec. 10, 1881), 427-428.
     Review of Mary Stuart.

321 "Mr. Swinburne's 'Mary Stuart.'" The Athenaeum, 78 (Dec.
     17, 1881), 814.

322 Nation (New York), 32 (Feb. 10, 1881), 98-99.
     Review of Studies in Song.

323 "Oleo-margarine." Punch, 80 (April 16, 1881), 174.

324 Pall Mall Gazette, Dec. 17, 1881, p. 19.
     Review of Mary Stuart.

325 Saturday Review (London), 52 (Dec. 3, 1881), 702-703.
     Review of Mary Stuart.

326 The Spectator, 54 (March 5, 1881), 316-317.
     Review of Studies in Song.

327 "Swinburne and Water." Punch, 81 (July 23, 1881), 26.

328 Tilley, Arthur. "Two Theories of Poetry." Macmillan's
     Magazine, 44 (Aug. 1881), 268-279.

329 [Watts, Theodore]. The Athenaeum, 77 (Jan. 15, 1881), 90-
     92.
     Review of Studies in Song.

330 _____. The Athenaeum, 78 (Dec. 10, 1881), 771-772.
     Review of Mary Stuart.

331 Westminster Review, 115 (April 1881), 615-616.
     Review of Studies in Song.

332 Wheeler, Alfred A. "Swinburne on Art and Life." Califor-
     nian, 3 (Feb. 1881), 129-131.

1882

Swinburne's Tristram of Lyonesse and Other Poems (hereafter referred to as Tristram) was published in 1882.

Books

333   Hamilton, Walter.   "Algernon Charles Swinburne."   The
        Aesthetic Movement in England.   London: Turner, 1882.
        pp. 61-68.

334   Hayne, Paul Hamilton.   "Sonnets to Algernon Charles Swin-
        burne."   Paul Hamilton Hayne.   Boston: 1882.   p. 269.
        Reprinted from Literary World, Jan. 17, 1880 (entry 290).

335   Shepard, William [pseudonym of William Shepard Walsh].
        "Swinburne and Oscar Wilde."   Pen Pictures of Modern
        Authors.   New York: Putnam, 1882.   pp. 202-215.

336   Traill, H. D.   Recaptured Rhymes: Political and Other Fu-
        gitives Arrested.   London: Blackwood, 1882.

Periodicals

337   American, 1 (Nov. 1882), 75-76.
        Review of Tristram.

338   Bayne, Thomas.   "Mr. Swinburne's Trilogy."   Fraser's Maga-
        zine, n. s. 26 (Oct. 1882), 469-479.
        Review of Mary Stuart.

339   British Quarterly Review, 75 (Jan. 1882), 225-226.
        Review of Mary Stuart.

340   British Quarterly Review, 76 (Oct. 1882), 476-478.
        Review of Tristram.

341   "Clowning and Classicism."   Punch, 82 (Jan. 7, 1882), 10-11.

342   Critic (New York), 2 (Aug. 12, 1882), 210.
        Review of Tristram.

343   Dial, 2 (Feb. 1882), 237-238.
        Review of Mary Stuart.

344   Earle, John Charles.   "The Vices of Agnostic Poetry."   Dub-
        lin Review, n. s. 39 (July 1882), 104-120.
        Swinburne discussed on pages 117-120.

345   "In Earnest."   Punch, 82 (Jan. 7, 1882), 12.

346   Lyttleton, Arthur Temple. "Modern Pagan Poetry." Church
Quarterly Review, 14 (July 1882), 367-390.
Discusses Swinburne and James Thomson. Well written.
Reprinted: Modern Poets of Faith, Doubt and Paganism
(entry 754).

347   "Mr. Swinburne's 'Mary Stuart.'" Literary World, 13 (Jan.
14, 1882), 3.
Review of Mary Stuart.

348   "Mr. Swinburne's New Volume." Pall Mall Gazette, July 29,
1882, p. 4.
Review of Tristram.

349   Nation (New York), 34 (April 27, 1882), 360.
Review of Mary Stuart.

350   "Oscar Interviewed." Punch, 82 (Jan. 14, 1882), 14.

351   "Les Poëtes S'amusent." Punch, 83 (Dec. 2, 1882), 261.

352   "A Poet's Day." Punch, 82 (Feb. 4, 1882), 58-59.

353   Saturday Review (London), 54 (July 29, 1882), 156-157.
Review of Tristram.

354   Simcox, G. A. "Mr. Swinburne's Trilogy." Fortnightly Re-
view, n. s. 31 (Feb. 1, 1882), 166-179.
Review of Mary Stuart.
Reprinted: Eclectic Magazine of Foreign Literature, 98
(April 1882), 166-179.

355   The Spectator, 55 (Aug. 12, 1882), 1055-1057.
Review of Tristram.

356   Stedman, Edmund Clarence. "Some London Poets." Harper's
Monthly Magazine, 64 (May 1882), 888-892.

357   "Swinburne's New Poems." Literary World, 13 (Sept. 9,
1882), 293-294.
Review of Tristram.

358   Symonds, John Addington. Academy, 22 (Aug. 5, 1882), 93-
94.
Review of Tristram.

359   Urban, Sylvanus. "Mr. Swinburne's New Poems." Gentleman's Magazine, 253 (Sept. 1882), 384.
Review of Tristram.

360   [Watts, Theodore]. The Athenaeum, 80 (July 22, 1882), 103-
105.
Review of Tristram.

361   Westminster Review, 118 (July 1882), 278.
          Review of Mary Stuart.

362   Westminster Review, 118 (Oct. 1882), 586-587.
          Review of Tristram.

1883

Swinburne published A Century of Roundels (hereafter referred to
as Roundels) in 1883.

Books

363   Gower, Ronald Sutherland.   My Reminiscences.   London:
          Kegan, Paul, Trench, 1883.
          Swinburne mentioned on pages 289-290.

364   Hazeltine, Mayo Williamson.   "Swinburne."   Chats About
          Books, Poets, and Novelists.   New York: 1883.   pp. 91-
          150.

365   Shepherd, Richard Herne.   The Bibliography of Swinburne: A
          Bibliographical List Arranged in Chronological Order of the
          Published Writings in Verse and Prose of Algernon Charles
          Swinburne (1857-1883).   [London: Billing, 1883.]
          This bibliography has been the source of some confusion for
          students of Swinburne, primarily because it is incomplete.
          Noted: Academy, Aug. 25, 1883 (entry 366).
          Reviewed: Notes and Queries, Sept. 15, 1883 (entry 379).

Periodicals

366   Academy, 24 (Aug. 25, 1883), 127.
          Notice of the publication of R. H. Shepherd's The Bibliog-
          raphy of Swinburne (entry 365).

367   American, 6 (July 28, 1883), 248-249.
          Review of Roundels.

368   British Quarterly Review, 78 (July 1883), 227-228.
          Review of Roundels.

369   Courtney, W. L.   "Poets of To-day."   Fortnightly Review,
          40 (Nov. 1883), 712-727.
          Swinburne discussed on pages 715-716.

370   Critic (New York), 3 (Oct. 13, 1883), 403-404.
          Review of Roundels.

371   Dial, 3 (March 1883), 255.
      Review of Tristram.

372   Ker, W. P. "Poetry." Contemporary Review, 44 (Sept.
          1883), 466-467.
      Review of Roundels.

373   Le Livre, 4 (Oct. 10, 1883), 617.
      Review of Roundels.

374   "Mr. Swinburne and Mary Stuart." Lippincott's Monthly Maga-
          zine, 32 (Nov. 1883), 506-512.
      Review of Mary Stuart.

375   "Mr. Swinburne's Century of Roundels." The Spectator, 56
          (July 28, 1883), 970.
      Review of Roundels.

376   "Mr. Swinburne's Roundels." Literary World, 14 (July 14,
          1883), 222-223.
      Review of Roundels.

377   "A New Poet." Blackwood's Magazine, 134 (Oct. 1883), 435.

378   Noble, James Ashcroft. Academy, 23 (June 23, 1883), 429-
          430.
      Review of Roundels.

379   Notes and Queries, 6th ser., 8 (Sept. 15, 1883), 220.
          Review of R. H. Shepherd's The Bibliography of Swinburne
          (entry 365).

380   Pall Mall Gazette, July 5, 1883, pp. 4-5.
      Review of Roundels.

381   Schovelin, T. A. Dial, 4 (Aug. 1883), 90-91.
      Review of Roundels.

382   Scottish Review, 2 (Sept. 1883), 398-399.
      Review of Roundels.

383   "Three Representative Poets: Mr. Tennyson, Mr. Swinburne,
          and Mr. Browning." Scottish Review, 2 (Sept. 1883), 334-
          358.
      Swinburne is discussed on pages 343-349.

384   The Times, June 6, 1883, pp. 4-5.
      Review of Roundels.

385   [Watts, Theodore]. The Athenaeum, 81 (June 16, 1883), 755-
          756.
      Review of Roundels.

1884

Swinburne published A Midsummer Holiday and Other Poems (hereafter referred to as A Midsummer Holiday) in 1884.

Books

386   Chiarini, Giuseppe. "A. Swinburne." Ombre e Figure:
        Saggi Critici. Rome: Sommaruga, 1884.
        Reprinted: Saggi di letterature Straniere. Livorno: Vigo,
        1905.

387   Lowell, James Russell. "Swinburne's Tragedies." My Study
        Windows. Boston: Houghton, Mifflin, 1884. pp. 210-226.
        Reprinted from North American Review, April 1866 (entry
        44).

388   Thomson, James. "The Swinburne Controversy." Satires and
        Profanities. London: Progressive, 1884. pp. 99-104.
        Reprinted from the National Reformer, Dec. 23, 1866
        (entry 71).

Periodicals

389   "Christmas Waits." Punch, 87 (Dec. 27, 1884), 303.

390   Critic, (New York), 5 (Nov. 1, 1884), 207.
        Review of Selections from the Poetical Works of A. C.
        Swinburne, ed. Richard Henry Stoddard (New York:
        Crowell, [1884]).

391   Gentleman's Magazine, 257 (Dec. 1884), 620.
        Review of A Midsummer Holiday.

392   "'Les Casquettes.'" Notes and Queries, 6th ser., 9 (March
        15, 1884), 205-206.

393   Literary World, 15 (Sept. 20, 1884), 307.
        Review of Selections from the Poetical Works of A. C.
        Swinburne, ed. Richard Henry Stoddard (New York:
        Crowell, [1884]).

394   Morshead, E. D. A. Academy, 26 (Dec. 6, 1884), 367-368.
        Review of A Midsummer Holiday.

395   "Mr. Swinburne's Debt to the Bible." Scottish Review, 3
        (April 1884), 266-285.

396   "Mr. Swinburne upon Charles Reade." Gentleman's Magazine,
        257 (Nov. 1884), 518-519.

397   The Nation (New York), 39 (Dec. 18, 1884), 527.
      Review of Selections from the Poetical Works of A. C.
      Swinburne, ed. Richard Henry Stoddard (New York:
      Crowell, [1884]).

398   Pall Mall Gazette, Nov. 22, 1884, pp. 4-5.
      Review of A Midsummer Holiday.

399   Payne, William Morton. "Swinburne's Poems." Dial, 5 (Oct.
      1884), 136-139.

400   Saturday Review (London), 58 (Nov. 29, 1884), 697-698.
      Review of A Midsummer Holiday.

401   The Spectator, 57 (Nov. 29, 1884), 1584-1585.
      Review of A Midsummer Holiday.

402   The Times, Nov. 12, 1884, p. 7.
      Review of A Midsummer Holiday.

403   [Watts, Theodore]. The Athenaeum, 84 (Nov. 22, 1884), 651-
      653.

1885

Swinburne published a drama in verse, Marino Faliero, in 1885.

Books

404   Galton, Arthur. "Mr. Swinburne." Urbana Scripta: Studies
      of Five Living Poets. London: Stock, 1885. pp. 108-131.

405   Sarrazin, Gabriel. Poètes Modernes de L'Angleterre. Paris:
      Ollendorf, 1885. pp. 273-348.

406   Shepard, William [pseudonym of William Shepard Walsh].
      "Algernon Charles Swinburne." Enchiridon of Criticism.
      Philadelphia: Lippincott, 1885. pp. 260-262.

Periodicals

407   Book Buyer, n. s. 2 (Feb. 1885), 19.
      Review of A Midsummer Holiday.

408   Book Buyer, n. s. 2 (July 1885), 150.
      Review of Marino Faliero.

409   British Quarterly Review, 81 (Jan. 1885), 212-214.
      Review of A Midsummer Holiday.

410   British Quarterly Review, 82 (July 1885), 207-208.
      Review of Marino Faliero.

411   [Collins, Churton]. "The Predecessors of Shakespeare."
      Quarterly Review, 161 (Oct. 1885), 335-337.

412   Courtney, W. L. "Mr. Swinburne's Poetry." Fortnightly Re-
      view, n. s. 37 (May 1885), 597-610.
      Reprinted: Eclectic Magazine of Foreign Literature, 105
      (July 1885), 119-128; and Studies New and Old (entry 473).

413   Dial, 6 (June 1885), 39-40.
      Review of A Midsummer Holiday.

414   Ker, W. P. The Contemporary Review, 47 (Jan. 1885), 144-
      145.
      Review of A Midsummer Holiday.

415   _____. The Contemporary Review, 48 (Aug. 1885), 287-288.
      Review of Marino Faliero.

416   Robertson, Eric. Academy, 27 (June 13, 1885), 412-414.
      Review of Marino Faliero.

417   Stead, William Taylor. "The Maiden Tribute of Modern Baby-
      lon." Pall Mall Gazette, July 6, 7, 8, and 10, 1885.

418   The Times, May 14, 1885, p. 12.
      Review of Marino Faliero.

419   [Watts, Theodore]. The Athenaeum, 85 (June 13, 1885), 751-
      753.
      Review of Marino Faliero.

420   Woodberry, G. E. Atlantic Monthly, 55 (April 1885), 564-565.
      Review of A Midsummer Holiday.

1886

Swinburne published criticism in 1886: Miscellanies and A Study of
Victor Hugo (hereafter referred to as Victor Hugo).

Books

421   Harrison, Frederic. "On the Choice of Books." The Choice

of Books. London: 1886.
Reprinted from Fortnightly Review, April 1, 1879 (entry
274).

422 Lang, Andrew. "To Lord Byron." Letters to Dead Authors.
New York: Scribner, 1886. pp. 205-215.
Poem.

Periodicals

423 Anderson, Melville B. "Swinburne the Critic." Dial, 7 (Nov.
1886), 156-158.
Review of Miscellanies.

424 "Babydom." Punch, 91 (Dec. 11, 1886), 281.

425 [Collins, Churton]. "Mr. Swinburne and the 'Quarterly Review.'" The Athenaeum, 88 (Nov. 13, 1886), 636.

426 Critic (New York), n. s. 5 (April 17, 1886), 192-193.
Review of Victor Hugo.

427 Dial, 6 (Jan. 1886), 248-249.
Review of Marino Faliero.

428 Dial, 6 (March 1886), 305.
Review of Victor Hugo.

429 Graham, P. Anderson. "Mr. Swinburne's Poetry." The Con-
temporary Review, 50 (Sept. 1886), 401-411.
Reprinted: Eclectic Magazine of Foreign Literature, 107
(Nov. 1886), 607-614.

430 Huss, H. C. O. Modern Language Notes, 1 (April 1886), 59-
60.
Review of Victor Hugo.

431 Literary World (Boston), 17 (April 3, 1886), 114.
Review of Victor Hugo.

432 Literary World (London), n. s. 33 (June 25, 1886), 613-615.
Review of Miscellanies.

433 London Quarterly Review, 65 (Jan. 1886), 247-250.
Review of A Midsummer Holiday.

434 Morshead, E. D. A. Academy, 29 (March 27, 1886), 211-212.
Review of Victor Hugo.

435 Nation (New York), 42 (Feb. 25, 1886), 175.
Review of Victor Hugo.

436 Notes and Queries, 7th ser., 2 (July 24, 1886), 79.
Review of Miscellanies.

437   Pall Mall Gazette, Feb. 27, 1886, p. 5.
      Review of Victor Hugo.

438   Pall Mall Gazette, June 7, 1886, p. 5.
      Review of Miscellanies.

439   Saturday Review (London), 62 (July 17, 1886), 100-101.
      Review of Miscellanies.

440   The Spectator, 59 (Sept. 18, 1886), 1248-1249.
      Review of Miscellanies.

441   The Times, March 6, 1886, p. 15.
      Review of Victor Hugo.

442   Urban, Sylvanus. "Mr. Swinburne on Victor Hugo." Gentle-
      man's Magazine, 261 (July 1886), 103.
      Review of Victor Hugo.

443   [Watts, Theodore]. The Athenaeum, 87 (March 13, 1886),
      351-353.
      Review of Victor Hugo.

444   _____. The Athenaeum, 87 (June 19, 1886), 803-805.
      Review of Miscellanies.

1887

The year 1887 was marked by Swinburne's publication of Locrine, a
play in verse.

Books

445   Bleibtrau, Karl. "Geschichte der englischen Literatur im
      neunzehnten Jahrhundert." Geschichte der Weltliteratur.
      Vol. II. Leipzig: Friedrich, [1887]. pp. 507-509.

446   Fockens, Pieter. Maria Stuart: eine literarhistorische Studie.
      Berlin: Schade, 1887.
      Publication of a dissertation (entry 448).

447   Gilchrist, Herbert Harlakenden. Anne Gilchrist. London:
      Unwin, 1887. p. 137.

Dissertation

448   Fockens, Pieter. Maria Stuart: eine literarhistorische Studie.

Leipzig, 1887.
Discusses Chastelard.
Published: Maria Stuart (entry 446).

Periodicals

449 "Bombastes Swinburneoso." Critic (New York), 11 (Aug. 27, 1887), 104-105.

450 Critic (New York), 11 (Oct. 1, 1887), 162.

451 Dowden, Edward. "Victorian Literature." Fortnightly Review, 47 (June 1887), 861-863.

452 Garrod, Herbert B. Academy, 32 (Dec. 10, 1887), 381-382. Review of Locrine.

453 "Havoc." Punch, 93 (Aug. 13, 1887), 61.

454 "Laus Veneris vs. Leaves of Grass." Public Opinion (New York), 3 (Aug. 20, 1887), 407.

455 Literary World (Boston), 18 (Oct. 1, 1887), 329.

456 Morshead, E. D. A. Academy, 32 (Sept. 3, 1887), 145-146.

457 "Mr. Swinburne's Politics." Pall Mall Gazette, Aug. 4, 1887, pp. 2-3.

458 Nation (New York), 45 (Aug. 4, 1887), 97.

459 Pall Mall Gazette, Nov. 16, 1887, p. 4.

460 Pall Mall Gazette, Nov. 18, 1887, p. 3. Review of Locrine.

461 Payne, W. M. Dial, 8 (Dec. 1887), 185.

462 "Pot and Kettle." Punch, 92 (May 21, 1887), 245.

463 Saturday Review (London), 64 (Dec. 3, 1887), 763-764. Review of Locrine.

464 Shepherd, Richard Herne. "Mr. Swinburne's 'Locrine.'" Gentleman's Magazine, 263 (Dec. 1887), 608-614. Review of Locrine.

465 Symonds, John Addington. "A Note on Whitmania." Fortnightly Review, n. s. 42 (Sept. 1887), 459-460.

466 "Thomas Dekker." Notes and Queries, 7th ser., 3 (April 23, 1887), 324-325.

467 The Times, Nov. 18, 1887, pp. 13-14.
     Review of Locrine.

468 Underhill, George F. "The Philosophical Poetry of Mr. Swin-
     burne." Book-Lore, 6 (Oct. 1887), 121-125.

469 [Watts, Theodore]. The Athenaeum, 89 (June 4, 1887), 727-
     729.

470 _____. The Athenaeum, 90 (Dec. 24, 1887), 856-859.
     Review of Locrine.

1888

Books

471 Adam, Villiers de l'Isle. "Le sadisme anglais." Histoire
     Insolites. Paris: 1888.

472 Clifford, William Kingdon. Cosmic Emotion. New York:
     Humbolt, 1888.
     Reprinted from Nineteenth Century, Oct. 1877 (entry 238).
     See entry 238 for other reprinting.

473 Courtney, W. L. "Mr. Swinburne's Poetry." Studies New
     and Old. London: Chapman, 1888. pp. 124-149.
     Reprinted from Fortnightly Review, May 1885 (entry 412).
     See entry 412 for other reprinting.

474 Taylor, Henry. Correspondence of Henry Taylor. Ed. Ed-
     ward Dowden. London: Longmans, Green, 1888. pp. 398-
     399, 406, 407, and 417-418.

Periodicals

475 "Another Ode to March." Punch, 94 (March 17, 1888), 125.

476 Bowker, R. R. "London as a Literary Center." Harper's
     Monthly Magazine, 76 (May 1888), 820.

477 Critic (New York), 13 (Nov. 17, 1888), 242.
     Review of Locrine.

478 Literary World (Boston), 19 (Feb. 18, 1888), 54.
     Review of Locrine.

479 Nation (New York), 46 (May 17, 1888), 410-411.
     Review of Locrine.

480   Parker, H. T. "A Study in Swinburne." The Harvard Month-
      ly, 6 (March 1888), 30-39.

481   Payne, W. M. Dial, 8 (Feb. 1888), 247.
      Review of Locrine.

482   The Spectator, 61 (Jan. 7, 1888), 16-17.
      Review of Locrine.

483   Westminster Review, 129 (March 1888), 392.
      Review of Locrine.

1889

Poems and Ballads: Third Series was published in 1889, as well
as a critical work, A Study of Ben Jonson (hereafter referred to
as Ben Jonson).

Books

484   Lang, Andrew. Letters on Literature. London: Longmans,
      Green, 1889. pp. 20-23.

485   Patmore, Coventry. "Mr. Swinburne's Selections." Principle
      in Art. London: Bell, 1889. pp. 112-117.

Periodicals

486   Book Buyer, n. s. 6 (Sept. 1889), 280-281.
      Review of Poems and Ballads: Third Series.

487   Cotterell, George. Academy, 35 (April 27, 1889), 279-280.
      Review of Poems and Ballads: Third Series.

488   Critic (New York), 15 (Nov. 16, 1889), 238-239.
      Review of Poems and Ballads: Third Series.

489   Davidson, John. Academy, 36 (Nov. 23, 1889), 331-332.
      Review of Ben Jonson.

490   "Mr. Swinburne's Poems and Ballads." Gentleman's Maga-
      zine, 267 (July 1889), 103-104.
      Review of Poems and Ballads: Third Series.

491   Literary World (Boston), 20 (July 6, 1889), 223.
      Review of Poems and Ballads: Third Series.

492   Nation (New York), 49 (Dec. 26, 1889), 522.
      Review of Poems and Ballads: Third Series.

493   "The New Swinburne." The Scots Observer, 1 (April 27,
      1889), 639-640.
      Review of Poems and Ballads: Third Series.

494   Payne, W. M. Dial, 10 (Sept. 1889), 103-104.
      Review of Poems and Ballads: Third Series.

495   Public Opinion, 7 (April 27, 1889), 67.
      Review of Poems and Ballads: Third Series.

496   Saturday Review (London), 67 (April 20, 1889), 482-483.
      Review of Poems and Ballads: Third Series.

497   The Spectator, 62 (June 1, 1889), 764-765.
      Review of Poems and Ballads: Third Series.

498   The Times, April 10, 1889, p. 16.
      Review of Poems and Ballads: Third Series.

499   The Times, Nov. 12, 1889, p. 3.
      Review of Ben Jonson.

500   Urban, Sylvanus. "Mr. Swinburne on Ben Jonson." Gentle-
      man's Magazine, 267 (Dec. 1889), 631-632.
      Review of Ben Jonson.

501   _____. "Mr. Swinburne's Poetic Awards." Gentleman's
      Magazine, 267 (Dec. 1889), 632.

502   [Watts, Theodore]. The Athenaeum, 93 (May 25, 1889), 655-
      658.
      Review of Poems and Ballads: Third Series.

503   Wilde, Oscar. Pall Mall Gazette, June 27, 1889, p. 3.
      Review of Poems and Ballads: Third Series.

1890

Books

504   Dawson, W. J. The Makers of Modern English. New York:
      1890.
      Listed in C. K. Hyder, Swinburne's Literary Career and
      Fame (entry 1761), page 343. Not examined.

505 Gildersleeve, Basil Lanneau. "The Legend of Venus." Es-
       says and Studies: Educational and Literary. Baltimore:
       Murray, 1890. pp. 161-205.
       Reprinted from Southern Review, April 1867 (entry 84).

506 Reid, T. Wemyss. The Life, Letters, and Friendships of
       Richard Monckton Milnes, First Lord Houghton. Vol. II.
       London: Cassell, 1890.

507 Sarrazin, Gabriel. La Renaissance de la Poésie Anglaise,
       1798-1889. Paris: Perrin, 1890.

508 Steuart, John A. "A. C. Swinburne." Letters to Living Au-
       thors. London: Sampson Low, Marston, 1890.
       Reviewed: The Speaker, Nov. 8, 1890 (entry 520).

Periodicals

509 "Algernon Charles Swinburne." The Speaker, 2 (Aug. 9,
       1890), 152-153.

510 "'The Big Gun': Poem." Punch, 98 (March 8, 1890), 114.

511 "The Coming Laureate." Public Opinion (New York), 8 (March
       22, 1890), 568.

512 Critic (New York), 16 (March 1, 1890), 101-102.
       Review of Ben Jonson.

513 Dial, 10 (April 1890), 341-342.
       Review of Ben Jonson.

514 Furniss, Henry. "Fancy Portrait of Algernon Charles Swin-
       burne." Punch, 99 (Aug. 16, 1890), 83.

515 Gladstone, W. E. "British Poetry of the Nineteenth Century."
       The Speaker, 1 (Jan. 11, 1890), 34.

516 "Modern Men: Algernon Charles Swinburne." Scots Observer,
       3 (March 8, 1890), 430-431.

517 "Mr. Swinburne's Lyrics." Edinburgh Review, 171 (April
       1890), 429-452.
       Discusses Poems and Ballads: Second Series and Poems
       and Ballads: Third Series.

518 Nation (New York), 50 (March 6, 1890), 208-209.
       Review of Ben Jonson.

519 Schelling, Felix E. Modern Language Notes, 5 (June 1890),
       183-185.
       Review of Ben Jonson.

520   The Speaker, 2 (Nov. 8, 1890), 530-531.
      Review of J. A. Steuart's Letters to Living Authors (entry
      508).

521   "Swinburne on Ben Jonson." Literary World (Boston), 21
      (March 15, 1890), 88-89.
      Review of Ben Jonson.

522   "Tennyson: and After?" Fortnightly Review, 53 (May 1,
      1890), 621-637.
      Swinburne discussed on pages 625-629 and mentioned again
      on page 637.

523   Urban, Sylvanus. "The Laureate and Mr. Swinburne."
      Gentleman's Magazine, 268 (April 1890), 431.

1891

Books

524   Maupassant, Guy de. "Notes sur Swinburne." Ballades et
      Poèmes de A. C. Swinburne. Trans. Gabriel Mourey.
      Paris: Albert Savine, 1891. pp. v-x.
      Guy de Maupassant's introduction to this French translation
      of Swinburne's poetry is of special interest to students
      of Swinburne's reputation; his view of the English poet
      helped to form French opinion.
      Excerpted: C. K. Hyder, Swinburne: The Critical Heri-
      tage (entry 2083), pages 185-187. English translation by
      Violette Lang.

525   Sharp, Amy. "Dante Gabriel Rossetti, William Morris, and
      Algernon Charles Swinburne." Victorian Poets. London:
      Methuen, 1891. pp. 157-185.
      Swinburne discussed on pages 178-185. Includes short
      chronology of Swinburne's works on page xvi.
      Reviewed: The Speaker, Aug. 15, 1891 (entry 528).
      Reprinted: Port Washington, N.Y., and London: Kennikat,
      1970.

Periodicals

526   Quesnel, Léo. "Algernon Charles Swinburne: poète et
      prosateur." Bibliothèque Universelle et Revue Suisse,
      3rd ser., 50 (April 1891), 152-172.

527   Shindler, Robert. "The Theology of Mr. Swinburne's Poems."

Gentleman's Magazine, n. s. 47 (Nov. 1891), 459-471.
Reprinted: Eclectic Magazine of Foreign Literature, 118
(Jan. 1892), 109-116.

528 The Speaker, 4 (Aug. 15, 1891), 206-207.
Review of Amy Sharp's Victorian Poets (entry 525).

1892

Swinburne's drama in verse The Sisters was published in 1892.
Tennyson died on October 6th, and Swinburne was among those
mentioned in the press as a possible successor to the Poet
Laureateship.

Books

529 Cheney, John Vance. "Six Minutes with Swinburne." The
     Golden Guess: Essays on Poetry and the Poets. Boston:
     Lee and Shepard, 1892. pp. 203-212.

530 Cochrane, Robert. "Algernon Charles Swinburne." The
     Treasury of Modern Biography. Edinburgh: Nimmo, Nay,
     and Mitchell, 1892. pp. 541-542.

531 Oliphant, Margaret. "Algernon Swinburne, 1837." The Vic-
     torian Age of English Literature. Vol. II. New York:
     Tait, [1892]. pp. 437-442.

532 Pain, Barry. "The Poets at Tea: III. Swinburne, Who Let
     It Get Cold." Playthings and Parodies. New York: Cas-
     sell, [1892]. p. 226.

533 Scott, William Bell. Autobiographical Notes of the Life of
     William Bell Scott. Ed. William Minto. London: Osgood,
     McIlvaine, 1892. Vol. II.
     Swinburne discussed on pages 14-20.

534 Stedman, Edmund Clarence. The Nature of Elements of Po-
     etry. Boston: Houghton, Mifflin, 1892.
     Swinburne on pages 131-133.

Periodicals

535 The Bookman (London), 2 (June 1892), 88.
     Review of The Sisters.

536 Cotterell, George. Academy, 42 (July 2, 1892), 5.
     Review of The Sisters.

537   Critic (New York), 21 (Oct. 15, 1892), 213.
        Mentions Swinburne as possibly the next Poet Laureate.

538   Critic (New York), 21 (Dec. 1892), 308.
        Review of The Sisters.

539   Gentleman's Magazine, 273 (Aug. 1892), 212.
        Review of The Sisters.

540   "The Laureateship." Critic (New York), 21 (Nov. 5, 1892),
        255-256.

541   "The Laureateship." Illustrated London News, 101 (Oct. 15,
        1892), 491.

542   "The Laureateship." The Spectator, 69 (Oct. 15, 1892), 517-
        518.

543   Literary Digest, 5 (June 18, 1892), 187.
        Review of The Sisters.

544   Literary World (Boston), 23 (July 16, 1892), 239-240.
        Review of The Sisters.

545   Minto, William. "Mr. W. B. Scott's Autobiography."
        Academy, 42 (Dec. 10, 1892), 541-542.
        This is a reply to Swinburne's and William Sharp's criti-
        cism of William Bell Scott's Autobiographical Notes (entry
        533). Swinburne's criticism appeared in Fortnightly Re-
        view, Dec. 1892, pages 830-833. Swinburne answered
        Minto in a letter published in the December 24th issue of
        the Academy, pages 590-591.

546   National Observer, 8 (May 28, 1892), 43-44.
        Review of The Sisters.

547   "The Next Laureate." Pall Mall Budget, 40 (Oct. 13, 1892),
        1514.

548   Payne, W. M. Dial, 13 (Sept. 16, 1892), 185-186.
        Review of The Sisters.

549   Public Opinion, 14 (Nov. 26, 1892), 193.
        Review of The Sisters.

550   Public Opinion, 14 (Dec. 10, 1892), 241.
        Review of Locrine.

551   "The Question of the Laureateship." The Bookman (London),
        3 (Nov. 1892), 52-55.

552   Saturday Review (London), 73 (May 21, 1892), 602.
        Review of The Sisters.

553   The Spectator, 69 (July 2, 1892), 19-21.
      Review of The Sisters.

554   The Times, May 12, 1892, p. 10.
      Review of The Sisters.

555   Urban, Sylvanus.   "Mr. Swinburne's Praise of Northumber-
      land."   Gentleman's Magazine, 273 (Aug. 1892), 212-213.

556   Walford, L. B.   "London Letter."   Critic (New York), 20
      (June 4, 1892), 317-318.
      Discusses The Sisters.

557   [Watts, Theodore].   The Athenaeum, 100 (July 2, 1892), 31-32.
      Review of The Sisters.

558   "Who Will Be Poet Laureate?"   Atlantic Monthly, 70 (Dec.
      1892), 855-856.

1893

Books

559   Myers, Frederic W. H.   "Modern Poets and the Meaning of
      Life."   Science and a Future Life.   London: Macmillan,
      1893.   pp. 166-210.
      Reprinted from Nineteenth Century, Jan. 1893 (entry 564).
      See entry 564 for other reprinting.

560   Watson, William.   "Some Literary Idolatries."   Excursions in
      Criticism.   London: Mathews and Lane, 1893.   pp. 1-22.

Periodicals

561   Archer, William.   "Webster, Lamb, and Swinburne."   New
      Review, 8 (Jan. 1893), 96-106.

562   "A. Swinburne."   Punch, 104 (May 13, 1893), 221.

563   "Contemporary Poets and Versifiers."   Edinburgh Review,
      178 (Oct. 1893), 469-499.
      Swinburne on page 471.

564   Myers, Frederic W. H.   "Modern Poets and the Meaning of
      Life."   Nineteenth Century, 33 (Jan. 1893), 93-111.
      Reprinted: Science and a Future Life (entry 559); and
      C. K. Hyder, Swinburne: The Critical Heritage (entry
      2083), pages 188-197.

1894

Swinburne published Astrophel and Other Poems (hereafter referred
to as Astrophel) and Studies in Prose and Poetry in 1894.

Books

565 Lowell, James Russell. Letters of James Russell Lowell.
        Ed. Charles Eliot Norton. New York: Harper, 1894.
        Vol. I.
        Swinburne mentioned on page 377.

566 Slater, J. H. Early Editions. London: Kegan, Paul, Trench,
        Trübner, 1894.
        Bibliography. Swinburne on pages 288-303.
        Reviewed: T. J. Wise, The Bookman (London), May 1894
        (entry 591).

567 Smith, C. Alphonso. "Repetition in the Poems of Algernon
        Charles Swinburne." Repetition and Parallelism in English
        Verse. New York: University Publishing Co., 1894. pp.
        57-76.

Periodicals

568 Book Buyer, n.s. 11 (July 1894), 296-297.
        Review of Astrophel.

569 The Bookman (London), 6 (June 1894), 74-76.
        Review of Astrophel.

570 The Bookman (London), 7 (Dec. 1894), 83-84.
        Review of Studies in Prose and Poetry.

571 Critic (New York), 25 (July 21, 1894), 35.
        Review of Astrophel.

572 Hankin, St. John. Academy, 46 (Dec. 29, 1894), 547-548.
        Review of Studies in Prose and Poetry.

573 Hannigan, D. F. "Mr. Swinburne as a Critic." Westminster
        Review, 142 (Aug. 1894), 142-145.

574 Henley, W. E. "The New Swinburne." Pall Mall Gazette,
        June 13, 1894, p. 4.
        Review of Astrophel.
        Reprinted: Critic (New York), 25 (July 21, 1894), 45-46.

575 Johnson, M. "The Poetry of Swinburne." The Primitive
        Methodist Quarterly Review, n.s. 16 (July 1894), 414-427.

576   Literary World (London), n. s. 50 (Dec. 21, 1894), 491-492.
      Review of Studies in Prose and Poetry.

577   Morshead, E. D. A. Academy, 45 (May 26, 1894), 429.
      Review of Astrophel.

578   "Mr. Swinburne's 'Astrophel.'" Saturday Review (London), 77
      (May 5, 1894), 472-473.
      Review of Astrophel.

579   "Mr. Swinburne's 'Astrophel.'" The Spectator, 72 (June 16,
      1894), 828-829.
      Review of Astrophel.

580   Poet Lore, 6 (June-July 1894), 375.
      Review of Astrophel.

581   Quiller-Couch, Arthur Thomas. "Mr. Swinburne's 'Astrophel.'"
      The Speaker, 9 (May 5, 1894), 500-502.
      Review of Astrophel.

582   Saturday Review (London), 78 (Nov. 17, 1894), 539-540.
      Review of Studies in Prose and Poetry.

583   "Swinburne and the 'Little Folk.'" The Speaker, 9 (May 12,
      1894), 529.

584   "Swinburne's New Poem." Literary World (London), n. s. 49
      (May 18, 1894), 451-452.
      Review of Astrophel.

585   Urban, Sylvanus. "Mr. Swinburne's New Poems." Gentle-
      man's Magazine, 276 (June 1894), 640-644.
      Review of Astrophel.

586   The Times, April 26, 1894, p. 6.
      Review of Astrophel.

587   The Times, Nov. 6, 1894, p. 13.
      Review of Studies in Prose and Poetry.

588   [Watts, Theodore]. The Athenaeum, 103 (June 2, 1894), 701-
      703.
      Review of Astrophel.

589   [Watts, Theodore]. The Athenaeum, 104 (Dec. 22, 1894),
      853-855.
      Review of Studies in Prose and Poetry.

590   Waugh, Arthur. "Reticence in Literature." The Yellow Book,
      1 (April 1894), p. 213.
      Reprinted: Reticence in Literature (entry 1209).

591   Wise, T. J. The Bookman (London), 6 (May 1894), 49-50.
      Review of J. H. Slater's Early Editions (entry 566).

592   "The Young Men." Contemporary Review, 65 (Feb. 1894), 178.

1895

Books

593   Hallard, James Henry. "The Poetry of Mr. Swinburne."
      Gallica: and Other Essays. London: Longmans, Green,
      1895. pp. 128-142.

594   Le Gallienne, Richard. "In a Copy of Mr. Swinburne's
      'Tristram of Lyonesse.'" English Poems. London: Lane,
      1895. p. 51.

595   Mourey, Gabriel. "Une visite à Algernon Charles Swinburne."
      Passé le Détroit: la vie et l'art à Londres. Paris:
      Ollendorff, 1895.

596   Nordau, Max. Degeneration. New York: Appleton, 1895.
      Swinburne on pages 94-98.

597   Rossetti, William Michael. Dante Gabriel Rossetti: His Fam-
      ily Letters with a Memoir. London: 1895.

598   Saintsbury, George. "Mr. Swinburne." Corrected Impres-
      sions: Essays on Victorian Writers. New York: Dodd,
      Mead, 1895.
      Reprinted: The Collected Essays and Papers of George
      Saintsbury, 1875-1920 (entry 1497); and C. K. Hyder,
      Swinburne: The Critical Heritage (entry 2083), pages 198-
      206.

599   [Skelton, John, writing as "Shirley"]. The Table-Talk of
      Shirley. Edinburgh and London: Blackwood, 1895.
      Swinburne on pages 136-137.

Periodicals

600   Coupe, Charles. "Mr. Swinburne's 'Studies in Prose and
      Poetry': A Critique." Dublin Review, 116 (April 1895),
      338-362.
      Review of Studies in Prose and Poetry.

601   Gentleman's Magazine, 278 (Jan. 1895), 105-108.
      Review of Studies in Prose and Poetry.

602 National Observer, 13 (March 2, 1895), 427.
     Review of Studies in Prose and Poetry.

603 Plowman, Thomas F. "The Aesthetes: The Story of a
     Nineteenth-Century Cult. " Pall Mall Magazine, 5 (Jan.
     1895), 27-44.

604 Pollock, Walter Herries. "The Laureateship. " National Ob-
     server, 13 (Jan. 12, 1895), 233-234.

605 "Swinburne's Mania for Alliteration. " Literary Digest, 11
     (May 25, 1895), 100.

606 "A Valediction to St. Valentine. " Punch, 108 (Feb. 23, 1895),
     95.
     Poem parodying Swinburne's "Dolores. "

607 "The Victorian Garden of Song. " Dial, 19 (Nov. 1, 1895), 238.
     Poem.

608 "Who Should Be Laureate?" The Idler, 7 (1895), 400-419.

1896

Swinburne's The Tale of Balen (hereafter referred to as Balen),
poetry, was published in 1896.

Books

609 Knight, William. Memoir of John Nichol. Glasgow:
     MacLehose, 1896.

610 Seaman, Owen. "A Song of Renunciation. " The Battle of the
     Bays. London: Lane, 1896. pp. 1-4.

Periodicals

611 [Anderson, Melville Best]. "To Swinburne: Poem. " Dial,
     21 (Oct. 1, 1896), 199.

612 Atlantic Monthly, 78 (Oct. 1896), 569-570.
     Review of Balen.

613 Book Buyer, n. s. 13 (June 1896), 307.
     Review of Balen.

614 The Bookman (New York), 3 (July 1896), 395-396.
     Review of Balen.

615   Critic (New York), 29 (July 4, 1896), 4-5.
      Review of Balen.

616   D'Esterre-Keeling, Elsa.   Academy, 49 (June 13, 1896), 481-
      482.
      Review of Balen.

617   "The Ethics of Mr. Swinburne's Poetry."   Saturday Review
      (London), 81 (Jan. 25, 1896), 95-97.

618   The Guardian, 51 (June 10, 1896), 905.
      Review of Balen.

619   Lang, Andrew.   Cosmopolis, 3 (July 1896), 69-70.
      Review of Balen.

620   Literary World (London), n. s. 53 (June 5, 1896), 536-537.
      Review of Balen.

621   Macdonell, Anne.   The Bookman (London), 10 (July 1896), 112.
      Review of Balen.

622   "Mr. Swinburne on Christianity."   Saturday Review (London),
      81 (March 21, 1896), 296-298.

623   Nation (New York), 63 (Oct. 8, 1896), 274.
      Review of Balen.

624   Payne, W. M.   Dial, 21 (Sept. 1, 1896), 119-120.
      Review of Balen.

625   Saturday Review (London), 82 (Aug. 15, 1896), 166-167.
      Review of Balen.

626   The Times, May 28, 1896, p. 12.
      Review of Balen.

627   Urban, Sylvanus.   Gentleman's Magazine, 281 (July 1896),
      106-108.
      Review of Balen.

628   [Watts, Theodore].   The Athenaeum, 107 (June 20, 1896),
      799-800.
      Review of Balen.

1897

Books

629 Guthrie, William Norman. "Algernon Charles Swinburne. "
       Modern Poet Prophets. Cincinnati: Clarke, 1897. pp.
       110-115.

630 Lowry, James M. "Spasmodeus in Swinburnia: A Fragment
       of Greek Tragedy. " The Keys "At Home": and Spasmodeus
       in Swinburnia. London: Simpkin, Marshall, 1897. pp. 65-
       78.

631 MacArthur, Henry. "A. C. Swinburne. " Realism and Ro-
       mance: and Other Essays. Edinburgh: Hunter, 1897.
       pp. 165-203.

632 Nencioni, Enrico. "Locrine di Swinburne. " Saggi critici di
       letteratura inglese. Firenze: Le Monnier, 1897. pp. 346-
       348.

633 Payne, William Morton. "Algernon Charles Swinburne. " Li-
       brary of the World's Best Literature. Ed. Charles Dudley
       Warner. New York: 1897.
       Reprinted: C. K. Hyder, Swinburne: The Critical Heri-
       tage (entry 2083), pp. 207-212.

634 Shorter, Clement King. Victorian Literature. New York:
       Dodd, Mead, 1897.
       Swinburne on pages 16-17.

635 Smith, Byron Caldwell. A Young Scholar's Letters: Being a
       Memoir of Byron Caldwell Smith. Ed. D. O. Kellogg.
       New York and London: Putnam, 1897.
       Swinburne mentioned on pages 73-75 and 99-101.

636 Tennyson, Hallam. Alfred Lord Tennyson: A Memoir by His
       Son. London: Macmillan, 1897.
       Swinburne mentioned on pages 425 and 496 in Volume I,
       and on page 285 in Volume II.
       Reprinted: New York: Greenwood, 1969.

637 Wise, T. J. A Bibliographical List of the Scarcer Works and
       Uncollected Writings of Algernon Charles Swinburne. Lon-
       don: T. J. Wise, 1897.

Periodicals

638 Academy, 52 (Nov. 27, 1897), 449; and 52 (Dec. 4, 1897),
       483.
       A letter from Swinburne on a proposed English Academy,

and further commentary.
See Academy, Nov. 6, 1897, below (entry 639).

639   "An Academy of Letters." Academy, 52 (Nov. 6, 1897), 376.
        See Academy, Nov. 27 and Dec. 4, 1897, above (entry
        638).

640   Gosse, Edmund William. "The Literature of the Victorian
        Era." The English Illustrated Magazine, 17 (July 1897),
        491.

641   "Mr. Swinburne's Frenzy." The Speaker, 16 (Nov. 27, 1897),
        603.

1898

---

642   Literary World (London), n. s. 58 (Dec. 16, 1898), 486.
        Review of Elizabeth Barrett Browning's Aurora Leigh, with
        a preface by Swinburne (London: Smith, Elder, 1898).

643   Phillips, Stephen. "The Poetry of Byron." Cornhill Maga-
        zine, n. s. 4 (Jan. 1898), 20.

1899

The year 1899 was marked by the publication of Swinburne's drama
in verse Rosamund: Queen of the Lombards, and the first dissertation devoted to Swinburne, that of Hermann Wollaeger (entry 649).

Books

644   Adams, Francis. "The Poetry and Criticism of Mr. Swin-
        burne." Essays in Modernity. London: Lane, 1899. pp.
        119-141.

645   Dawson, William James. "Algernon Charles Swinburne."
        The Makers of Modern Poetry. London: 1899.

646   Gosse, Edmund. Locrine. [London: privately printed, 1899].
        Four-page brochure.

647 Scudder, Vida D. The Life of the Spirit in the Modern Eng-
       lish Poets. Boston: Houghton, Mifflin, 1899.
       Swinburne on pages 278-280.

648 Wollaeger, Hermann Wilhelm Franz. Studien über Swinburnes
       poetischen Stil. Heidelberg: Geisendörfer, 1899.
       Publication of dissertation (entry 649), below.

Dissertation

649 Wollaeger, Hermann Wilhelm Franz. Studien über Swinburnes
       poetischen Stil. Heidelberg, 1899.

Periodicals

650 Academy, 57 (Oct. 14, 1899), 417.

651 Academy, 57 (Nov. 11, 1899), 529.

652 B. M. R. "To Mr. Swinburne." Academy, 57 (Nov. 18, 1899),
       578.
       Poem.

653 "Caricature." Academy, 56 (June 24, 1899), 686-687.

654 "Classic or Romantic." Literature, 5 (Nov. 4, 1899), 431-
       432.
       Review of Rosamund: Queen of the Lombards.

655 Dean, Jonathan. "For an Anthology of Parody." Academy,
       57 (Nov. 18, 1899), 578.

656 Independent, 51 (Dec. 21, 1899), 3431-3432.
       Review of Rosamund: Queen of the Lombards.

657 Literary World (Boston), n. s. 60 (Nov. 10, 1899), 351-352.
       Review of Rosamund: Queen of the Lombards.

658 Macdonell, Anne. The Bookman (London), 17 (Dec. 1899), 86.
       Review of Rosamund: Queen of the Lombards.

659 "Mr. Swinburne's New Tragedy." The Speaker, n. s. 1 (Nov.
       4, 1899), 118-120.
       Review of Rosamund: Queen of the Lombards.
       Reprinted: Public Opinion, 27 (Dec. 7, 1899), 723-724.

660 "The New Swinburne." Academy, 57 (Nov. 11, 1899), 534-
       535.
       Review of Rosamund: Queen of the Lombards.

661 "Pegasus on the War-Path." Truth (London), 46 (Nov. 30,
       1899), 1329.

662   Saturday Review (London), 88 (Nov. 11, 1899), 619-620.
      Review of Rosamund: Queen of the Lombards.

663   "Swinburne's New Drama." Literary Digest, 19 (Dec. 16,
      1899), 737.
      Review of Rosamund: Queen of the Lombards.

664   "'Wan Legends': Mr. Swinburne on the Stage." Academy,
      56 (March 25, 1899), 362-363.
      About Locrine.

665   [Watts, Theodore]. The Athenaeum, 114 (Oct. 28, 1899), 579.
      Review of Rosamund: Queen of the Lombards.

666   "Wherein the Clergy Have Failed." Review of Reviews (Lon-
      don), 20 (Nov. 1899), 444.

1900

Books

667   Benson, Arthur Christopher. The Diary of Arthur Christopher
      Benson. Ed. Percy Lubbock. London: Hutchinson, [19--?].
      Swinburne on pages 64-68.

668   Chiarini, Giuseppe. "Algernon Charles Swinburne 1879."
      Studi e Ritratti Letterari. Livorno: 1900. pp. 219-239.

669   Franke. W.   Algernon Charles Swinburne als dramatiker.
      Ostern: Bitterfield, Schenke, [1900].

670   Kassner, Rudolf. "Swinburne." Die Mystik die Künstler und
      das Leben. Leipzig: Diederichs, 1900. pp. 159-192.

671   Tinsley, William. Random Recollections of an Old Publisher.
      Vol. I. London: Simpkin, Marshall, Hamilton, Kent, 1900.
      Swinburne on pages 232-234.

672   Wratislaw, Theodore. Algernon Charles Swinburne: A Study.
      London: Greening, 1900.
      Assesses Swinburne as a great poet, both in thought and
      expression.
      Reviewed: Academy (entry 697); The Athenaeum (entry 700);
      The Bookman (London) (entry 701); Literary World (entry
      706); and Literature (entry 707).

Periodicals

673   The Bookman (New York), 10 (Jan. 1900), 495.
      Review of Rosamund: Queen of the Lombards.

674   Breymann, Hans.   "Algernon Charles Swinburne."   Liter-
      arisches Centralblatt für Deutschland, 51 (April 7, 1900),
      640-641.

675   Brownell, W. C.   Book Buyer, n. s. 20 (Feb. 1900), 54-55.
      Review of Rosamund: Queen of the Lombards.

676   Chesterton, Gilbert Keith.   "The Literary Portraits of G. F.
      Watts, R. A."   The Bookman (London), 19 (Dec. 1900), 82.

677   Douglas, James.   "Mr. Swinburne as a Metrist."   The Book-
      man (London), 18 (June 1900), 75-79.

678   _____.   "Algernon Charles Swinburne."   The Bookman (New
      York), 11 (July 1900), 435-439.

679   Gentleman's Magazine, 288 (Jan. 1900), 101-103.
      Review of Rosamund: Queen of the Lombards.

680   Hood, Arthur.   "Is Swinburne a 'Great Poet'?"   Literature, 7
      (Oct. 20, 1900), 303.

681   Literature, 6 (Jan. 20, 1900), 74.

682   "Living English Poets."   Current Literature, 29 (Sept. 1900),
      268-269.

683   "Mr. Swinburne S'Amuse."   Punch, 119 (Sept. 26, 1900), 224.

684   Nation (New York), 70 (May 10, 1900), 361.
      Review of Rosamond: Queen of the Lombards.

685   Noyes, Alfred.   "Is Swinburne a 'Great Poet'?"   Literature,
      7 (Sept. 29, 1900), 241; and 7 (Oct. 13, 1900), 280-281.

686   _____.   "Swinburne."   Literature, 7 (Oct. 27, 1900), 328;
      and 7 (Nov. 17, 1900), 398.

687   Payne, W. M.   Dial, 28 (Jan. 16, 1900), 48-49.
      Review of Rosamund: Queen of the Lombards.

688   Poet Lore, 12 (Jan. -March 1900), 134-136.
      Review of Rosamund: Queen of the Lombards.

689   Sewanee Review, 8 (Jan. 1900), 106-109.
      Review of Rosamund: Queen of the Lombards.

690   The Spectator, 84 (Feb. 3, 1900), 173-174.
      Review of Rosamund: Queen of the Lombards.

691   Sillard, P. A. "Is Swinburne a 'Great Poet'?" Literature,
        7 (Oct. 6, 1900), 262.

692   _____. "Swinburne." Literature, 7 (Nov. 3, 1900), 352.

693   Thomas, Edith M. Critic (New York), 36 (Feb. 1900), 152-
        153.
        Review of Rosamund: Queen of the Lombards.

1901

Books

694   Beers, Henry Augustin. A History of English Romanticism in
        the Nineteenth Century. New York: Holt, 1901.
        Swinburne on pages 339-351.

695   Layard, George Somes. Mrs. Lynn Linton: Her Life, Let-
        ters, and Opinions. London: Methuen, 1901.
        Swinburne on pages 239-240.

696   Murray, Henry. "Algernon Charles Swinburne." Robert Bu-
        chanan: A Critical Appreciation, and Other Essays. Lon-
        don: Wellby, 1901. pp. 116-127.
        Reviewed: Academy (entry 698).

Periodicals

697   Academy, 60 (March 23, 1901), 267-268.
        Review of T. Wratislaw's Algernon Charles Swinburne
        (entry 672).

698   Academy, 61 (July 20, 1901), 50.
        Review of H. Murray's Robert Buchanan (entry 696).

699   Armstrong, William. "Mr. Swinburne and Mr. Watts-Dunton
        at 'The Pines.'" Critic (New York), 39 (Dec. 1901), 512-
        522.

700   The Athenaeum, 117 (March 16, 1901), 330.
        Review of T. Wratislaw's Algernon Charles Swinburne
        (entry 672).

701   The Bookman (London), 19 (March 1901), 200.
        Review of T. Wratislaw's Algernon Charles Swinburne
        (entry 672).

702 Fisher, W. E. Garrett. "Algernon Charles Swinburne."
     Literature, 9 (Oct. 5, 1901), 313-315.

703 Gwynn, Stephen. "Mr. Swinburne on Boer Tyranny."
     Saturday Review (London), 92 (Nov. 16, 1901), 622.

704 Hauser, Otto. "Algernon Charles Swinburne." Westermanns
     Illustrierte Deutsche Monatshefte, 90 (Sept. 1901), 796-805.

705 Hille, Peter. "Bei Algernon Swinburne." Die Geschellschaft,
     17 (Dec. 1901), 342-345.

706 Literary World (London), n. s. 63 (March 1, 1901), 205-206.
     Review of T. Wratislaw's Algernon Charles Swinburne
     (entry 672).

707 Literature, 8 (Feb. 16, 1901), 119.
     Review of T. Wratislaw's Algernon Charles Swinburne
     (entry 672).

708 Literature, 9 (Oct. 5, 1901), 315-316.
     Swinburne bibliography.

709 Marble, Annie Russell. "Messages of the Nineteenth Century
     Poets." Dial, 30 (Feb. 16, 1901), 99.

710 McVarish, Duncan C. "Mr. Swinburne on Boer Tyranny."
     Saturday Review (London), 92 (Nov. 16, 1901), 621; and 92
     (Nov. 23, 1901), 642.
     Discusses Swinburne's poem "The Transvaal."

711 Ortensi, Ulisse. "Letterati Contemporanei: Algernon Charles
     Swinburne." Emporium, 13 (March 1901), 202-210.

712 The Rambler, 2 (Nov. 23, 1901), 1419-1422.
     About Swinburne's poem "The Transvaal."

713 [Seaman, Owen]. "Watchman, What of the Knight?" Punch,
     120 (Jan. 9, 1901), 26.

714 Sharp, William. "A Literary Friendship: Mr. A. C. Swin-
     burne and Mr. Watts-Dunton at the Pines." Pall Mall Maga-
     zine, 25 (Dec. 1901), 435-448.

715 Wood, Joanna E. "Algernon Charles Swinburne: An Apprecia-
     tion." The Canadian Magazine, 17 (May 1901), 3-10.

1902

Books

716   Gower, Ronald Sutherland.   Old Diaries, 1881-1901.   New
         York: Scribner, 1902.
         Swinburne on page 44.

717   Payne, William Morton.   "Algernon Charles Swinburne."
         Library of the World's Best Literature.   Ed. C. D.
         Warner. New York: Hill, [1902]. Vol. XXXVI. pp.
         14289-14293.

718   Shindler, Robert.   "Swinburne, Meredith." On Certain As-
         pects of Recent English Literature.   Leipzig: Teubner,
         1902.   pp. 38-47.
         Neuphilologische Vorträge und Abhandlungen II.

Periodicals

719   "The Appreciations of Algernon."   Punch, 123 (Aug. 6, 1902),
         79.
         Parody.

720   "An Austrian Appreciation of Swinburne."   Literary Digest, 24
         (Jan. 18, 1902), 76-77.

721   Bayne, Thomas.   "Carlyle, Coleridge and Swinburne." Notes
         and Queries, 9th ser., 10 (Oct. 11, 1902), 296.

722   Colles, Ramsay.   "Mr. Swinburne's First Drama." Gentle-
         man's Magazine, n. s. 68 (March 1902), 301-310.

723   Cresswell, Lionel.   "Royal Descent of Algernon Charles Swin-
         burne." Genealogical Magazine (London), 6 (Dec. 1902),
         358-360.

724   Davray, Henry D.   Mercure de France, 42 (June 1902), 840-
         842.

725   Gosse, Edmund William.   "Mr. Swinburne." Century Illus-
         trated Monthly Magazine, 64 (May 1902), 100-106.

726   Harper's Weekly, 46 (Sept. 6, 1902), 1237.
         Discusses Swinburne's "Charles Dickens" (The Quarterly
         Review, July 1902, pp. 20-39).

727   Hirsch, Charles Henry.   Mercure de France, 41 (Feb. 1902),
         511-513.
         Discusses Swinburne and Rudyard Kipling.

728   "An Imaginary Correspondence." Punch, 123 (July 30, 1902),
      60.
      Reprinted: C. K. Hyder, Swinburne: The Critical Heri-
      tage, pages 213-214 (entry 2083).

729   Kaluza, M.   Zeitschrift für Französischen und Englischen
      Unterricht, 1 (1902), 441.
      Discusses Atalanta in Calydon.

730   Lang, Andrew. "The First Word o' Flyting." Morning Post
      (London), July 12, 1902, p. 3.

731   Linton, E. Knox. "'A Year's Letters.'" Academy, 63 (Sept.
      13, 1902), 275.
      Thomas B. Mosher of Portland, Maine, published an edi-
      tion of A Year's Letters in 1901.

732   Literary Digest, 25 (Aug. 16, 1902), 188-190.
      Discusses Swinburne's "Charles Dickens" (The Quarterly
      Review, July 1902, pp. 20-39).

733   "Mrs. Boythorn and Her Canary." Academy, 63 (July 10,
      1902), 87-88.

734   "Mr. Swinburne on Dickens." Times Literary Supplement,
      July 25, 1902, p. 219.
      Discusses Swinburne's "Charles Dickens" (The Quarterly
      Review, July 1902, pp. 20-39).

735   "'The Pity of It.'" Academy, 63 (Dec. 20, 1902), 686.

736   Saturday Review (London), 94 (July 26, 1902), 112-113.
      Discusses Swinburne's "Charles Dickens" (The Quarterly
      Review, July 1902, pp. 20-39).

1903

Books

737   Douglas, James. English Literature: Algernon Charles Swin-
      burne.   Philadelphia: Lippincott, 1903.

738   Jay, Harriett. "The Fleshly School of Poetry, 1870."
      Robert Buchanan. London: Unwin, 1903. pp. 159-168.

Periodicals

739   Colles, Ramsay. "Mr. Swinburne's Early Dramas and Po-
        ems." Gentleman's Magazine, 295 (July 1903), 128-150.

740   "A Double-Barrelled Hero." Punch, 124 (May 13, 1903),
        341-342.

741   Hake, Thomas St. E. "How Authors Work Best." T.P.'s
        Weekly, 2 (Oct. 16, 1903), 630.

742   Hankin, St. John. "Swinburne." Punch, 125 (Nov. 11, 1903),
        330.
        Reprinted: Lost Masterpieces (entry 753).

743   Maxwell, Patrick. "Translations, Good and Bad." Notes and
        Queries, 9th ser., 12 (Oct. 10, 1903), 285.

744   "Mr. Swinburne as Critic." Academy, 64 (March 21, 1903),
        281-282.

745   Powell, Frederick York. "Algernon Charles Swinburne." The
        English Illustrated Magazine, 29 (April 1903), 84 and 90;
        and 29 (May 1903), 213-214.
        Lists Swinburne's contributions to periodicals, with evalua-
        tion.
        Reprinted: Frederick York Powell (entry 861).

746   Sigma. "Personalia." Blackwood's Magazine, 174 (Sept.
        1903), 304-307.

747   Stringer, Arthur. "When Closing Swinburne." The Bookman
        (New York), 17 (April 1903), 159.
        Poem.

748   "Swinburne." Literary World (London), n.s. 67 (Feb. 20,
        1903), 175.

749   Teall, Gardner C. "Whistler and Swinburne." The Bookman
        (New York), 18 (Sept. 1903), 69-70.

1904

In 1904, Swinburne's A Channel Passage and Other Poems (hereafter referred to as A Channel Passage) was published, but the
work that most interested the critics was The Poems of Algernon
Charles Swinburne. It was brought out in both England and the

United States and included prefatory remarks by Swinburne. With
the publication of the six-volume edition came renewed interest in
Swinburne's Poems and Ballads of 1866.

Books

750   Burne-Jones, Georgina.   Memorials of Edward Burne-Jones.
      New York: Macmillan, 1904.
      Swinburne on page 269.

751   Douglas, James.   "Algernon Charles Swinburne."   Chambers's
      Cyclopaedia of English Literature.   Philadelphia: Lippin-
      cott, 1904.   Vol. III.   pp. 672-680.

752   Dunn, Henry Treffry.   Recollections of Dante Gabriel Rossetti
      and His Circle.   London: 1904.

753   Hankin, St. John.   "Swinburne."   Lost Masterpieces: and
      Other Verses.   London: Constable, 1904.   pp. 22-26.
      Reprinted from: Punch, Nov. 11, 1903 (entry 742).

754   Lyttelton, Arthur Temple.   "Modern Pagan Poetry (Swinburne
      and James Thomson)."   Modern Poets of Faith, Doubt and
      Paganism: and Other Essays.   London: Murray, 1904.
      pp. 212-245.
      Lyttelton remarks, "Mr. Swinburne is at the head of that
      class of English poets who seem to have taken for their
      motto, Ars est ostentare artem" (p. 213).
      Reprinted from the Church Quarterly Review, July 1882
      (entry 346).

755   More, Paul Elmer.   "Swinburne."   Shelburne Essays.   11
      volumes.   New York: Houghton, Mifflin, 1904-1921.   Vol.
      III.   pp. 100-123.

756   Pughe, F. H.   Führende dichter im zeitalter der Königin
      Viktoria.   Vienna: Konegen, 1904.

757   Reul, Paul de.   Swinburne et la France: Essai de Littérature
      comparée.   Brussels: Lefèvre, 1904.
      Reprinted from Revue de l'Université de Bruxelles, Jan.
      1904 (entry 782).
      See entry 782 for other reprinting.
      Reviewed by: Saturday Review (London) (entry 785).

Periodicals

758   Academy, 67 (Dec. 24, 1904), 638.
      Review of The Poems of Algernon Charles Swinburne.

759   "A. C. Swinburne."   Notes and Queries, 10th ser., 1 (March
      5, 1904). 198.

760 Agresti, A. "Un nuovo libro di versi di A. Swinburne."
     Italia Moderna, 3rd ser., 2 (Dec. 1904), 1679-1686.
     Review of A Channel Passage.

761 The Athenaeum, 123 (June 18, 1904), 775-776.
     Review of Volume I of The Poems of Algernon Charles
     Swinburne (Poems and Ballads).

762 The Athenaeum, 124 (Oct. 8, 1904), 475-476.
     Review of A Channel Passage.

763 Blackwood's Magazine, 176 (July 1904), 123-126.
     Review of The Poems of Algernon Charles Swinburne.

764 "A Channel Passage and Other Poems." The Monthly Review,
     17 (Nov. 1904), 165-170.
     Review of A Channel Passage.

765 Critic (New York), 45 (Sept. 1904), 196.

766 Davray, H. D. Mercure de France, 51 (Sept. 1904), 818-820.
     Discusses Poems and Ballads, Songs Before Sunrise, and
     Songs of Two Nations.

767 _____. Mercure de France, 52 (Nov. 1904), 528-529.
     Review of A Channel Passage.

768 _____. Mercure de France, 52 (Dec. 1904), 803-804.
     Review of The Poems of Algernon Charles Swinburne.

769 Douglas, James. "Swinburne." The Bookman (London),
     (July 1904), 130-132.
     Review of Volume I of The Poems of Algernon Charles
     Swinburne (Poems and Ballads).

770 _____. The Bookman (London), 26 (Sept. 1904), 213.
     Review of The Poems of Algernon Charles Swinburne.

771 Eclectic Magazine of Foreign Literature, 143 (Oct. 1904),
     555-560.
     Review of Volume I of The Poems of Algernon Charles
     Swinburne (Poems and Ballads).

772 Elton, Oliver. "Mr. Swinburne's Poems--Old and New."
     The Speaker, n.s. 10 (Sept. 10, 1904), 541-543; and n.s.
     11 (Feb. 18, 1905), 488-490 (entry 818).
     Review of The Poems of Algernon Charles Swinburne.

773 Hauser, Otto. "Swinburne's Lyrik." Zeitschrift für
     vergleichende Literaturgeschichte, n.s. 15 (1904), 206-232.

774 Literary World (London), n.s. 70 (Sept. 16, 1904), 195-196.
     Review of A Channel Passage.

775   Literary World (London), n. s. 70 (Sept. 23, 1904), 220.
      Review of The Poems of Algernon Charles Swinburne.

776   Living Age, 242 (Aug. 13, 1904), 438-443.
      Review of The Poems of Algernon Charles Swinburne.

777   Newcomer, Alphonso G.   "The Poe-Chivers Tradition Re-
      Examined. " Sewanee Review, 12 (Jan. 1904), 20-35.

778   Notes and Queries, 10th ser., 1 (June 25, 1904), 518-519.
      Review of Volume I of The Poems of Algernon Charles
      Swinburne (Poems and Ballads).

779   Notes and Queries, 10th ser., 2 (Sept. 17, 1904), 240.
      Discusses Songs Before Sunrise.

780   "The Old and the New Swinburne. " Saturday Review (Lon-
      don), 98 (Sept. 17, 1904), 365-366.
      Review of A Channel Passage.

781   "The Poems of Algernon Charles Swinburne. " The Athenaeum,
      124 (Aug. 27, 1904), 264-265.
      Review of The Poems of Algernon Charles Swinburne.

782   Reul, Paul de.   "Swinburne et la France: Essai de littérature
      comparée. " Revue de l'Université de Bruxelles, 9 (Jan.
      1904), 267-322.
      Reprinted: La Grande Revue, 32 (Dec. 15, 1904), 496-520;
      and Swinburne et la France (entry 757).

783   Rhys, E.   The Bookman (London), 27 (Oct. 1904), 23-24.
      Review of A Channel Passage.

784   Saturday Review (London). 98 (July 2, 1904), 17-18.
      Review of Volume I of The Poems of Algernon Charles
      Swinburne (Poems and Ballads).

785   Saturday Review (London), 98 (Dec. 31, 1904), 828-829.
      Review of P. de Reul's Swinburne et la France (entry 757).

786   Seaman, Owen.   "Sweet Uses of Obesity. " Punch, 126 (April
      27, 1904), 290.

787   _____ .   "A Channel Record. " Punch, 127 (Sept. 14, 1904),
      182.
      Poem parodying A Channel Passage.

788   The Spectator, 93 (July 16, 1904), 88-89.
      Review of Volume I of The Poems of Algernon Charles
      Swinburne (Poems and Ballads).

789   The Spectator, 93 (Sept. 17, 1904), 393-394.
      Review of A Channel Passage.

790   "Swinburne as Parodist." Saturday Review (London), 98 (Dec.
        3, 1904), 699-700.

791   "Swinburne on Himself." Literary World (London), n. s. 69
        (June 17, 1904), 580-581.
        Review of Volume I of The Poems of Algernon Charles
        Swinburne (Swinburne's prefatory note).

792   "Swinburne's Early Poems." Literary Digest, 29 (Aug. 20,
        1904), 225-226.
        Review of Volume I of The Poems of Algernon Charles
        Swinburne.

793   Thompson, Francis. Academy, 66 (June 25, 1904), 680-681.
        Review of Volume I of The Poems of Algernon Charles
        Swinburne (Poems and Ballads).

794   _____. Academy, 67 (Sept. 17, 1904), 196.
        Review of A Channel Passage.

795   Times Literary Supplement, July 8, 1904, pp. 209-210.
        Review of The Poems of Algernon Charles Swinburne.

796   Times Literary Supplement, Sept. 2, 1904, pp. 265-266.
        Review of A Channel Passage.

797   Urban, Sylvanus. Gentleman's Magazine, 297 (Sept. 1904),
        309-312.
        Review of The Poems of Algernon Charles Swinburne.

1905

Swinburne's novel Love's Cross-Currents (originally titled A Year's
Letters) was published in 1905 by Chatto and Windus.   Also published by Chatto and Windus was the five-volume edition, The Tragedies of Algernon Charles Swinburne, which appeared under Harper's
imprint in the United States.   Also appearing in the United States
was the Selected Poems of Algernon Charles Swinburne, edited by
William Morton Payne (hereafter referred to as Selected Poems,
Payne).

Books

798   Carman, Bliss. "Mr. Swinburne's Poetry." The Poetry of
        Life. Boston: Page, 1905. pp. 177-190.

799   Ruskin, John. Letters of John Ruskin to Charles Eliot Norton.

Ed. Charles Eliot Norton.   Boston: Houghton,   Mifflin,
1904.
Swinburne mentioned in Volume I, page 57.

800   Symons, Arthur.   "Algernon Charles Swinburne."   The Poets
and the Poetry of the Nineteenth Century.   Ed. Alfred H.
Miles.   London: Routledge, 1905.   Vol. VI.   pp. 281-288.

801   Taine, H.   Sa Vie et sa correspondance.   4 volumes.   Paris:
1905-1914.   pp. 3 and 145.
Noted in P. Henderson's Swinburne (entry 2166), page 293.
Not examined.

802   Taylor, Marie Hansen.   On Two Continents.   London: Smith,
Elder, 1905.
Swinburne on page 174.

803   Thomson, Joseph Charles.   Bibliographical List of the Writings of Algernon Charles Swinburne.   Wimbledon: J.
Thomson and Walter T. Spencer, 1905.
This is an unreliable listing.   Among other problems, it
lists as Swinburne's work poems published in Fraser's
Magazine in 1848, 1849, 1851, and 1856.   The works were
signed "A.C.S." for Anthony Cunningham Sterling.   Swinburne turned eleven years old in 1848.

804   Wesley, E. A.   "The Poetical Works of Algernon Charles
Swinburne Critically Considered."   Proceedings of the Lit-
erary and Philosophical Society of Liverpool during the
Ninety-Fourth Session, 1904-1905.   London: 1905.
Listed in C. K. Hyder's Swinburne's Literary Career and
Fame (entry 1761), page 377.   Not examined.

805   Woodberry, George Edward.   Swinburne.   New York:
McClure, Phillips, 1905.
Contemporary Men of Letters.
Reprinted: New York: Macmillan, 1912.
Reviewed: Critic (New York) (entry 870); F. Greenslet
Nation (New York) (entry 875); Lewis N. Chase, New York
Times Saturday Review (entry 811); and Review of Reviews
(entry 891).

Periodicals

806   The Athenaeum, 126 (Aug. 5, 1905), 165-166.
Review of Love's Cross-Currents.

807   Barlow, George.   "On the Spiritual Side of Mr. Swinburne's
Genius."   Contemporary Review, 88 (Aug. 1905), 231-250.

808   Barry, W.   The Bookman (London), 28 (Aug. 1905), 159-160.
Review of Love's Cross-Currents.

809   Boynton, H. W.   "Algernon Charles Swinburne."   Critic (New
       York), 47 (July 1905), 58-61.

810   Brocklehurst, J. H.   "Algernon Charles Swinburne."   The
       Manchester Quarterly, 24 (1905), 404-430.

811   Chase, Lewis N.   New York Times Saturday Review, 10 (Dec.
       16, 1905), 889.
       Review of G. E. Woodberry's Swinburne (entry 805).

812   Contemporary Review, 88 (Sept. 1905), 454-455.
       Review of Love's Cross-Currents.

813   "Crossing the Channel."   Punch, 129 (Aug. 16, 1905), 115.

814   Davray, H. D.   Mercure de France, 53 (Feb. 15, 1905), 637.
       Review of The Poems of Algernon Charles Swinburne.

815   _____.   Mercure de France, 58 (Nov. 15, 1905), 299-301.
       Review of The Tragedies of Algernon Charles Swinburne.

816   Dunbar, Olivia Howard.   Critic (New York), 47 (Nov. 1905),
       452.
       Review of Love's Cross-Currents.

817   "The Early Swinburne."   Saturday Review (London), 100 (July
       8, 1905), 54-55.
       Review of The Tragedies of Algernon Charles Swinburne.

818   Elton, Oliver.   "Mr. Swinburne's Poems--Old and New."
       The Speaker, n. s. 11 (Feb. 18, 1905), 488-490; and n. s.
       10 (Sept. 10, 1904), 541-543 (entry 772).
       Review of The Poems of Algernon Charles Swinburne.

819   Gaines, C. H.   Harper's Weekly, 49 (Aug. 12, 1905), 1160.
       Review of Love's Cross-Currents.

820   Gilman, Lawrence.   "The New Swinburne."   Harper's Weekly,
       49 (Jan. 7, 1905), 23.

821   Greenslet, Ferris.   Atlantic Monthly, 96 (Sept. 1905), 415-416.
       Review of The Poems of Algernon Charles Swinburne.

822   Hoffsten, Ernest Godfrey.   "Swinburne's Poetic Theory and
       Practice."   Sewanee Review, 13 (Jan. 1905), 54-60.

823   Independent, 58 (June 22, 1905), 1420-1421.
       Review of The Poems of Algernon Charles Swinburne.

824   Independent, 59 (Sept. 7, 1905), 582.
       Review of Love's Cross-Currents.

825   "Mazzini and Swinburne."   T. P. 's Weekly, 5 (June 30, 1905),
       817.

826   Meyerfeld, M.   Das Literarische Echo, 7 (Jan. 1, 1905),
        472-473.
        Review of A Channel Passage.

827   "Mr. Swinburne's Novel." Punch, 129 (July 5, 1905), 2.

828   Murray, Gilbert.   "The Plays of a Great Poet." The Speaker,
        n. s. 12 (Sept. 16, 1905), 570-572.
        Review of The Tragedies of Algernon Charles Swinburne.
        Reprinted: Living Age, 247 (Oct. 28, 1905), 244-248.

829   Nation (New York), 80 (April 13, 1905), 292-293.
        Review of The Poems of Algernon Charles Swinburne.

830   Nation (New York), 81 (Aug. 3, 1905), 96.
        Review of Selected Poems, ed. W. M. Payne.
        Very positive review.

831   Nation (New York), 81 (Aug. 17, 1905), 147.
        Review of Love's Cross-Currents.

832   "The New Swinburne." Outlook, 80 (June 10, 1905), 388-390.
        Review of The Poems of Algernon Charles Swinburne.

833   New York Times Saturday Review, 10 (July 15, 1905), 465.
        Review of Love's Cross-Currents.

834   New York Times Saturday Review, 10 (Aug. 12, 1905), 525.
        Review of Selected Poems, ed. W. M. Payne.
        Very positive review.

835   Notes and Queries, 10th ser., 4 (July 8, 1905), 39; 4 (Nov.
        18, 1905), 418; 4 (Dec. 16, 1905), 497; and 5 (Feb. 10,
        1906), 118 (entry 883).
        Reviews of The Tragedies of Algernon Charles Swinburne.

836   "The Novel of a Great Poet." Literary Digest, 31 (Sept. 30,
        1905), 449.
        Review of Love's Cross-Currents.

837   Outlook, 80 (July 29, 1905), 838.
        Review of Love's Cross-Currents.

838   Payne, William Morton.   "The Poetry of Mr. Swinburne."
        Dial, 38 (March 1, 1905), 152-154.
        Review of The Poems of Algernon Charles Swinburne.
        Note Payne's selective edition of Swinburne's poems, as
        mentioned in the introductory comments to the 1905 section
        of the present bibliography.

839   _____.   Dial, 39 (Sept. 1, 1905), 112-113.
        Review of Love's Cross-Currents.

840   "A Poet as Novelist." Saturday Review (London), 100 (Aug.

     5, 1905), 184-185.
     Review of Love's Cross-Currents.

841 "The Poetry and Criticism of Mr. Swinburne." Quarterly Re-
     view, 203 (Oct. 1905), 525-547.

842 "A Poet's Retrospect." Dial, 38 (Feb. 16, 1905), 111-113.

843 Punch, 129 (Aug. 2, 1905), 90.
     About Love's Cross-Currents.

844 Radford, George. "Swinburne on Sea." Gentleman's Maga-
     zine, 299 (Aug. 1905), 198-202.
     Review of The Poems of Algernon Charles Swinburne.

845 "Resurrection Pie." Academy, 69 (July 15, 1905), 726-727.
     Review of Love's Cross-Currents.

846 Review of Reviews, 32 (Dec. 1905), 759.
     Review of Love's Cross-Currents.

847 Rhys, Ernest. "Swinburne's Collected Poems." Fortnightly
     Review, 83 (Jan. 1905), 150-157.
     Review of The Poems of Algernon Charles Swinburne.
     Reprinted: Poems by Algernon Charles Swinburne.
     New York: Boni and Liveright, n.d. pp. vii-xvi.

848 Ross, Robert. "Swinblake: a Prophetic Book, with Home
     Zarathrusts." Academy, 71 (Sept. 29, 1905), 307-309.

849 The Spectator, 95 (July 29, 1905), 157.
     Review of Love's Cross-Currents.

850 "Spiritual Side of Swinburne's Genius." Literary Digest, 31
     (Nov. 4, 1905), 650-651.

851 "Swinburne." Harper's Weekly, 49 (Feb. 25, 1905), 269.

852 Times Literary Supplement, June 30, 1905, p. 208.
     Review of The Tragedies of Algernon Charles Swinburne.

853 Times Literary Supplement, July 14, 1905, p. 225.
     Review of Love's Cross-Currents.

1906

Chatto and Windus reprinted Swinburne's critical essay William
Blake in 1906, and Crowell of New York published an edition of

Swinburne's poems, edited by Arthur Beatty (hereafter referred to
as Poems, Beatty).

Books

854 Benn, Alfred William. The History of English Rationalism in
     the Nineteenth Century. London: Longmans, Green, 1906.
     Swinburne in volume III, pages 286-289.

855 Elton, Oliver. Frederick York Powell: A Life and a Selec-
     tion from His Letters and Occasional Writings. Vol. II.
     London: Oxford University Press (Clarendon Press), 1906.
     See also F. Y. Powell, "Algernon Charles Swinburne"
     (entry 861), below.

856 Grappe, Georges. "A. C. Swinburne." Essai sur la poésie
     anglaise au XIXe siècle. Paris: Sansot, 1906. pp. 59-65.

857 Hill, George Birkbeck. Letters of George Birkbeck Hill.   Ed.
     Lucy Crump. London: 1906.
     Swinburne on pages 65-66.

858 Myall, Laura Hain [Friswell]. In the Sixties and Seventies:
     Impressions of Literary People and Others. Boston:
     Turner, 1906.
     Swinburne on pages 73-83.
     Reviewed: P. F. Bicknell, Dial (entry 866).

859 Öfterning, Michael. "Algernon Charles Swinburne." Fest-
     schrift zum zwölften allgemeinen deutschen Neuphilologen-
     tage in München. Erlangen: Junge, 1906. pp. 146-174.

860 Perry, Bliss. Walt Whitman. Boston: Houghton, Mifflin,
     [1906].
     American Men of Letters.
     Swinburne on pages 260-261.

861 Powell, Frederick York. "Algernon Charles Swinburne."
     Frederick York Powell: A Life and a Selection from His
     Letters and Occasional Writings. Ed. Oliver Elton. Lon-
     don: Oxford University Press (Clarendon Press), 1906.
     Vol. II. pp. 311-313.
     Reprinted from The English Illustrated Magazine, April
     1903 (entry 745).

862 Rossetti, William Michael. Some Reminiscences. London:
     Brown, Langham, 1906.
     Swinburne in Volume I, pages 218-221.
     Reviewed: The Bookman (London) (entry 867).

Periodicals

863 Arena, 36 (Dec. 1906), 685.
     Review of Poems, Beatty.

864   The Athenaeum, 128 (Aug. 11, 1906), 149-150.
      Review of William Blake.

865   [Bailey, John]. "Swinburne's Scotch Trilogy." Times Liter-
      ary Supplement, Feb. 2, 1906), 33-34.
      Review of The Tragedies of Algernon Charles Swinburne.
      Reprinted: Poets and Poetry (entry 1119).

866   Bicknell, P. F.   Dial, 40 (March 16, 1906), 188-190.
      Review of L. H. Myall's In the Sixties and Seventies
      (entry 858).

867   The Bookman (London), 31 (Dec. 1906), 156.
      Review of W. M. Rossetti's Some Reminiscences (entry
      862).

868   Clutton-Brock, Arthur.   "A Literary Causerie: The Later
      Poetry of Mr. Swinburne." Academy, 71 (Oct. 20, 1906),
      397-398.

869   Critic (New York), 48 (March 1906), 201-203.

870   Critic (New York), 48 (May 1906), 459.
      Review of G. E. Woodberry's Swinburne (entry 805).

871   Dial, 40 (May 16, 1906), 330-331.
      Review of The Tragedies of Algernon Charles Swinburne.

872   Dial, 41 (Nov. 16, 1906), 330.
      Review of Poems, Beatty.

873   Dial, 41 (Dec. 1, 1906), 400.
      Review of William Blake.

874   "The First of Living Poets." Current Literature, 40 (March
      1906), 268-270.

875   [Greenslet, F.].   Nation (New York), 82 (Jan. 18, 1906), 58-
      59.
      Review of G. E. Woodberry's Swinburne (entry 805).

876   Hellman, George S.   New York Times Saturday Review, 11
      (May 19, 1906), 320.
      Review of The Tragedies of Algernon Charles Swinburne.

877   Le Gallienne, Richard.   "Swinburne's Lyrical Poems." North
      American Review, 183 (Oct. 19, 1906), 792-795.

878   Lyall, Alfred Comyn.   "Characteristics of Mr. Swinburne's
      Poetry." Edinburgh Review, 204 (Oct. 1906), 468-487.
      Reprinted: Studies in Literature and History (entry 1206).

879   Mehring, Sigmar.   "Algernon Charles Swinburne." Das
      literarische Echo, 8 (June 1906), 1199-1212.

880 Michaelides, C. C. "Mr. Swinburne and the Sea." The Inde-
      pendent Review, 8 (Jan. 1906), 69-80.

881 Moss, Mary. Atlantic Monthly, 97 (Jan. 1906), 58.
      Review of Love's Cross-Currents.

882 Nation (New York), 82 (May 10, 1906), 382.
      Review of The Tragedies of Algernon Charles Swinburne.

883 Notes and Queries, 10th ser., 5 (Feb. 10, 1906), 118.
      For related reviews, see entry 835.
      Review of The Tragedies of Algernon Charles Swinburne.

884 Noyes, Alfred. The Bookman (London), 30 (May 1906), 57-62.
      Review of The Tragedies of Algernon Charles Swinburne.

885 Outlook, 83 (June 23, 1906), 483.
      Review of The Tragedies of Algernon Charles Swinburne.

886 Pancoast, Henry S. "Mr. Swinburne's Poetry." Dial, 40
      (Jan. 16, 1906), 36.

887 _____. "A Final Word About Swinburne as 'a Love Poet.'"
      Dial, 40 (Feb. 16, 1906), 112-113.

888 "A Performance of Swinburne's Greatest Tragedy." Current
      Literature, 41 (Aug. 1906), 188-189.

889 "A Poet for Poets." Dial, 40 (Jan. 1, 1906), 3-5.

890 "Pre-Raphaelitism in Outline: Algernon Charles Swinburne."
      Book News Monthly, 24 (June 1906), 698.

891 Review of Reviews, 33 (March 1906), 383.
      Review of G. E. Woodberry's Swinburne (entry 805).

892 "Swinburne as a Dramatist." Saturday Review (London), 101
      (Feb. 24, 1906), 238-239.
      Review of The Tragedies of Algernon Charles Swinburne.

893 Symons, Arthur. Saturday Review (London), 102 (Aug. 25,
      1906), 231.
      Review of William Blake.

894 Times Literary Supplement, 5 (Aug. 10, 1906), 276.
      Review of William Blake.

895 Williams, Francis Howard. "Mr. Swinburne as 'a Love
      Poet.'" Dial, 40 (Feb. 1, 1906), 79.

896 World To-Day, 11 (Nov. 1906), 1221.
      Review of Poems, Beatty.

1907

Books

897   Allingham, William. William Allingham: A Diary. Ed. H.
      Allingham and D. Radford. London: Macmillan, 1907.

898   Douglas, James. Theodore Watts-Dunton. New York: Lane,
      [1907?].
      Swinburne on pages 268-274 and 279-284.

899   Elton, Oliver. "Mr. Swinburne's Poems." Modern Studies.
      London: Arnold, 1907. pp. 208-227.
      Reprinted: C. K. Hyder, Swinburne: The Critical Heri-
      tage (entry 2083), pages 218-232.

900   Golther, Wolfgang. Tristan und Isolde in den Dichtungen des
      Mittelalters und der neuen Zeit. Leipzig: 1907.

901   Jiriczek, O. Viktorianische dichtung. Heidelberg: 1907.
      Swinburne on pages 396-441.

902   Kipka, Karl. Maria Stuart im Drama der Weltliteratur
      vormehmlich des 17. und 18. Jahrhunderts: Ein Beitrag
      zur vergleichenden Literaturgeschichte. Leipzig: 1907.
      Breslauer Beiträge zur Literaturgeschichte IX.

903   More, Paul Elmer. "Swinburne." Shelburne Essays: Third
      Series. New York: Putnam, 1907. pp. 100-123.

904   Nicoll, William Robertson, and Thomas Seccombe. History of
      English Literature. New York: Dodd, Mead, 1907.
      Swinburne in volume III, pages 1250-1257.

905   Payne, William Morton. "Algernon Charles Swinburne."
      The Greater English Poets of the Nineteenth Century. New
      York: Holt, 1907. pp. 348-383.
      Reprinted: Freeport, N. Y.: Books for Libraries, 1967.

906   Sewell, Elizabeth M. The Autobiography of Elizabeth M.
      Sewell. Ed. Eleanor L. Sewell. London: Longmans,
      Green, 1907.
      Swinburne on pages 105-109.

907   Smith, Arnold. "Swinburne." The Main Tendencies of Vic-
      torian Poetry. London: Simpkin, Marshall, Hamilton,
      Kent, 1907. pp. 147-182.

908   Viereck, George Sylvester. "To Swinburne." Nineveh and
      Other Poems. New York: Moffat, Yard, 1907.
      Reprinted from Century Illustrated Monthly Magazine, Jan.
      1907 (entry 929). See entry 929 for other reprinting.

Periodicals

909 A. L. A. Booklist, 3 (March 1907), 86.
       Review of William Blake.

910 Academy, 72 (April 13, 1907), 355.

911 Brooks, Van Tyne. "The Lyric Origins of Swinburne."
       Poet Lore, 18 (Winter 1907), 468-477.

912 Current Literature, 42 (Feb. 1907), 169.
       Review of William Blake.

913 Ebsworth, Joseph Woodfall. "Joseph Knight on the Laureate-
       ship." Notes and Queries, 10th ser., 8 (Oct. 19, 1907),
       311.

914 Fletcher, Robert Huntington. "The Metrical Forms Used by
       Victorian Poets." Journal of English and Germanic Phi-
       lology, 7 (1907), 87-91.

915 Galletti, Alfredo. "Carlo Algernon Swinburne." Nuova
       Antologia di Lettere, Science ed Arti, 212 (April 1, 1907),
       419-440.

916 "Has England Outgrown Swinburne?" Literary Digest, 34 (May
       11, 1907), 763-764.

917 Jaggard, William. "The Children of the Chapel." Notes and
       Queries, 10th ser., 7 (May 11, 1907), 378.

918 "Mr. Swinburne's Birthday." The Spectator, 98 (April 13,
       1907), 568-569.

919 Murdoch, W. G. Blaikie. "Random Recollections of Swin-
       burne: With Notes Toward a Bibliography of Swinburne
       Criticism." Book-Lover's Magazine, 7 (1907), 108-110;
       and 7 (1908), 144-152 (entry 956).

920 [Nevinson, Henry Woodd]. "A Poet's Youth." Nation (Lon-
       don), 1 (April 13, 1907), 267-268.
       Reprinted: Essays in Freedom (entry 1125).

921 Noyes, Alfred. "A Seventieth Birthday." North American
       Review, 184 (April 5, 1907), 740-741.
       Also: Fortnightly Review, 87 (April 1907), 571-572.

922 "'Othello' V, ii, and Swinburne." Notes and Queries, 10th
       ser., 8 (Aug. 31, 1907), 164.

923 Outlook, 85 (March 2, 1907), 527.
       Review of William Blake.

924   Pierpoint, Robert.   "Joseph Knight on the Laureateship. "
        Notes and Queries, 10th ser. , 8 (Oct. 5, 1907), 267.

925   "The Putney Pageant. "   Punch, 132 (April 3, 1907), 251.

926   Russell, Charles Edward.   "Swinburne and Music. "   North
        American Review, 186 (Nov. 1907), 427-441.

927   Seaman, Owen.   "Another Poet of the Channel. "   Punch, 132
        (May 8, 1907), 326.

928   Talbot, Ethel.   "Tennyson or Another ?"   Academy, 73 (July
        6, 1907), 654.

929   Viereck, George Sylvester.   "To Swinburne. "   Century Illus-
        trated Monthly Magazine, 73 (Jan. 1907), 464.
        Reprinted: Nation (New York), 85 (July 11, 1907), 36; and
        Nineveh and Other Poems (entry 908).

1908

In 1908, Swinburne published The Duke of Gandia, a play in verse,
and The Age of Shakespeare, a critical work.

Books

930   Caine, Hall.   My Story.   London: Heinemann, 1908.

931   Carr, Joseph William Comyns.   "Some Victorian Poets. "
        Some Eminent Victorians.   London: Duckworth, 1908.
        Swinburne on pages 208-212 and 215-219.
        Reviewed: P. F. Bicknell, Dial (entry 994).

932   James, Henry.   "Swinburne's Essays. "   Views and Reviews.
        Boston: Ball, 1908.   pp. 49-59.
        Reprinted from Nation (New York), July 29, 1875 (entry
        197).

933   Lindau, P.   A. C. Swinburne.   Hamburg: 1908.
        Nachrichten, No. 48.

934   Rossetti, Christina Georgina.   The Family Letters of Christina
        Georgina Rossetti.   Ed. William Michael Rossetti.   London:
        1908.   New York: Scribner, 1908.

Dissertation

935   Richter, Ludwig.   Swinburne Verhältnis zu Frankreich und

Italien.   Munich, 1908.
Published in 1910 (entry 1100).

Periodicals

936   "Algernon Charles Swinburne."   Book News Monthly, 26
        (March 1908), 533-536.

937   The Athenaeum, 131 (April 18, 1908), 469-470.
        Review of The Duke of Gandia.

938   The Athenaeum, 132 (Nov. 28, 1908), 674-675.
        Review of The Age of Shakespeare.

939   Bensly, Edward.   "Swinburne Translations."   Notes and
        Queries, 10th ser., 9 (May 9, 1908), 375.

940   Cooper, Frederic Taber.   "Mr. Swinburne as Critic."
        Forum, 40 (Oct. 1908), 405-409.
        Review of The Age of Shakespeare.

941   Current Literature, 45 (Dec. 1908), 661-663.
        Review of The Age of Shakespeare.

942   "The Danger of Overdoing It."   Punch, 135 (Sept. 30, 1908),
        244.

943   Davray, H. de.   Mercure de France, 73 (May 1, 1908), 166.
        Review of The Duke of Gandia.

944   Dithmar, E. A.   New York Times Saturday Review, 13 (Oct.
        31, 1908), 633.
        Review of The Age of Shakespeare.

945   Dowden, Edward.   "Mr. Swinburne as Eulogist."   Nation (Lon-
        don), 3 (Sept. 26, 1908), 909-910.
        Review of The Age of Shakespeare.

946   Fletcher, R. H.   "The Metrical Forms Used by Certain Vic-
        torian Poets."   Journal of English and Germanic Philology,
        8 (1908).

947   Hille, Peter.   "Algernon Swinburne."   Gegenwart, no. 27
        (1908).

948   Independent, 65 (Dec. 3, 1908), 1310.
        Review of The Age of Shakespeare.

949   "The Later Course of English Prose."   Academy, 75 (Sept.
        12, 1908), 254.

950   Literary Digest, 37 (Dec. 5, 1908).
        Review of The Age of Shakespeare.

951   Living Age, 257 (May 2, 1908), 305-308.
      Review of The Duke of Gandia.

952   "A Master's Work." The Bookman (London), 34 (May 1908),
      72-73.
      Review of The Duke of Gandia.

953   "More Messages from the Dead." Punch, 135 (Oct. 7, 1908),
      265.

954   "Mr. Swinburne's New Book." T. P. 's Weekly, 12 (Sept. 2,
      1908), 341.

955   "Mr. Swinburne's Tragedy." Academy, 74 (April 18, 1908),
      685-686.
      Review of The Duke of Gandia.

956   Murdoch, W. G. Blaikie.   "Random Recollections of Swin-
      burne: With Notes Toward a Bibliography of Swinburne
      Criticism." Book-Lover's Magazine, 7 (1908), 144-152;
      and 7 (1907), 108-110 (entry 919).

957   Nation (New York), 86 (April 9, 1908), 339.
      Review of The Duke of Gandia.

958   Nation (New York), 87 (Nov. 5, 1908), 445-446.
      Review of The Age of Shakespeare.

959   New York Times Saturday Review, 13 (April 18, 1908), 226.
      Review of The Duke of Gandia.

960   Outlook, 89 (May 30, 1908), 264.
      Review of The Duke of Gandia.

961   Payne, W. M. Dial, 45 (Aug. 1, 1908), 60-61.
      Review of The Duke of Gandia.

962   Saturday Review (London), 105 (April 25, 1908), 532-533.
      Review of The Duke of Gandia.

963   Saturday Review (London), 106 (Oct. 3, 1908), 422-423.
      Review of The Age of Shakespeare.

964   Schuyler, Montgomery. The Bookman (New York), 28 (Nov.
      1908), 265.
      Review of The Age of Shakespeare.

965   The Spectator, 101 (July 4, 1908), 20.
      Review of The Duke of Gandia.

966   The Spectator, 101 (Oct. 3, 1908), 502-503.
      Review of The Age of Shakespeare.

967   Times Literary Supplement, Sept. 24, 1908, p. 305.
        Review of The Age of Shakespeare.

1909

Swinburne died on April 10, 1909. Most of the following listings
are eulogies and memorials. His critical work Shakespeare was
published in this year. Harper and Brothers, of New York, took
three of his essays on Shakespeare that had appeared in Harper's
Monthly Magazine and published them as Three Plays of Shakespeare. Arthur Beatty's edition of Swinburne's plays, Swinburne's
Dramas, was also published in 1909.

Books

968   Gabrielson, Arvid. Rime as a Criterion of the Pronunciation
        of Spenser, Pope, Byron, and Swinburne. Uppsala: Alm-
        qvist and Wikselle, 1909.

969   Gosse, Edmund. Swinburne: Personal Recollections.
        London: privately printed, 1909.

970   Herlet, Bruno. Versuch eines Kommentars zu Swinburnes
        "Atalanta." 2 volumes. Bamberg: Nagengast, 1909-1910.

971   Kellner, Leon. Die englische Literatur im Zeitalter der
        königen Viktoria. Leipzig: Tauchnitz, 1909.
        Swinburne on pages 483-496.

972   Mackail, John William. Swinburne: A Lecture. Oxford:
        Clarendon Press, 1909.
        Reviewed: North American Review (entry 1046) and The
        Spectator (entry 1068).
        Reprinted: Studies in English Poets (entry 1553).

973   Magnus, Laurie. "Algernon Charles Swinburne." English
        Literature in the Nineteenth Century: An Essay in Criti-
        cism. New York: Putnam, 1909. pp. 327-332.

974   Maupassant, Guy de. "L'anglais d'Etretat." Oeuvres Com-
        plètes. Paris: Conard, 1909. Vol. XV. pp. 255-263.

975   Nichols, Wallace Bertram. Date Lilia: An Elegy on Alger-
        non Charles Swinburne. London: Burleigh, [1909].

976   Noyes, Alfred. In Memory of Swinburne. Cleveland: Marion,

1909.
Reprinted from Nation (New York), May 1909 (entry 1047).
See entry 1047 for other reprinting.

977 [Sargent, George Henry]. Writings of Swinburne. [Boston: 1909].
Four-page pamphlet.

978 Svanberg, Harold. Swinburne: En Studie. Göteborg: V. Zachrissons Boktrycheri, 1909.

Periodicals

979 Academy, 76 (April 17, 1909), 3.
Notice of Swinburne's death.

980 A. L. A. Booklist, 6 (Dec. 1909), 149.
Review of Swinburne's Dramas, ed. A. Beatty.

981 "Algernon Charles Swinburne." Academy, 76 (April 17, 1909), 5-7.
Memorial essay.

982 "Algernon Charles Swinburne." Living Age, 261 (May 29, 1909), 556-561.

983 "Algernon Charles Swinburne." Nation (New York), 88 (April 15, 1909), 378-379.

984 "Algernon Charles Swinburne." The Times, April 12, 1909, p. 7.

985 "Algernon Charles Swinburne." Times Literary Supplement, April 15, 1909, 141-142.

986 "Algernon Charles Swinburne: Born April 5, 1837: Died April 10, 1909." English Review, 2 (May 1909), 193-194.

987 American Monthly Review of Reviews, 39 (June 1909), 768.
Review of Three Plays of Shakespeare.

988 "American Views of Swinburne." Literary Digest, 38 (April 24, 1909), 694-696.

989 The Athenaeum, 133 (Feb. 27, 1909), 254.
Review of Three Plays of Shakespeare.

990 The Athenaeum, 134 (Sept. 11, 1909), 289-290.
Review of Shakespeare.

991 Barral, Octave de. "Swinburne et son oeuvre poétique." Revue Hebdomadaire, April 24, 1909.

992 [Bennett, Arnold, writing as "Jacob Tonson"]. New Age,
       April 22, 1909.
       Reprinted: Books and Persons (entry 1239).

993 Bensly, Edward. "Swinburne and Maupassant." Notes and
       Queries, 10th ser., 11 (June 26, 1909), 505.

994 Bicknell, P. F. Dial, 46 (March 1, 1909), 134-135.
       Review of J. W. C. Carr's Some Eminent Victorians
       (entry 931).

995 Bird, Alice L., and Ernest Rhys. "Two Evenings with
       Swinburne." Bibliophile, 3 (July 1909), 238-241.

996 Blake, W. B. "Swinburne and Maupassant." Dial, 47 (Aug.
       1, 1909), 63.

997 "Bonchurch, April 15, 1909." Academy, 76 (April 17,
       1909), 5.
       Poem.

998 Bonnerjee, R. C. "Swinburne and Meredith: the Last Two
       Great Victorians." The Hindustan Review, 20 (1909), 72-
       81.

999 Book News Monthly, 27 (Aug. 1909), 938.

1000 Brand, Wilhelm F. "Algernon Swinburne." Illustrierte
        Zeitung, 132 (April 22, 1909), 803.

1001 Brandes, George Morris Cohen. "The Genius and Influence
        of Swinburne." The Bookman (London), 36 (June 1909), 131.

1002 Brocklehurst, J. H. Papers of the Manchester Literary Club,
        35 (1909), 358-370.
        Review of The Age of Shakespeare.

1003 Burton, Richard. "The Passing of Algernon Charles Swin-
        burne and Frances Marion Crawford--Poet and Novelist."
        The Bellman, 6 (April 24, 1909), 516.

1004 Chassé, Charles. "Algernon Charles Swinburne." Mercure
        de France, 79 (May 1909), 5-13.

1005 Conrad, H. "A. C. Swinburne." Allgemeine Zeitung, no.
        16 (1909).

1006 Convers, Royall. "A Poet and a Critic." Harper's Weekly,
        53 (Oct. 2, 1909), 6.

1007 Cornish, Blanche Warre. "Swinburne and Eton." The Book-
        man (London), 36 (June 1909), 123-126.

1008   Crane, William. "The Genius and Influence of Swinburne."
       The Bookman (London), 36 (June 1909), 128.

1009   Davison, W. T. "Poetic Agnosticism: Meredith and Swin-
       burne." London Quarterly Review, 112 (July 1909), 127-
       130.

1010   "The Death of Mr. Swinburne." Literary World (London),
       n. s. 75 (April 15, 1909), 103.

1011   Dial, 46 (Jan. 16, 1909), 53-54.
       Review of The Age of Shakespeare.

1012   Dial, 46 (June 1, 1909), 358-359.

1013   Dial, 47 (Nov. 16, 1909), 391.
       Review of Swinburne's Dramas, ed. A. Beatty.

1014   The Dickensian, 5 (May 1909), 115-116.
       On Swinburne's death.

1015   Douglas, James. "Algernon Charles Swinburne." The
       Athenaeum, 133 (April 17, 1909), 463-465.

1016   _____. "Swinburne and His Circle." The Bookman (Lon-
       don), 36 (June 1909), 117-123.

1017   Foote, G. W. "Swinburne as a Free-Thinker." Freethinker,
       April 18 and 25, 1909.

1018   Fuller, E. The Bookman (New York), 29 (Aug. 1909), 636.
       Review of Three Plays of Shakespeare.

1019   "Funeral of Mr. Swinburne." The Times, April 16, 1909,
       p. 9.
       For further comments, see: The Times, April 19, 1909,
       p. 11; and May 13, 1909, p. 10.

1020   Gaines, C. H. "Algernon Charles Swinburne: An Apprecia-
       tion." Harper's Weekly, 53 (April 24, 1909), 10.

1021   "The Genius and Influence of Swinburne." The Bookman
       (London), 36 (June 1909), 126-131.
       Includes articles by E. W. Gosse (entry 1023), W. M.
       Rossetti (entry 1061), W. Crane (entry 1008), I. Zangwill
       (entry 1089), A. S. Kok (entry 1031), G. B. Shaw (entry
       1066), J. Todhunter (entry 1083), R. W. Gilder (1022),
       and G. M. C. Brandes (entry 1000).

1022   Gilder, Richard Watson. "The Genius and Influence of
       Swinburne." The Bookman (London), 36 (June 1909), 130-
       131.

1023   Gosse, Edmund William. "The Genius and Influence of Swin-
       burne." The Bookman (London), 36 (June 1909), 126-127.

1024   _____. "Swinburne, 1837-1909." Fortnightly Review, 91
       (June 1909), 1019-1039.
       Reprinted: Living Age, 262 (July 3, 1909), 3-17; and
       Portraits and Sketches (entry 1136).

1025   _____. "Swinburne: Traduit par Henry D. Davray."
       Mercure de France, 80 (July 1909), 43-68.

1026   Henry, A. S. Book News Monthly, 27 (Jan. 1909), 357-358.
       Review of The Duke of Gandia.

1027   Independent, 67 (July 8, 1909), 90.
       Review of Three Plays of Shakespeare.

1028   Independent, 67 (Oct. 14, 1909), 884.
       Review of Swinburne's Dramas, ed. A. Beatty.

1029   Kellett, Ernest Edward. "Swinburne." London Quarterly
       Review, 112 (July 1909), 8-24.
       Reprinted: Reconsiderations (entry 1616).

1030   Keys, Florence V. "The Elizabethans and Mr. Swinburne."
       North American Review, 189 (Jan. 1909), 53-60.

1031   Kok, Abraham Seyne. "The Genius and Influence of Swin-
       burne." The Bookman (London), 36 (June 1909), 128-129.

1032   Lang, Andrew. "Impressions of Swinburne." Nation (New
       York), 88 (May 20, 1909), 506-507.

1033   "The Last of the Giants." Harper's Weekly, 53 (April 24,
       1909), 6.

1034   "The Laureateship of the Sea (Algernon Charles Swinburne)."
       The Bookman (London), 36 (July 1909), 172-175.

1035   Macdonald, J. F. "The Poetry of Swinburne." Queen's
       Quarterly, 17 (July-Sept. 1909), 1-7.

1036   Marquis, Don. "Swinburne." Putnam's Magazine, 6 (June
       1909), 317.

1037   Medhurst, Francis. "To Algernon Charles Swinburne."
       Harper's Weekly, 53 (April 24, 1909), 6.

1038   Meynell, Alice Christina. "Swinburne's Lyrical Poetry."
       Dublin Review, 145 (July 1909), 172-183.
       Reprinted: Living Age, 262 (Aug. 28, 1909), 534-541; and
       Hearts of Controversy (entry 1244).

1039   "A Modern Rhapsodist." Outlook, 91 (April 24, 1909), 909-
       912.

1040   More, Paul Elmer. "Algernon Charles Swinburne." Nation
       (New York), 88 (April 15, 1909), 378-379.

1041   "Mr. Swinburne as a Master of Metre." The Spectator, 102
       (April 17, 1909), 605-606.
       Reprinted: Living Age, 261 (May 8, 1909), 372-376.

1042   Museus. "The Function of Poets." Contemporary Review,
       95 (May 1909), supplement 1-5.

1043   Nation (New York), 89 (Oct. 28, 1909), 411.
       Review of Shakespeare.

1044   Nation (New York), 89 (Nov. 25, 1909), 517.
       Review of Swinburne's Dramas, ed. A. Beatty.

1045   Nicoll, William Robertson. "Algernon Charles Swinburne."
       Contemporary Review, 95 (May 1909), 527-538.
       Reprinted: A Bookman's Letters (entry 1160).

1046   North American Review, 190 (Sept. 1909), 409.
       Review of J. W. Mackail's Swinburne (entry 972).

1047   Noyes, Alfred. "In Memory of Swinburne." Nation (New
       York), 88 (May 6, 1909), 460.
       Also: Blackwood's Magazine, 185 (May 1909), 733-734.
       Reprinted: In Memory of Swinburne (entry 976).

1048   Öfterning, Michael. "A. C. Swinburne." Hochland, 7 (July
       1909), 444-453.

1049   Peck, Harry Thurston. "Swinburne and the Swinburnians."
       The Bookman (New York), 29 (June 1909), 374-384.

1050   Phillpotts, Eden. "Swinburne." The Athenaeum, 133 (April
       24, 1909), 496.
       Poem.
       Reprinted: Living Age, 261 (June 19, 1909).

1051   Pizzagalli, A. M. "Il mito di Atalanta e Algernon Charles
       Swinburne." Atene e Roma, 12 (Nov.-Dec. 1909), 331-347.

1052   "'Placing' Swinburne." Literary Digest, 38 (May 8, 1909),
       800-801.

1053   "A Poet's Mind." Dial, 47 (July 1, 1909), 5-7.

1054   "The Poet of Pain." Nation (London), 5 (April 17, 1909),
       82-83.

1055 "The Poet Swinburne." Outlook, 91 (April 17, 1909), 854-855.

1056 Price, Warwick James. "The Last of the Great Poets." Sewanee Review, 17 (Oct. 1909), 409-417.

1057 "The Religion of Swinburne." Current Literature, 47 (Aug. 1909), 179-182.

1058 Rhys, Ernest. "A Tribute to Swinburne." Nineteenth Century and After, 65 (June 1909), 965-979.

1059 "The Riddle of Swinburne." Current Literature, 47 (Oct. 1909), 411-412.

1060 Robinson, Perry. "Reminiscences of Swinburne." The Bellman, 6 (May 15, 1909), 596.

1061 Rossetti, William Michael. "The Genius and Influence of Swinburne." The Bookman (London), 36 (June 1909), 127-128.

1062 Saintsbury, George. "Algernon Charles Swinburne." The Bookman (London), 36 (June 1909), 113-116.

1063 [Seaman, Owen]. "In Memoriam: Algernon Charles Swinburne." Punch, 136 (April 21, 1909), 272.

1064 Seccombe, Thomas. "Algernon Charles Swinburne." Readers' Review, 2 (May 1909), 55-56.

1065 Sharp, William. "Algernon Charles Swinburne: The Story of a Literary Friendship." Pall Mall Magazine, 43 (June 1909), 689-697.

1066 Shaw, George Bernard. "The Genius and Influence of Swinburne." The Bookman (London), 36 (June 1909), 129.

1067 Shorter, Clement King. "From Literary London." Dial, 47 (Dec. 16, 1909), 504-505.

1068 The Spectator, 102 (May 29, 1909), 865. Review of J. W. Mackail's Swinburne (entry 972).

1069 "Swinburne." Dial, 46 (May 1, 1909), 281-283.

1070 "Swinburne." Saturday Review (London), 107 (April 17, 1909), 484-485.

1071 "Swinburne Again." Independent, 66 (April 22, 1909), 878.

1072 "Swinburne and Eton." The Times, April 14, 1909, p. 8.

1073   "Swinburne and Meredith. "   Westminster Review, 172 (July
           1909), 29-35.

1074   "Swinburne and Meredith: The Last Victorians. "
           Chautauquan, 55 (July 1909), 160-162.

1075   "Swinburne as a Metrician. "   Academy, 76 (April 24, 1909),
           32-33.

1076   "Swinburne's 'Hymn of Man' and Carducci's 'Inno a Satana. ' "
           New Age, n. s. 6 (Dec. 30, 1909), 210-211.

1077   "Swinburne's Prose. "   Academy, 76 (April 17, 1909), 7-10.

1078   "Swinburne, the Improvisatore. "   Collier's Weekly, 43 (May
           8, 1909), 29-30.

1079   "Swinburne: The Last of the Giants. "   Current Literature,
           46 (June 1909), 640-643.

1080   "Swinburne: The Last of the Victorian Poets. "   Review of
           Reviews and World's Work (New York), 39 (May 1909),
           637-638.

1081   Teasdale, Sara.   "On the Death of Swinburne. "   Current Lit-
           erature, 46 (June 1909), 687.
           Poem.

1082   Thompson, Silvanus P.   "Swinburne's Use of Bouts-Rimés. "
           Saturday Review (London), 107 (April 24, 1909), 529.

1083   Todhunter, John.   "The Genius and Influence of Swinburne. "
           The Bookman (London), 36 (June 1909), 129-130.

1084   Tellemacher, Lionel A.   "Swinburne, the Laureateship, and
           Tennyson. "   The Guardian, 64 (May 12, 1909), 763.

1085   Weygandt, Cornelius.   "The Last of the Victorian Poets. "
           Book News Monthly, 27 (July 1909), 839-843.

1086   Willcox, Louise.   "The Fortifying Principle in Swinburne. "
           North American Review, 190 (July 1909), 93-100.

1087   "A Wizard of Words. "   Independent, 66 (April 15, 1909),
           822-823.

1088   "Writings of Swinburne: Little Known Facts of the Poet's
           Bibliography. "   Boston Evening Transcript, April 21, 1909.

1089   Zangwill, I.   "The Genius and Influence of Swinburne. "   The
           Bookman (London), 36 (June 1909), 128.

1910

McKay published a two-volume edition of Swinburne's works in 1910.

Books

1090   Austin, Alfred. "A Vindication of Tennyson. " The Bridling
       of Pegasus: Prose Papers on Poetry. London: Macmil-
       lan, 1910. pp. 197-217.
       Reprinted from Macmillan's Magazine, March 1881 (entry
       313).
       Reprinted: Freeport, N. Y. : Books for Libraries, 1967.

1091   Belloc, Hilaire. "On a Poet. " On Anything. New York:
       Dutton, 1910. pp. 54-62.
       Reprinted: Freeport, N. Y. : Books for Libraries, 1969.

1092   Browning, Oscar. Memories of Sixty Years. London: Lane,
       1910.
       Swinburne on pages 108-109.

1093   Chapman, Edward Mortimer. "Heyday of Minor Poetry. "
       English Literature in Account with Religion. Boston:
       Houghton Mifflin, 1910. pp. 468-474.

1094   Hill, Walter M. List of the Original Manuscripts of A. C.
       Swinburne. Chicago: Hill, [1910].
       A bookseller's catalogue.

1095   Kado, Maria. Swinburnes Verkunst. Berlin: Felber, 1910.
       Publication of a dissertation (entry 1106).

1096   Laurent, Raymond. "Le préraphaélisme en angleterre:
       introduction à l'étude du préraphaélisme anglais. " Etudes
       anglaises. Paris: Grasset, 1910. pp. 35-138.

1097   Leith, Mary. The Children of the Chapel. London: Chatto
       and Windus, 1910.

1098   Morton, Edward Payson. The Technique of English Non-
       Dramatic Blank Verse. Chicago: Donnelley, 1910.
       Swinburne on pages 126-129.
       Publication of a dissertation (entry 1107).

1099   Murdoch, W. G. Blaikie. Memories of Swinburne: With
       Other Essays. Edinburgh: J. and J. Gray, the St. James
       Press, 1910.

1100   Richter, Ludwig. Swinburnes Verhältnis zu Frankreich und
       Italien. Naumburg: Lippert, 1910.
       Publication of a dissertation (entry 935).

1101   Saintsbury, George. "The Pre-Raphaelite School. " A History
       of English Prosody from the Twelfth Century to the Present
       Day. London: Macmillan, 1910. Vol. III. pp. 334-352.
       See also pages 549-551.
       Reprinted: New York: Russell and Russell, 1961.

1102   Sattler, Edward. Algernon Charles Swinburne als Naturdichter.
       Bonn: Foppen, 1910.
       Publication of a dissertation (entry 1108).

1103   Serner, Gunnar. On the Language of Swinburne's Lyrics and
       Epics: A Study. Lund: Berlingska Boktryckeriet, 1910.
       Publication of a dissertation (entry 1109).

1104   Stedman, Laura, and George M. Gould. Life and Letters of
       Edmund Clarence Stedman. 2 volumes. New York: Mof-
       fat, Yard, 1910.

1105   Whiting, Lilian. Louise Chandler Moulton, Poet and Friend.
       Boston: Little, Brown, 1910.
       Swinburne on pages 85-86 and 114.

Dissertations

1106   Kado, Maria. Swinburnes Verkunst. Königsberg, 1910.
       Published: entry 1095.

1107   Morton, Edward Payson. The Techniques of English Non-
       Dramatic Blank Verse. University of Chicago, 1910.
       Published: entry 1098.

1108   Sattler, Eduard. Algernon Charles Swinburne als Naturdichter.
       Munich, 1910.
       Published: entry 1102.

1109   Serner, Martin G. On the Language of Swinburne's Lyrics
       and Epics. Lund, 1910.
       Published: entry 1103.

Periodicals

1110   Hardy, Thomas. "A Singer Asleep (Algernon Charles Swin-
       burne, 1837-1909). " English Review, 5 (April 1910), 1-3.
       Reprinted: Collected Poems of Thomas Hardy (entry 1693).

1111   Katscher, Leopold. "Swinburne als Dramatiker. " Bühne und
       Welt, 12 (July 1910), 841-845.

1112   Kernahan, Coulson. "Conversations with Mr. Swinburne. "
       London Quarterly Review, 113 (Jan. 1910), 22-45.

1113   Leith, Mary. "The Boyhood of Algernon Charles Swinburne. "
       Contemporary Review, 97 (April 1910), 385-398.

1114   New York Times Saturday Review, 15 (Nov. 26, 1910), 672.
        Review of the McKay edition of Swinburne's works.

1115   Reul, Paul de. "La poésie révolutionnaire et l'idéalisme de
        Swinburne. " Revue de l'Université de Bruxelles, (Nov. -
        Dec. 1910), 113-156.

1116   "Some Poets of the Victorian Era: VII--Swinburne. "
        Academy, 79 (Sept. 3, 1910), 221-224.

1117   "The Swinburne Question. " Nation (London), 26 (May 4,
        1910), 118.

1911

Books

1118   Austin, Alfred. The Autobiography of Alfred Austin, Poet
        Laureate, 1835-1910. Vol. II. London: Macmillan, 1911.
        Swinburne on pages 2-4.
        Reprinted: New York: AMS, 1973.

1119   Bailey, John. "Swinburne's Scotch Trilogy. " Poets and Po-
        etry: Being Articles Reprinted from the Literary Supple-
        ment of "The Times. " London: Oxford University Press,
        1911. pp. 181-186.
        Reprinted from the Times Literary Supplement, Feb. 2,
        1906 (entry 866).

1120   Barre, André. Le Symbolisme. 2 volumes. Paris: Jouve,
        1911.
        Swinburne in Volume I, page 11.

1121   Cook, E. T. The Life of John Ruskin. 2 volumes. London:
        Allen, 1911. New York: Macmillan, 1911.
        Swinburne in Volume II, pages 74-76.
        Reprinted: New York: Haskell House, 1968; and Philadel-
        phia: Richard West, 1973.

1122   Ford, Ford Madox. Ancient Lights and Certain New Reflec-
        tions, Being the Memoirs of a Young Man. London:
        Chapman and Hall, 1911.

1123   _____ . Memories and Impressions. New York: Harper,
        1911.

1124   Munro, John. Frederick James Furnivall: A Volume of

Personal Records. London: Frowde, 1911.
Swinburne on pages lvi-lviii.

1125   Nevinson, Henry Woodd. "A Poet's Youth." Essays in
       Freedom. London: 1911. pp. 37-42.
       Reprinted from Nation, April 13, 1907 (entry 920).

Periodicals

1126   Donkin, H. Bryan. "Swinburne's Greek Elegiacs on Landor."
       The Spectator, 107 (Oct. 14, 1911), 593.

1127   Gossaert, G. "A. C. Swinburne." Mannen en Vrouwen v.
       Beteekenis, no. 10 (Aug. 1911).

1128   Jonson, G. C. Aston. "A Plea for Experiments." The
       Drama, 1 (Nov. 1911), 236-241.
       The staging of Atalanta in Calydon.

1129   New York Times Book Review, 16 (May 28, 1911), 328.
       Review of a new edition of selections of Swinburne's works
       published by Harper.

1130   North American Review, 193 (June 1911), 931.
       Review of a new edition of selections of Swinburne's works
       published by Harper.

1131   Olivero, Federico. "Il paesaggio nei 'Poems and Ballads' di
       Algernon Charles Swinburne." Nuova Antologia di Lettere,
       Scienze ed Arti, 156 (Dec. 1, 1911), 435-448.
       Reprinted: Saggi di Letteratura Inglese (entry 1162).

1132   Prideaux, William Francis. "Swinburne's 'Unpublished
       Verses.'" The Athenaeum, 137 (March 11, 1911), 278.

1912

Books

1133   Collins, L. C. Life and Memories of John Churton Collins:
       Written and Compiled by His Son. London: Lane, 1912.

1134   Douady, Jules. La mer et les poètes anglais. Paris:
       Hachette, 1912. pp. 359-386.

1135   Gosse, Edmund, and Lord Redesdale. The Life of Swin-
       burne. London: Chiswick, 1912.

1136 _____. "Swinburne, 1837-1909." Portraits and Sketches.
London: Heinemann, 1912. pp. 1-58.
Reprinted from the Fortnightly Review (entry 1024).
See entry 1024 for other reprinting.
Reviewed: Nation (New York) (entry 1174); and J. Bailey
in Quarterly Review (entry 1254).

1137 Meredith, George. Letters of George Meredith. Ed. W. M.
Meredith. New York: Scribner, 1912.
Swinburne in Volume I, pages 55, 182-183, 188-190, and
240; and in Volume II, page 634.

1138 Pollen, Anne. John Hungerford Pollen. London: 1912.

1139 Saintsbury, George. A History of English Prose Rhythm.
London: Macmillan, 1912.
Swinburne on pages 427-435.

1140 Sharp, William. "Algernon Charles Swinburne." Papers
Critical and Reminiscent. New York: Duffield, 1912.
pp. 281-320.

1141 Thomas, Edward. Algernon Charles Swinburne: A Critical
Study. London: Secker, 1912. New York: Kennerly,
1912.
Reviewed: The Athenaeum (entry 1142); New York Times
Book Review (entry 1143); North American Review (entry
1177); Saturday Review (London) (entry 1180); The Spectator
(entry 1181); and T. P.'s Weekly (entry 1186).

Periodicals

1142 The Athenaeum, 140 (Dec. 7, 1912), 684.
Review of E. Thomas's Algernon Charles Swinburne (entry
1141).

1143 B., H. W. New York Times Book Review, 17 (Dec. 29, 1912),
796.
Review of E. Thomas's Algernon Charles Swinburne.

1144 Bunner, Henry Cuyler. "The Great Swinburnian Hoax." The
Bookman (New York), 36 (Dec. 1912), 425-429.

1145 Falzon, Paul L. "Reminiscences of Swinburne in D'Annunzio." Notes and Queries, 11th ser., 5 (March 16, 1912),
201-203.

1146 Gosse, Edmund. "Swinburne et Etretat." Cornhill Magazine,
3rd ser., 33 (Oct. 1912), 457-468.

1147 Jones, Dora M. "English Writers and the Making of Italy."
London Quarterly Review, 118 (July 1912), 98.

1148 "A Phrase of Swinburne's: 'The Morn.'" Notes and Queries,
      11th ser., 6 (Sept. 14, 1912), 216.

1149 Reul, Paul de. "Les tragédies antiques de Swinburne."
      Revue de l'Université de Bruxelles, 17 (Feb. 1912), 369-
      407.

1150 Wilson, W. E. "A Phrase of Swinburne's: 'The Morn.'"
      Notes and Queries, 11th ser., 6 (Aug. 24, 1912), 147.

1913

In 1913, Chatto and Windus published Swinburne's essay Charles
Dickens in one volume. Badger of Boston published four of Swinburne's essays in A Pilgrimage of Pleasure.

Books

1151 Chesterton, Gilbert Keith. "Great Victorian Poets." The
      Victorian Age in Literature. New York: Holt, [1913].
      pp. 181-188.
      Home University Library of Modern Knowledge, No. 61.

1152 Collins, Mortimer. "'If'" and "Salad." A Century of Par-
      ody and Imitation. Ed. Walter Jerrold and R. M. Leonard.
      London: Oxford University Press, 1913. pp. 286-287.
      Two poems.

1153 Cook, Edward. The Life of Florence Nightingale. 2 volumes.
      London: Macmillan, 1913.
      Swinburne in volume II, pages 95 and 228.

1154 Drinkwater, John. Swinburne: An Estimate. London and
      Toronto: Dent, 1913. New York: Dutton, 1913.
      An intelligently written study, which considers Swinburne's
      works in three parts: lyric poetry, drama, and criticism.
      Reprinted: Folcroft, Pa.: Folcroft, 1969.
      Reviewed: Academy (entry 1166); A. L. A. Booklist (entry
      1167); Nation (New York) (entry 1175); New York Times
      Book Review (entry 1176); The Spectator (entry 1182); and
      T. P.'s Weekly (entry 1186).

1155 Gosse, Edmund. "Algernon Charles Swinburne." The Dic-
      tionary of National Biography. Second Supplement, I. [c.
      1913].
      This article's accuracy is questionable.

1156   Hilton, Arthur Clement.   "Octopus, by Algernon Charles Sin-
       burn. " A Century of Parody and Imitations.   Ed. Walter
       Jerrold and R. M. Leonard.   London: Oxford University
       Press, 1913.   pp. 363-364.

1157   Lang, Andrew.   "Ballade of Cricket" and "The Palace of
       Bric-à-brac. " A Century of Parody and Imitation.   Ed.
       Walter Jerrold and R. M. Leonard.   London: Oxford
       University Press, 1913.   pp. 354 and 355-356, respec-
       tively.
       Two poems.

1158   Livingston, Luther Samuel.   First Editions of Algernon Swin-
       burne: The Bibliographical Description of a Collected Set
       of the First Editions of the Writings of the Last of the
       Great Victorian Poets: With the Manuscript of "A Midsum-
       mer Holiday. "   New York: Dodd and Livingston, [1913].
       Mentioned in J. Carter and G. Pollard, The Firm of
       Charles Ottley (entry 1854), page 21, as part of their
       general investigation of forgeries of Swinburne first edi-
       tions.

1159   Lytton, Earl of.   The Life of Edward Bulwer, First Lord
       Lytton.   London: Macmillan, 1913.
       Swinburne in Volume II, pages 431-439.

1160   Nicoll, William Robertson.   "Algernon Charles Swinburne. "
       A Bookman's Letters.   London: Hodder and Stoughton,
       1913.   pp. 235-254.
       Reprinted from Contemporary Review, May 1909 (entry
       1045).

1161   O'Brien, Edward J.   "A Bibliography of the Works of Alger-
       non Charles Swinburne. "   A Pilgrimage of Pleasure: Es-
       says and Studies.   By Algernon Charles Swinburne.   Bos-
       ton: Badger, 1913.   pp. 153-181.
       Reviewed: Dial (entry 1172).

1162   Olivero, Federico.   "Il paesaggio nei 'Poems and Ballads' di
       Algernon Charles Swinburne. " Saggi di Letteratura Inglese.
       Bari: Laterza, 1913.
       Reprinted from Nuova Antologia, Dec. 1, 1911 (entry 1131).

1163   Rhys, Ernest.   Lyric Poetry.   London: Dent, 1913.
       Swinburne on pages 339-346.

1164   Schelling, Felix E.   The English Lyric.   Boston: Houghton
       Mifflin, 1913.
       Swinburne on pages 239-248.

1165   Turquet-Milnes, Gladys.   "Swinburne. "   The Influence of
       Baudelaire in France and England.   London: Constable,
       1913.   pp. 222-229.

Periodicals

1166   Academy, 84 (June 7, 1913), 715.
       Review of J. Drinkwater's Swinburne (entry 1154).

1167   A. L. A. Booklist, 10 (Sept. 1913), 11.
       Review of J. Drinkwater's Swinburne (entry 1154).

1168   The Bookman (London), 44 (May 1913), 86-87.
       Review of Charles Dickens.

1169   Bickley, Francis. "Swinburne Byways." Academy, 84 (Jan.
       11, 1913), 47-48.

1170   Chesterton, G. K.   Nation (London), 12 (March 29, 1913),
       1068.
       Review of Charles Dickens.

1171   de Wyzewa, T.   Revue des Deux Mondes, 6th ser., 15 (May
       15, 1913), 457-468.
       Review of Charles Dickens.

1172   Dial, 55 (Nov. 1, 1913), 364.
       Review of A Pilgrimage of Pleasure.

1173   Helston, John.   "To Algernon Charles Swinburne."   Literary
       Digest, 46 (April 26, 1913), 963-964.
       Also: English Review, 14 (April 1913), 13-16.

1174   Nation (New York), 96 (March 27, 1913), 312-313.
       Review of E. W. Gosse's Portraits and Sketches (entry
       1136).

1175   Nation (New York), 97 (Nov. 27, 1913), 510-511.
       Review of J. Drinkwater's Swinburne (entry 1154).

1176   New York Times Book Review, 18 (July 6, 1913), 388.
       Review of J. Drinkwater's Swinburne (entry 1154).

1177   North American Review, 197 (Feb. 1913), 281-283.
       Review of E. Thomas's Algernon Charles Swinburne (entry
       1141).

1178   O'Brien, Edward J.   "Swinburne Bibliography."   Dial, 55
       (Dec. 1, 1913), 468.

1179   Pound, Olivia.   "On the Application of the Principles of
       Greek Lyric Tragedy in the Classical Dramas of Swin-
       burne."   The University Studies of the University of
       Nebraska, 13 (1913), 341-360.

1180   Saturday Review (London), 115 (April 5, 1913), 426.
       Review of E. Thomas's Algernon Charles Swinburne
       (entry 1141).

1181 The Spectator, 110 (Jan. 25, 1913), 131.
      Review of E. Thomas's Algernon Charles Swinburne (entry
      1141).

1182 The Spectator, 110 (May 24, 1913), 889.
      Review of J. Drinkwater's Swinburne (entry 1154).

1183 "The Secret of Swinburne's Power." Current Opinion, 54
      (March 1913), 233-234.

1184 "Swinburne on Dickens." The Athenaeum, 141 (March 8,
      1913), 277-278.
      Review of Charles Dickens.

1185 Swinburne, Isabel, and Edmund Gosse. Times Literary Sup-
      plement, April 5, 1913, pp. 11-12 and 14-16, respectively.
      Two letters regarding Gosse's errors in mentioning Swin-
      burne's juvenilia in his article in the Dictionary of National
      Biography (entry 1155).

1186 T. P.'s Weekly, 21 (May 23, 1913), 647.
      Review of Charles Dickens, E. Thomas's Algernon Charles
      Swinburne (entry 1141), and J. Drinkwater's Swinburne
      (entry 1154).

1914

Books

1187 Charles Scribner's Sons. Superb Collected Sets of the First
      Editions of Eliot, Milton, Coleridge, Swinburne, Words-
      worth. New York: Scribner, 1914.
      Swinburne on page 88.

1188 Dowden, Edward. The Letters of Edward Dowden and His
      Correspondents. Ed. John Eglinton. London: Dent, 1914.
      New York: Dutton, 1914.
      Swinburne on pages 140-144.

1189 Hunt, Theodore Whitfield. "The Poetry of Swinburne."
      English Literary Miscellany: Second Series. Oberlin,
      Ohio: Bibliotheca Sacra, 1914. pp. 293-316.

1190 The Swinburne Manuscripts. [Boston: Bibliophile Society,
      1914].
      This pamphlet is rare.
      Reprinted: A Suppressed Critique of Wise's Swinburne
      Transactions (entry 2081).

1190a Vaughan, C. E. "Bibliography of the Works of A. C. Swin-
       burne." Bibliographies of Swinburne, Morris and Rossetti.
       London: Oxford University Press (Hart), 1914. pp. 3-6.
       Reprinted: Folcroft, Pa.: Folcroft, 1969.

1191   Welby, T. Earle. Swinburne: A Critical Study. London:
       Mathews, 1914.
       A predecessor of Welby's A Study of Swinburne (entry
       1557).
       Reviewed: The Athenaeum (entry 1213); and The Spectator
       (entry 1216).

Dissertation

1192   Bausenwein, Josef. Die poetischen Bearbeitungen der Balin-
       und Balan-sage von Tennyson und Swinburne und ihr Ver-
       hältnis zu Malory. Heidelberg, 1914.
       This dissertation is listed in R. D. Altick and R. Mat-
       thews's Guide to Doctoral Dissertations in Victorian Lit-
       erature 1886-1958 (Urbana: University of Illinois Press,
       1960) and has not been examined by the present bibliogra-
       pher. Alice Galimberti lists the same dissertation for the
       year 1894 in her L'Aedo d'Italia (entry 1524).

Periodicals

1193   Bensly, Edward. "Swinburne as Polyglot Author." Notes
       and Queries, 11th ser., 9 (Feb. 21, 1914), 156-157.

1194   Gosse, Edmund. "Swinburne's Unpublished Writings." Fort-
       nightly Review, 102 (Aug. 1914), 255-267.

1195   Hoops, J. "Swinburnes Tale of Balen und Malorys Mort
       d'Arthur [sic]." Festschrift zum XVI Neuphilologentag in
       Bremen, 1 (June 1914), 1-44.

1196   "A Literary Curiosity." The Spectator, 112 (May 2, 1914),
       732-733.
       About Victor Hugo.

1197   Lux, Jacques. "Un ami de Swinburne." Revue Politique et
       Littéraire, 52 (July 4, 1914), 32.

1198   Malmstedt, A. "Om Swinburne's liv och diktning." Studier
       i Modern Språkvetenskap, 5 (1914), 47-86.

1199   Moore, Charles Leonard. "Poetic Expression." Dial, 56
       (Feb. 16, 1914), 131-132.

1200   Pearson, Edmund Lester. "Swinburne." Nation (New York),
       98 (March 26, 1914), 329-330.

1201   Simpson, Selwyn G. "Algernon Charles Swinburne." East
       and West, 13 (Jan. 1914), 30-44.

1915

Books

1202 Bell, A. F. "Rossetti, Morris, and Swinburne." Leaders in English Literature. London: Bell, 1915. pp. 214-223. Rare.

1203 Dodd, Robert H. Algernon Charles Swinburne: First Editions and an Autograph Manuscript: Offered by R. H. Dodd. New York: Dodd, 1915.

1204 Galletti, Alfredo. Saggi e Studi. Bologna: 1915.

1205 Hearn, Lafcadio. "Swinburne's 'Hertha.'" Interpretations of Literature. Ed. J. Erskine. New York: Dodd, Mead, 1915. Vol. I. pp. 362-370. Sensible evaluation of "Hertha."

1206 Lyall, Alfred Comyn. "Characteristics of Mr. Swinburne's Poetry." Studies in Literature and History. London: Murray, 1915. pp. 263-290. Reprinted from the Edinburgh Review, Oct. 1906 (entry 879).

1207 Mitford, Algernon Bertram (Lord Redesdale). Memories. London: Hutchinson, 1915. Swinburne in Volume I, pages 68-74, and in Volume II.

1208 Sélincourt, Ernest de. "English Poetry Since 1815." English Poets and the National Ideal. London: Oxford University Press, 1915. Swinburne on pages 107-108 and 110-112.

1209 Waugh, Arthur. "Reticence in Literature." Reticence in Literature and Other Papers. London: Wilson, [1915]. pp. 17-20. Reprinted from The Yellow Book, April 1894 (entry 590). Reviewed: Times Literary Supplement (entry 1217).

1210 Williamson, Claude C. H. "Algernon Charles Swinburne." Writers of Three Centuries, 1789-1914. Philadelphia: Jacobs, [c. 1915]. pp. 284-303.

Dissertations

1211 Heilbrunn, Stella. Elizabethan Influence on Swinburne's Dramas. University of Chicago, 1915.

1212 Henderson, Walter B. D. Swinburne and Landor: A Study of Their Spiritual Relationship and Its Effect on Swinburne's

Moral and Poetic Development.   Princeton, 1915.
Published: entry 1315.

Periodicals

1213 The Athenaeum, 145 (Feb. 6, 1915), 113.
      Review of T. E. Welby's Swinburne (entry 1191).

1214 Ayscough, John. "Last Giants." Catholic World, 100
      (March 1915), 776-779.

1215 "Poseidon and Athene." Notes and Queries, 11th ser., 9
      (May 15, 1915), 377-378.

1216 The Spectator, 115 (July 24, 1915), 114-115.
      Review of T. E. Welby's Swinburne (entry 1191).

1217 Times Literary Supplement, April 16, 1915, p. 132.
      Review of A. Waugh's Reticence in Literature (entry 1209).

1916

Books

1218 Clark, John Scott. "Algernon Charles Swinburne." A Study
      of English and American Writers. New York: Row, Peter-
      son, [1916].   pp. 582-592.

1219 Hake, Thomas, and Arthur Compton-Rickett. The Life and
      Letters of Theodore Watts-Dunton. 2 volumes. London:
      Jack, 1916. New York: Putnam, 1916.
      Theodore Watts-Dunton played an enormously important role
      in Swinburne's life. The poet lived the last three decades
      of his life under the care of Watts-Dunton.
      Reviewed: The Athenaeum (entry 1229); W. H. Chesson in
      Saturday Review (London) (entry 1230); E. F. E. in Boston
      Evening Transcript (entry 1264); New York Times Book Re-
      view (entry 1284); The Spectator (entry 1237); and Times
      Literary Supplement (entry 1238).

1220 Hearn, Lafcadio. "Studies in Swinburne." Appreciations of
      Poetry. Ed. J. Erskine. New York: Dodd, Mead, 1916.
      pp. 126-171.

1221 Lucas, E. V. At 'The Pines': A Visit to A. C. Swinburne.
      London: Shorter, [1916].
      Rare edition.

Reprinted from New Statesman, March 25, 1916 (entry 1233).

1222 Quayle, William Alfred. "Selfish Womanhood." Recovered Yesterdays in Literature. New York: Abingdon, 1916. pp. 74-87.

1223 Sotheby, Wilkinson and Hodge. Catalogue of the Library of A. C. Swinburne, deceased: Sold by Order of the Executors of the Late W. T. Watts-Dunton Esq.: Comprising First Editions of Eminent English Authors. [London: Dryden (J. Davy), 1916].
Catalogues most of the books Swinburne owned.

1224 Symons, Arthur. "Algernon Charles Swinburne." Figures of Several Centuries. New York: Dutton, 1916. pp. 153-200.

1225 Thompson, Alexander Hamilton. "Algernon Charles Swinburne." Cambridge History of English Literature. Ed. A. W. Ward and A. R. Waller. Cambridge: Cambridge University Press, 1916. Vol. XIII. pp. 129-138.

1226 Watts-Dunton, Theodore. Poets and the Renascence of Wonder. London: Jenkins, 1916.

1227 Whistler, James McNeill. "Ten O'clock." Portland, Me.: Mosher, 1916.

Periodicals

1228 Amram, Beaulah B. "Swinburne and Carducci." Yale Review, n.s. 5 (Jan. 1916), 365-381.

1229 The Athenaeum, 148 (Dec. 1916), 575.
Review of T. Hake and A. Compton-Rickett's The Life and Letters of Theodore Watts-Dunton (entry 1219).

1230 Chesson, W. H. Saturday Review (London), 122 (Dec. 30, 1916), 623.
Review of T. Hake and A. Compton-Rickett's The Life and Letters of Theodore Watts-Dunton (entry 1219).

1231 De Gourcuff, Olivier. "Un essai de Swinburne sur le 'Roi Lear.'" Mercure de France, 115 (May 1916), 373-376.

1232 Littell, Philip. "Books and Things." New Republic, 8 (Sept. 9, 1916), 145.

1233 Lucas, Edward Verrall. "At 'The Pines': A Visit to A. C. Swinburne." New Statesman, 6 (March 25, 1916), 593-595.
Reprinted: At "The Pines" (entry 1221).

1234   Moore, Charles Leonard.   "The Passionate Victorians."
        Dial, 60 (June 8, 1916), 524.

1235   "Poetry and the Intuition of Immortality."   Times Literary
        Supplement, Sept. 14, 1916, pp. 433-434.

1236   Reinach, S.   "Thinking in French."   Notes and Queries, 12th
        ser., 1 (March 11, 1916), 207.

1237   The Spectator, 117 (Dec. 16, 1916), 771.
        Review of T. Hake and A. Compton-Rickett's The Life and
        Letters of Theodore Watts-Dunton (entry 1219).

1238   Times Literary Supplement, Nov. 9, 1916, 535.
        Review of T. Hake and A. Compton-Rickett's The Life and
        Letters of Theodore Watts-Dunton (entry 1219).

1917

In 1917, some previously uncollected Swinburne poems were published in Posthumous Poems, edited by Edmund Gosse and T. J.
Wise.

Books

1239   Bennett, Arnold.   "Mallarmé, Bazin, Swinburne" and "Swin-
        burne."   Books and Persons: Being Comments on a Past
        Epoch: 1908-1911.   London: Chatto and Windus, 1917.
        New York: Doran, 1917.   pp. 65-67 and 123-129, respec-
        tively.
        "Swinburne" reprinted from the New Age, April 22, 1909
        (entry 992).
        Bennett laments the misunderstanding of Swinburne by Eng-
        lish critics and readers.

1240   Gosse, Edmund.   The Life of Algernon Charles Swinburne.
        London: Macmillan, 1917.   New York: Macmillan, 1917.
        Reprinted as Volume XIX of the Bonchurch edition of Swin-
        burne's works (years 1925-1927).
        Gosse was not a careful researcher, and thus his biography
        of Swinburne contains many errors of fact.   He was prone
        to take the word of unreliable witnesses, without verifica-
        tion.
        Reviewed: A. L. A. Booklist (entry 1248); American Review
        of Reviews (entry 1250); The Athenaeum (entry 1251); J.
        Bailey in Quarterly Review (entry 1254); L. Binyon in The
        Bookman (London) (entry 1255); Catholic World (entry 1259);

S. C. Chew in Modern Language Notes (entry 1321); Cleveland Open Shelf (entry 1260); G. I. Colbron in The Bookman (New York) (entry 1261); Contemporary Review (entry 1262); E. F. E. in Boston Evening Transcript (entry 1265); Independent (1271), C. Kernahan in London Quarterly Review (1273); B. I. Kinne in Dial (entry 1274); Nation (London) (entry 1280); Nation (New York) (entry 1281); New York Times Book Review (1285); Pittsburgh Monthly Bulletin (entry 1289); E. Pound in Poetry (entry 1334); Pratt Institute Quarterly Book List (entry 1290); A. Quiller-Couch in Edinburgh Review (entry 1291); Saturday Review (London) (entry 1293); The Spectator (entry 1295); Times Literary Supplement (entry 1305); and C. B. Tinker in Yale Review (entry 1306).

1241 Gwynn, Stephen, and Gertrude M. Tuckwell.   The Life of the Rt. Hon. Sir Charles W. Dilke, Bart., M. P.   London: 1917.

1242 Kernahan, Coulson. "A. C. Swinburne." In Good Company. London: Lane, 1917. pp. 1-31.

1243 Leith, Mary. The Boyhood of Algernon Charles Swinburne: Personal Recollections by His Cousin, Mrs. Disney Leith: With Extracts from Some of His Private Letters.   London: Chatto and Windus, 1917. New York: Putnam, 1917. Mary Leith (then Mary Gordon) knew Swinburne as a child. Her book includes letters by Swinburne, but her texts and datings, as well as her insights, cannot be entirely trusted. Reviewed: J. Bailey in Quarterly Review (entry 1254); Boston Evening Transcript (entry 1257); S. C. Chew in Modern Language Notes (entry 1321); Dial (entry 1263); Independent (entry 1270); Nation (London) (entry 1280); Nation (New York) (entry 1282); New York Times Book Review (entry 1286); North American Review (entry 1287); Saturday Review (London) (entry 1292); The Spectator (entry 1296); Times Literary Supplement (entry 1303); and C. B. Tinker in Yale Review (entry 1307).

1244 Meynell, Alice Christina. "Swinburne's Lyrical Poetry." Hearts of Controversy. New York: Scribner, 1917. pp. 53-75. Reprinted from Dublin Review, July 1909 (entry 1038). See entry 1037 for other reprinting.

1245 Morley, John. Recollections. New York: Macmillan, 1917. Swinburne in Volume I, pages 40-44.

1246 [Squire, John Collings, writing as "Solomon Eagle"]. "If Swinburne Had Written 'The Lay of Horatius.'" Tricks of the Trade. New York: Putnam, 1917. pp. 51-53. Reprinted: Collected Parodies (entry 1440).

1247   Thomas, Edward. "Swinburne." Literary Pilgrim in Eng-
       land. New York: Dodd, 1917. pp. 263-269.

Periodicals

1248   A. L. A. Booklist, 14 (Nov. 1917), 57.
       Review of E. Gosse's The Life of ACS (entry 1240).

1249   "Algernon Swinburne as the Peter Pan of the Victorian Po-
       ets." Current Opinion, 63 (July 1917), 51-52.

1250   American Review of Reviews, 56 (July 1917), 103.
       Review of E. Gosse's The Life of ACS (entry 1240).

1251   The Athenaeum, 153 (May 1917), 256.
       Review of E. Gosse's The Life of ACS (entry 1240).

1252   The Athenaeum, 154 (July 1917), 362.
       Review of Posthumous Poems.

1253   Aubry, G. Jean. "Baudelaire et Swinburne." Mercure de
       France, 124 (Nov. 16, 1917), 265-281.

1254   Bailey, John. Quarterly Review, 228 (July 1917), 228-248.
       Review of E. Gosse's Portraits and Sketches (entry 1136),
       E. Gosse's The Life of ACS (entry 1240), Mary Leith's
       The Boyhood of ACS (entry 1243), and Posthumous Poems.

1255   Binyon, Lawrence. The Bookman (London), 52 (May 1917),
       35-37.
       Review of E. Gosse's The Life of ACS (entry 1240).

1256   _____. "Gleanings from Swinburne." The Bookman (Lon-
       don), 52 (Aug. 1917), 145-147.
       Review of Posthumous Poems.

1257   Boston Evening Transcript, June 23, 1917, p. 6.
       Review of M. Leith's The Boyhood of ACS (entry 1243).

1258   Campbell, Archibald Young. "Swinburne's Criticism." New
       Statesman, 9 (May 5, 1917), 110-111.

1259   Catholic World, 106 (Nov. 1917), 259.
       Review of E. Gosse's The Life of ACS (entry 1240).

1260   Cleveland Open Shelf, Sept. 1917, p. 115.
       Review of E. Gosse's The Life of ACS (entry 1240).

1261   Colbron, G. I. The Bookman (New York), 45 (May 1917),
       290.
       Review of E. Gosse's The Life of ACS (entry 1240).

1262   Contemporary Review, 111 (May 1917), 651-653.
       Review of E. Gosse's The Life of ACS (entry 1240).

1263 Dial, 63 (Sept. 27, 1917), 275-276.
      Review of M. Leith's The Boyhood of ACS (entry 1243).

1264 E. , E. F. Boston Evening Transcript, Jan. 27, 1917, p. 8.
      Review of T. Hake and A. Compton-Rickett's The Life of
      Theodore Watts-Dunton (entry 1219).

1265 _____. Boston Evening Transcript, May 23, 1917, p. 6.
      Review of E. Gosse's The Life of ACS (entry 1240).

1266 Fehr, Bernhard. "Zu Swinburnes literarischer Biographie. "
      Archiv für das Studium der neueren Sprachen und Litera-
      turen Brunswick, 136 (May 1917), 240-248.

1267 Gosse, Edmund. "Swinburne and Music. " The Spectator,
      118 (May 5, 1917), 516.

1268 _____. "Swinburne's 'Death of Franklin.' " Times Lit-
      erary Supplement, July 26, 1917, p. 357.

1269 Hagberg, Karl August. "Dolores: En af Swinburnes
      märkligaste dikter. " Finsk Tidskrift, 83 (1917), 9-14.

1270 Independent, 92 (Oct. 6, 1917), 64.
      Review of M. Leith's The Boyhood of ACS (entry 1243).

1271 Independent, 92 (Oct. 6, 1917), 65.
      Review of E. Gosse's The Life of ACS (1240).

1272 Jones, Gwen Ann. "Notes on Swinburne's 'Song of Italy.' "
      Modern Language Notes, 32 (April 1917), 200-207.

1273 Kernahan, Coulson. "Swinburne and Mr. Gosse. " London
      Quarterly Review, 128 (July 1917), 91-101.
      Review of E. Gosse's The Life of ACS (entry 1240).

1274 Kinne, B. I. Dial, 63 (June 28, 1917), 21-23.
      Review of E. Gosse's The Life of ACS (entry 1240).

1275 Latham, F. L. "The Newdigate of 1858, and Swinburne's
      Poem on the Death of Sir John Franklin. " Times Liter-
      ary Supplement, July 19, 1917, p. 345; and Aug. 16, 1917,
      p. 393.

1276 Leith, Mary. "Swinburne's 'Death of Franklin.' " Times
      Literary Supplement, Aug. 2, 1917, p. 369; and Sept. 6,
      1917, p. 429.

1277 McDowall, A. S. "Swinburne and Mary Stuart. " Times
      Literary Supplement, May 31, 1917, p. 261.

1278 "A Mid-Victorian Literary Tempest. " Literary Digest, 54
      (June 16, 1917), 1851.

1279 "Mr. Swinburne's Posthumous Poems. " Contemporary Review,
      112 (July 1917), 106-107.
      Review of Posthumous Poems.

1280 Nation (London), 21 (April 14, 1917), 42-44.
      Review of E. Gosse's The Life of ACS (entry 1240) and
      M. Leith's The Boyhood of ACS (entry 1243).

1281 Nation (New York), 105 (Aug. 23, 1917), 201.
      Review of E. Gosse's The Life of ACS (entry 1240).

1282 Nation (New York), 105 (Aug. 23, 1917), 206.
      Review of M. Leith's The Boyhood of ACS (entry 1243).

1283 Nation (New York), 105 (Sept. 27, 1917), 345.
      Review of Posthumous Poems.

1284 New York Times Book Review, 22 (Jan. 28, 1917), 25.
      Review of T. Hake and A. Compton-Rickett's The Life of
      Theodore Watts-Dunton (entry 1219).

1285 New York Times Book Review, 22 (May 6, 1917), 181.
      Review of E. Gosse's The Life of ACS (entry 1240).

1286 New York Times Book Review, 22 (June 24, 1917), 240.
      Review of M. Leith's The Boyhood of ACS (entry 1243).

1287 North American Review, 206 (Aug. 1917), 314.
      Review of M. Leith's The Boyhood of ACS (entry 1243).

1288 Pellegrini, Carlo. "The Eternal Boy. " Current Opinion,
      63 (July 1917), 52.

1289 Pittsburgh Monthly Bulletin, 22 (Nov. 1917), 745.
      Review of E. Gosse's The Life of ACS (entry 1240).

1290 Pratt Institute Quarterly Book List, Oct. 1917, p. 48.
      Review of E. Gosse's The Life of ACS (entry 1240).

1291 Quiller-Couch, Arthur. "Swinburne. " Edinburgh Review,
      225 (April 1917), 249-268.
      Review of E. Gosse's The Life of ACS (1240).
      Reprinted: Studies in Literature (entry 1358).

1292 Saturday Review (London), 123 (April 28, 1917), 392.
      Review of M. Leith's The Boyhood of ACS (entry 1243).

1293 Saturday Review (London), 124 (July 7, 1917), sup. 3.
      Review of E. Gosse's The Life of ACS (entry 1240).

1294 Saturday Review (London), 124 (July 7, 1917), sup. 4.
      Review of Posthumous Poems.

1295 The Spectator, 118 (April 21, 1917), 462-463; and 118 (April
        18, 1917), 490-491.
        Review of E. Gosse's The Life of ACS (entry 1240).

1296 The Spectator, 118 (April 28, 1917), 491.
        Review of M. Leith's The Boyhood of ACS (entry 1243).

1297 Swinburne, Evelyn C. "Swinburne's Ancestry." The Specta-
        tor, 118 (May 5, 1917), 516.

1298 "Swinburne and Mary Stuart." Times Literary Supplement,
        June 14, 1917, p. 285; and June 21, 1917, p. 297.
        See also entry 1277.

1299 "Swinburne Copyrights." Times Literary Supplement, April
        5, 1917, p. 166.

1300 "Swinburne's Posthumous Poems." The Spectator, 118 (June
        23, 1917), 701-702.
        Review of Posthumous Poems.

1301 "Swinburne's Visit to Paris in 1882." Times Literary Sup-
        plement, April 26, 1917, p. 203.

1302 Symons, Arthur. "Algernon Charles Swinburne: With Some
        Unpublished Letters." Fortnightly Review, 107 (May 1917),
        795-804.
        Reprinted: Living Age, 293 (June 16, 1917), 666-673.

1303 Times Literary Supplement, March 22, 1917, p. 139.
        Review of M. Leith's The Boyhood of ACS (entry 1243).

1304 Times Literary Supplement, June 21, 1917, p. 295.
        Review of Posthumous Poems.

1305 Times Literary Supplement, June 28, 1917, p. 309; and July
        12, 1917, pp. 333-334.
        Review of E. Gosse's The Life of ACS (entry 1240).

1306 Tinker, C. B. Yale Review, n.s. 7 (Oct. 1917), 195.
        Review of E. Gosse's The Life of ACS (entry 1240).

1307 _____. Yale Review, n.s. 7 (Oct. 1917), 195.
        Review of M. Leith's The Boyhood of ACS (entry 1243).

1308 Tollemache, Lionel A. "Swinburne." The Spectator, 118
        (April 28, 1917), 488.

1309 Tynan, Katharine. "Poets of Yesterday and To-day."
        Studies, 6 (Dec. 1917), 708-709.
        Review of Posthumous Poems.

1918

In 1918, Edmund Gosse published a selection of poems from four of Swinburne's books, under the title The Springtide of Life: Poems of Childhood (hereafter referred to as The Springtide of Life). Gosse and T. J. Wise also published a two-volume edition of Swinburne's letters, The Letters of Algernon Charles Swinburne (London: Heinemann, 1918). This edition will hereafter be referred to as The Letters of ACS, edited by E. Gosse and T. J. Wise. Thomas Hake and Arthur Compton-Rickett published their edition of Swinburne's letters, The Letters of Algernon Charles Swinburne: With Some Personal Recollections (London: Murray, 1918). This edition will hereafter be referred to as The Letters of ACS, edited by T. Hake and A. Compton-Rickett. Neither of these editions of letters is useful in the study of Swinburne, although they are interesting for the study of Swinburne's reputation. Both suffer from poor editing, hidden deletions for what Wise called "editorial discretion" (when complaining about the Hake and Compton-Rickett edition), and confusing commentaries. The Hake and Compton-Rickett edition may be useful for its "personal recollections."

Books

1310   Adams, Henry.   The Education of Henry Adams.   Boston and
         New York: Houghton Mifflin, 1918.
         Swinburne on pages 139-141.   Often quoted in Swinburne
         studies.
         Reprinted: C. K. Hyder, Swinburne: The Critical Heri-
         tage (entry 2083), pages 3-5.

1311   Beers, Henry A.   History of English Romanticism in the
         Nineteenth Century.   New York: Holt, 1918.

1312   Fehr, Bernhard.   "Auf Swinburnes Spuren."   Studien zu
         Oscar Wildes Gedichten.   Berlin: Mayer und Muller, 1918.
         pp. 52-104.
         Untersuchen und Texte aus der deutschen und englischen
         Philologie.   Palaestra 100.

1313   Galletti, Alfredo.   "Algernon Carlo Swinburne."   Studi di
         Letteratura Inglese.   Bologna: Zanichelli, 1918.   pp. 239-
         289.

1314   Gosse, Edmund.   "Algernon Charles Swinburne."   The Eng-
         lish Poets.   Ed. T. H. Ward.   New York: Macmillan,
         1918.   Vol. V.   pp. 368-375.

1315   Henderson, W. Brooks Drayton.   Swinburne and Landor: A
         Study of Their Spiritual Relationship and Its Effect on Swin-
         burne's Moral and Poetic Development.   London: Macmil-
         lan, 1918.   New York: Macmillan, 1918.

Publication of a dissertation (entry 1212).
Reviewed: A. L. A. Booklist (entry 1364); The Athenaeum
(entry 1343); W. S. B. in Boston Evening Transcript (entry
1320); S. C. Chew in Modern Language Notes (entry 1371);
H. A. L. in New Republic (entry 1382); Nation (New York)
(entry 1328); Times Literary Supplement (entries 1344 and
1345); S. Wheeler in The Bookman (London) (entry 1349);
and The Spectator (entry 1340).

1316   Olivero, Federico. "Atalanta in Calydon di A. C. Swin-
        burne." Nuova Saggi di Letteratura Inglese. Torino:
        Libreria Editice Internazionale, [c. 1918]. pp. 222-235.
        Reviewed: Times Literary Supplement (entry 1346).

1317   Vettermann, E. Balen--dichtungen und ihre Quellen. Halle an
        der Saale: 1918.
        Zeitschrift für Romanische Philologie, Beih. 60.

Dissertation

1318   Wier, Marion C. The Influence of Aeschylus and Euripides
        on the Structure and Content of Swinburne's Atalanta in
        Calydon and Erechtheus. University of Michigan, 1918.
        Published in 1920 (entry 1412).

Periodicals

1319   Aiken, C. Dial, 65 (July 18, 1918), 70.
        Review of Posthumous Poems.

1320   B., W. S. Boston Evening Transcript, Nov. 23, 1918, p. 9.
        Review of W. B. D. Henderson's Swinburne and Landor
        (entry 1315).

1321   Chew, S. C. Modern Language Notes, 33 (April 1918),
        224-236.
        Review of E. Gosse's The Life of ACS (entry 1240), Boy-
        hood of ACS (entry 1243), and Posthumous Poems.

1322   Collins, Nelson. "The Poet of This War." Century Monthly
        Illustrated Magazine, 97 (Dec. 1918), 219-225.

1323   Colum, Padraic. "Swinburne." New Republic, 16 (Aug. 24,
        1918), 101-103.
        Review of Posthumous Poems.

1324   Kernahan, C. The Bookman (London), 54 (May 1918), 64-66.
        Review of The Letters of ACS, ed. T. Hake and A.
        Compton-Rickett.

1325   Living Age, 297 (May 25, 1918), 498-500.
        Review of The Letters of ACS, ed. E. Gosse and T. J.
        Wise.

1326   Loewenberg, J.   "The Prophetic Songs of Swinburne. "   The
       University of California Chronicle, 20 (Jan. 1918), 106-115.

1327   Lynd, Robert.   "Swinburne. "   Nation (London), 23 (May 4,
       1918), 118.

1328   Nation (New York), 107 (Nov. 30, 1918), 665.
       Review of W. B. D. Henderson's Swinburne and Landor
       (entry 1315).

1329   Neff, Marietta.   "Swinburne as a Poet of Enthusiasm. "
       North American Review, 208 (Nov. 1918), 762-773.

1330   New York Times Book Review, 23 (Dec. 29, 1918), 584.
       Review of The Springtide of Life.

1331   "The Other Swinburne. "   Times Literary Supplement, Nov.
       28, 1918, p. 581.
       Review of The Letters of ACS, ed. E. Gosse and T. J.
       Wise.

1332   Phillips, T. M.   "Nature in Modern English Poetry. "   Man-
       chester Quarterly, 37 (Oct. 1918), 268-271.

1333   _____ .   "Colour in George Meredith and Other Modern
       English Poets. "   Papers of the Manchester Literary Club,
       44 (1918), 193-195.

1334   Pound, Ezra.   "Swinburne Versus His Biographers. "   Poetry,
       11 (March 1918), 322-329.
       Review of E. Gosse's The Life of ACS (entry 1240).
       Reprinted: Literary Essays (entry 1914).

1335   Russell, A. L. N.   "Swinburnian Foreknowledge. "   The
       Spectator, 120 (June 1, 1918), 562.

1336   Saturday Review (London), 126 (Dec. 14, 1918), 1164.
       Review of The Springtide of Life.

1337   Shackford, Martha Hale.   "Swinburne and Delavigne. "   PMLA,
       33 (March 1918), 85-95.

1338   Shanks, E.   Dial, 64 (April 25, 1918), 396-398.
       Review of The Letters of ACS, ed. T. Hake and A.
       Compton-Rickett.

1339   [Shorter, Clement King].   "A Literary Letter: Chatter About
       Swinburne. "   Sphere, 73 (April 13, 1918), 36.

1340   The Spectator, 120 (June 29, 1918), 679.
       Review of W. B. D. Henderson's Swinburne and Landor
       (entry 1315).

1341   "Swinburne as a Letter Writer." Saturday Review (London),
       126 (Dec. 28, 1918), 1204.
       Review of The Letters of ACS, ed. E. Gosse and T. J.
       Wise.

1342   "Swinburne's Swat at Lowell and Emerson." Boston Evening
       Transcript, Oct. 16, 1918, p. 4.

1343   "Swinburniana." The Athenaeum, 151 (May 1918), 233-234.
       Review of W. B. D. Henderson's Swinburne and Landor
       (entry 1315) and The Letters of ACS, ed. T. Hake and
       A. Compton-Rickett.

1344   Times Literary Supplement, April 18, 1918, p. 186.
       Notice of W. B. D. Henderson's Swinburne and Landor
       (entry 1315).

1345   Times Literary Supplement, May 2, 1918, p. 207.
       Review of W. B. D. Henderson's Swinburne and Landor
       (entry 1315).

1346   Times Literary Supplement, Sept. 19, 1918, p. 451.
       Review of F. Olivero's Nuova Saggi di Letteratura Inglese
       (entry 1316).

1347   Times Literary Supplement, Dec. 12, 1918, p. 614.
       Review of The Springtide of Life.

1348   Waugh, Arthur. "The Swinburne Letters and Our Debt to the
       Victorian Era." Nineteenth Century and After, 84 (Dec.
       1918), 1021-1034.
       Reprinted: Living Age, 300 (Jan. 11, 1919), 102-112; and
       Tradition and Change (entry 1361).

1349   Wheeler, S. The Bookman (London), 54 (June 1918), 96-97.
       Review of W. B. D. Henderson's Swinburne and Landor
       (entry 1315).

1919

Edmund Gosse and T. J. Wise, who by 1919 had become a Swinburne industry, edited two gatherings of Swinburne's works for 1919:
Contemporaries of Shakespeare, which contains nine of Swinburne's
essays on Elizabethan authors, and Selections from A. C. Swinburne.

Books

1350   Bennett, Arnold. "Poet and His People." Modern Book of

Criticism. Ed. Ludwig Lewisohn. New York: Boni, 1919.
pp. 122-125.

1351   Borchardt, Rudolf. Swinburne. Berlin: 1919.

1352   Browning, Robert. Critical Comments on Algernon Charles
Swinburne and D. G. Rossetti: With an Anecdote Relating
to W. M. Thackeray. [Ed. T. J. Wise]. London: Clay,
1919.
One of many T. J. Wise limited editions of thirty copies
or less. Rare.

1353   Ellis, Stuart Marsh. George Meredith: His Life and Friends
in Relation to His Work. London: Richards, 1919. New
York: Dodd, 1920.
Swinburne on pages 148-151.

1354   Gosse, Edmund. A Catalogue of the Works of A. C. Swinburne in the Library of Mr. Edmund Gosse. London:
Chiswick, 1919.

1355   Kernahan, Coulson. Swinburne as I Knew Him: With Some
Unpublished Letters from the Poet to His Cousin the Hon.
Lady Henniker Heaton. London: Lane, 1919.
Reviewed: The Athenaeum (entry 1368); Booklist (entry
1415); Boston Evening Transcript (entry 1417); Catholic
World (entry 1418); Nation (New York) (entry 1430); Times
Literary Supplement (entry 1399); and R. M. Weaver in
The Bookman (New York) (entry 1436).

1356   Littell, Philip. "Swinburne." Books and Things. New York:
Harcourt, Brace and Howe, 1919. pp. 187-193.

1357   Lynd, Robert. "Swinburne." Old and New Masters. New
York: Scribner, 1919. pp. 188-199.

1358   Quiller-Couch, Arthur Thomas. "Swinburne." Studies in
Literature. New York: Putnam, 1919. Cambridge:
Cambridge University Press, 1920. pp. 246-273.
Reprinted from the Edinburgh Review, April 1917 (entry
1291).

1359   Ruskin, John, William Morris, Edward Burne-Jones, and
Dante Gabriel Rossetti. Letters Addressed to Swinburne.
Ed. T. J. Wise. London: Clay, 1919.
A short (sixteen pages) T. J. Wise production, of which
only thirty copies were printed.

1360   Walker, Hugh, and Mrs. Hugh Walker. Outlines of Victorian
Literature. Cambridge: Cambridge University Press, 1919.
Swinburne on pages 88-91.

1361   Waugh, Arthur. "The Swinburne Letters and Our Debt to the

Victorian Era. " Tradition and Change: Studies in Contemporary Literature. London: Chapman and Hall, 1919.
pp. 180-203.
Reprinted from Nineteenth Century and After, Dec. 1918
(entry 1348).
See entry 1348 for other reprinting.

1362 Wright, Thomas. The Life of John Payne. London: Fisher
and Unwin, [1919].

Dissertation

1363 Kerstein, Margarete. Swinburnes Tristram of Lyonesse.
Königsberg, 1919.

Periodicals

1364 A. L. A. Booklist, 15 (Jan. 1919), 134.
Review of W. B. D. Henderson's Swinburne and Landor
(entry 1315).

1365 A. L. A. Booklist, 15 (Feb. 1919), 172.
Review of The Springtide of Life.

1366 A. L. A. Booklist, 15 (May 1919), 311.
Review of The Letters of ACS, ed. E. Gosse and T. J.
Wise.

1367 American Review of Reviews, 60 (July 1919), 110.
Review of The Letters of ACS, ed. E. Gosse and T. J.
Wise.

1368 The Athenaeum, 154 (Nov. 28, 1919), 1275.
Notice of C. Kernahan's Swinburne as I Knew Him (entry
1355).

1369 Boni, Giacomo. "Iris Dalmatica. " Nuovo Antologia di
Lettere, Scienze ed Arti, 285 (June 1, 1919), 279-285.

1370 Boston Evening Transcript, April 26, 1919, p. 8.
Review of The Letters of ACS, ed. E. Gosse and T. J.
Wise.

1371 Chew, S. C. Modern Language Notes, 34 (June 1919),
362-367.
Review of W. B. D. Henderson's Swinburne and Landor
(entry 1315).

1372 [_____]. Nation (New York), 108 (April 5, 1919), 505-
506.
Review of The Letters of ACS, ed. E. Gosse and T. J.
Wise.

1373 _____. "Swinburne After Ten Years." Nation (New York),
        108 (April 26, 1919), 659-660.

1374 [Compton-Rickett, Arthur]. "Rossetti and Swinburne." Times
        Literary Supplement, Oct. 16, 1919, pp. 565-566; and Oct.
        23, 1919, p. 591.
        Presents nine letters from Rossetti to Swinburne.
        Reprinted: Portraits and Personalities (entry 1808).

1375 Current Opinion, 67 (July 1919), 48-49.
        Review of The Letters of ACS, ed. E. Gosse and T. J.
        Wise.

1376 Dial, 66 (June 14, 1919), 612-614.
        Review of The Letters of ACS, ed. E. Gosse and T. J.
        Wise.

1377 Gosse, Edmund. "The First Draft of Swinburne's Anactoria."
        Modern Language Review, 14 (July 1919), 271-277.
        Discusses Swinburne's approaches to composing.
        Reprinted: Aspects and Impressions (entry 1463).

1378 Grierson, Herbert. "Lord Byron, Arnold, and Swinburne."
        British Academy, 9 (1919), 431-461.
        Reprinted: Lord Byron, Arnold and Swinburne (entry 1442);
        and The Background of English Literature (entry 1550).

1379 Harding, Anna Trail. "Shelley's Adonais and Swinburne's
        Ave atque Vale." Sewanee Review, 27 (Jan. 1919), 32-42.

1380 Kernahan, C. The Bookman (London), 55 (Jan. 1919), 128-
        129.
        Review of The Letters of ACS, ed. E. Gosse and T. J.
        Wise.

1381 _____. "Swinburne and Watts-Dunton: A Last Chapter."
        London Quarterly Review, 132 (July 1919), 26-39.

1382 L., H. A. New Republic, 18 (Feb. 15, 1919), 96.
        Review of W. B. D. Henderson's Swinburne and Landor
        (entry 1315).

1383 "The Letters of A. C. Swinburne." Blackwood's Magazine,
        205 (Jan. 1919), 138-140.
        Review of The Letters of ACS, ed. E. Gosse and T. J.
        Wise.

1384 Nation (New York), 108 (April 5, 1919), 505.
        Review of The Letters of ACS, ed. E. Gosse and T. J.
        Wise.

1385 North American Review, 209 (June 1919), 851.
        Review of The Letters of ACS, ed. E. Gosse and T. J.
        Wise.

1386 Outlook, 121 (Jan. 8, 1919), 75.
      Review of The Springtide of Life.

1387 Outlook, 122 (May 28, 1919), 162.
      Review of The Letters of ACS, ed. E. Gosse and T. J.
      Wise.

1388 Payrn-Payne, De V. "Poèmes français de Swinburne."
      Mercure de France, 134 (Aug. 1919), 765.

1389 Salt, Henry S. "Swinburne at Eton." Times Literary Sup-
      plement, Dec. 25, 1919, p. 781.

1390 Savage, Henry. "A Bookman's Lost Atlantis." Bookman's
      Journal, 1 (Dec. 12, 1919), 142.

1391 Siebold, Erica von. "Synästhesien in der englischen Dichtung
      des neunzehnten Jahrhunderts." Englische Studien, 53
      (1919), 303-313.

1392 The Spectator, 122 (Jan. 4, 1919), 13-14.
      Review of The Letters of ACS, ed. E. Gosse and T. J.
      Wise.

1393 The Spectator, 123 (Sept. 27, 1919), 407-408.
      Review of Contemporaries of Shakespeare.

1394 Strachey, James. "Drama: Swinburne and Mr. Yeats."
      The Athenaeum, 153 (June 6, 1919), 438.

1395 "Swinburne and Watts-Dunton." Times Literary Supplement,
      Nov. 27, 1919, p. 696.

1396 "Swinburne as Critic." Times Literary Supplement, Sept. 11,
      1919, p. 483.

1397 "Swinburne's Letters." The Athenaeum, 153 (Jan. 1919), 22-
      23.
      Review of The Letters of ACS, ed. E. Gosse and T. J.
      Wise.

1398 Thorndike, A. H. New York Times Book Review, 24 (May
      18, 1919), 281.
      Review of The Letters of ACS, ed. E. Gosse and T. J.
      Wise.

1399 Times Literary Supplement, Dec. 11, 1919, p. 730.
      Review of C. Kernahan's Swinburne as I Knew Him (entry
      1355).

1400 Times Literary Supplement, Dec. 11, 1919, p. 732.
      Review of Selections from A. C. Swinburne, ed. E. Gosse
      and T. J. Wise.

1920

Books

1401   Clutton-Brock, A. "Algernon Charles Swinburne" and "The
       Wonderful Visitor." Essays on Books. London: Methuen,
       1920. Reprinted: Freeport, N. Y.: Books for Libraries,
       1968.
       Both essays heavily praise Swinburne, with "The Wonderful
       Visitor" also praising Gosse for his biography of Swinburne.

1402   Eliot, T. S. "Swinburne as Critic" and "Swinburne as Poet."
       The Sacred Wood. London: Methuen, 1920. New York:
       Knopf, 1921. pp. 17-24 and 144-150, respectively.
       Eliot argues that Swinburne is misunderstood and that Swin-
       burne's poetry has qualities that can only come from genius.
       On Swinburne's criticism, he remarks, "With all his just-
       ness of judgment, however, Swinburne is an appreciator and
       not a critic" (page 19).
       "Swinburne as a Poet" was reprinted in Selected Essays
       (New York: Harcourt, Brace and World, 1932, 281-285).

1403   Elton, Oliver. "Algernon Charles Swinburne." A Survey of
       English Literature, 1830-1880. London: Arnold, 1920.
       Vol. II. pp. 55-84.
       This is a fine essay, which has suffered little from the pas-
       sage of time.

1404   Harris, Frank. "Swinburne: The Poet of Youth and Revolt."
       Contemporary Portraits. New York: Brentano's, 1920.
       pp. 228-239.
       This essay is primarily an account of Harris's encounters
       with ACS. The account and point of view are interesting,
       although a reader should keep in mind that Harris was al-
       most as eccentric in his way as was Swinburne, and that
       Harris was wont to claim an intimacy with great writers
       that he did not really enjoy.

1405   Hutchinson, H. G. "Swinburne and Meredith." Portraits of
       the Eighties. London: Unwin, 1920. pp. 188-193.

1406   Kassner, Rudolf. "A. C. Swinburne." Englische Dichter.
       Leipzig: Insel, 1920. pp. 124-142.

1406a Livingston, Flora V. Swinburne's Proof Sheets and Ameri-
       can First Editions: Bibliographical Data Relating to a Few
       of the Publications of Algernon Charles Swinburne: With
       Notes on the Priority of Certain Claimants to the Distinc-
       tion of "Editio Princeps." Cambridge, Mass.: privately
       printed, 1920.
       Livingston, a librarian at Harvard, reveals that some

publications of Swinburne's works that T. J. Wise asserted
were first editions could not possibly be.
See J. Carter and G. Pollard, The Firm of Charles Ottley
(entry 1854), for more information on Wise's forgeries.

1407   McCabe, Joseph Martin. A Biographical Dictionary of Mod-
        ern Rationalists. London: Watts, 1920.
        Swinburne on pages 774-775.

1408   Mallock, William H. Memoirs of Life and Literature. New
        York: Harper, 1920.
        Swinburne on pages 72-78.

1409   Powell, Charles. The Poets in the Nursery. London: Lane,
        1920.
        Swinburne on pages 42-44.

1410   [Squire, John Collings, writing as "Solomon Eagle"]. "Swin-
        burne's Vocabulary" and "Mutual Compliments." Books in
        General. New York: Knopf, 1920. pp. 66-68 and 75-76,
        respectively.
        Squire asserts that Swinburne was weak in judgment and
        needed to follow other people's opinions. He remarks that
        Swinburne's poems, when "a lot of them" are read together,
        "are tiring and monotonous to a degree unequalled by any
        verse of similar standing" (page 66).

1411   Wier, Marion Clyde. The Influence of Aeschylus and Eurip-
        ides on the Structure and Content of Swinburne's "Atalanta
        in Calydon" and "Erechtheus." Ann Arbor, Mich.: Wahr,
        1920.
        Publication of a dissertation from 1918 (entry 1318).

1412   Wise, Thomas J. A Bibliography of the Writings in Prose
        and Verse of Algernon Charles Swinburne. 2 volumes.
        London: Clay, 1920.
        Although this bibliography is still the standard reference
        for book collectors, it presents problems that make it an
        unsatisfactory research tool. Wise brazenly lists his for-
        geries of Swinburne as genuine first editions. His listings
        are confusing--for instance, the titles of poems published
        in periodicals are not distinguished from first lines of sim-
        ilarly published poems, thus making the first lines appear
        like titles. Wise frequently censures Swinburne for writing
        distasteful works, which he persistently declares will not be
        included in "any" collected works of Swinburne--thus putting
        into question the completeness of the Bonchurch collection
        of Swinburne's writings (1925), with which Wise was associ-
        ated. All in all, a careful researcher will not trust Wise's
        bibliography. Those who use the bibliography should con-
        sult J. Carter and G. Pollard, An Enquiry (entry 1781).
        Reprinted as Volume XX of the Bonchurch Complete Works
        (1925-1927).

Reviewed: W. G. Partington in <u>Bookman's Journal</u> (entry 1456).

1413   Woodberry, George Edward. "Swinburne." <u>Literary Essays.</u>
New York: Harcourt, Brace and Howe, 1920.   pp. 289-338.

Periodicals

1414   Beerbohm, Max. "No. 2.   The Pines." <u>Fortnightly Review,</u>
114 (Aug. 1920), 246-261.
Reprinted: <u>And Even Now</u> (entry 1437).

1415   <u>Booklist,</u> 17 (Oct. 1920), 29.
Review of C. Kernahan's <u>Swinburne as I Knew Him</u> (entry 1355).

1416   <u>Booklist,</u> 17 (Dec. 1920), 107.
Review of <u>Selections from A. C. Swinburne,</u> ed. E. Gosse and T. J. <u>Wise.</u>

1417   <u>Boston Evening Transcript,</u> May 15, 1920, p. 11.
Review of C. Kernahan's <u>Swinburne as I Knew Him</u> (entry 1355).

1418   <u>Catholic World,</u> 111 (Sept. 1920), 831.
Review of C. Kernahan's <u>Swinburne as I Knew Him</u> (entry 1355).

1419   Chew, Samuel Claggett.   "Swinburne's Contributions to The <u>Spectator</u> in 1862." <u>Modern Language Notes,</u> 35 (Feb. 1920), 118-119.
This article has been largely superseded by W. D. Paden's "Swinburne, <u>The Spectator</u> in 1862, and Walter Bagehot" (entry 1989).

1420   E., T.S. [T. S. Eliot?]. <u>The Athenaeum,</u> 155 (Jan. 16, 1920), 72.
Review of <u>Selections from A. C. Swinburne,</u> ed. E. Gosse and T. J. <u>Wise.</u>

1421   Fehr, B.   Beiblatt zur Anglia, 31 (May 1920), 97-106.
Review of <u>The Letters of ACS,</u> ed. E. Gosse and T. J. Wise.

1422   Fiedler, H. G.   "Swinburne's Mystifications." <u>Times Literary Supplement,</u> Aug. 19, 1920, p. 536.

1423   Gillet, Louis.   "Les Lettres de Swinburne." <u>Revue des Deux Mondes,</u> 6th ser., 57 (June 15, 1920), 890-901.
Review of <u>The Letters of ACS,</u> ed. E. Gosse and T. J. Wise.

1424   Gosse, Edmund.   "Swinburne and Kirkup." <u>London Mercury,</u> 3 (Dec. 1920), 156-165.

1425   _____. "Matthew Arnold and Swinburne." Times Literary Supplement, Aug. 12, 1920, p. 517.

1426   Heinemann, William. "Swinburne, Watts-Dunton, and the New Volume of Swinburne Selections." The Athenaeum, 155 (Jan. 2, 1920), 25.

1427   Independent, 104 (Nov. 13, 1920), 248.
     Review of Selections from A. C. Swinburne, ed. E. Gosse and T. J. Wise.

1428   Marks, Jeanette. "Swinburne: A Study in Pathology." Yale Review, n. s. 9 (Jan. 1920), 349-365.

1429   Nation (London), 26 (Feb. 7, 1920), 652.
     Review of Selections from A. C. Swinburne, ed. E. Gosse and T. J. Wise.

1430   Nation (New York), 110 (June 26, 1920), 861.
     Review of C. Kernahan's Swinburne as I Knew Him (entry 1355).

1431   Pearson, E. L. Weekly Review, 3 (Oct. 20, 1920), 345.
     Review of Selections from A. C. Swinburne, ed. E. Gosse and T. J. Wise.

1432   Renauld, C. "A. C. Swinburne et l'Italie." Nouvelle Revue d'Italie, 1920.

1433   The Spectator, 124 (April 3, 1920), 463.
     Review of Selections from A. C. Swinburne, ed. E. Gosse and T. J. Wise.

1434   Spencer, W. T. "Books and the Man." Bookman's Journal, 2 (June 4, 1920), 85.

1435   Tinker, C. B. Yale Review, n. s. 9 (Jan. 1920), 446.
     Review of The Letters of ACS, ed. E. Gosse and T. J. Wise.

1436   Weaver, R. M. The Bookman (New York), 51 (July 1920), 569.
     Review of C. Kernahan's Swinburne as I Knew Him (entry 1355).

1921

Books

1437 Beerbohm, Max. "No. 2. The Pines." And Even Now.
London: Heinemann, 1921. New York: Dutton, 1921.
pp. 55-88.
This anecdotal account was written in 1914 in response to
a request from Edmund Gosse for a description of Swinburne as Beerbohm knew him.
Reprinted from Fortnightly Review, Aug. 1920 (entry 1414).
Reprinted: C. K. Hyder, Swinburne: The Critical Heritage (entry 2083), pages 233-249.

1438 Blunt, Wilfred Scawen. My Diaries. New York: Knopf,
1921.
Swinburne on pages 114, 212, and 333.

1439 [Butler, Edward K.]. A Catalogue of the First Editions of
the Works of A. C. Swinburne in the Library of Edward K.
Butler. Boston: privately printed, 1921.

1440 [Squire, John Collings, writing as "Solomon Eagle"]. "If
Swinburne Had Written 'The Lay of Horatius.'" Collected
Parodies. London: Hodder and Stoughton, [c. 1921].
pp. 77-78.
Reprinted from Tricks of the Trade (entry 1246).

1441 Gosse, Edmund. "Poet Among the Cannibals." Books on
the Table. New York: Scribner, 1921. pp. 61-66.
About Swinburne's "The Cannibal Catechism."

1442 Grierson, H. J. C. Lord Byron, Arnold and Swinburne.
London: Oxford University Press, 1921.
The British Academy Warton Lecture on English Poetry,
No. 11.
Reprinted from British Academy, 1919 (entry 1378).
See entry 1378 for other reprinting.

1443 James, Henry. "Swinburne's 'Chastelard.'" Notes and
Reviews. Cambridge, Mass.: Dunster House, 1921.
pp. 132-138.
Reprinted from Nation (New York), Jan. 18, 1866 (entry
41).

1444 Kellner, Leon. Die englische Literatur der neuesten Zeit.
Leipzig: Tauchnitz, 1921.
Swinburne on pages 271-280.

1445 Kilmer, Joyce. "Swinburne and Francis Thompson." Cir-
cus, and Other Essays: and Fugitive Pieces. New York:
Doran, 1921. pp. 253-267.

1446 Olivero, Federico. "On Swinburne's Atalanta in Calydon."
      Studies in Modern Poetry. London: Milford, 1921. pp.
      36-53.

1447 Pennell, Elizabeth Robins, and Joseph Pennell. The Whistler
      Journal. Philadelphia: Lippincott, 1921.
      Swinburne on pages 23-28.

1448 Rossetti, Dante Gabriel. Letters from Dante Gabriel Rossetti
      to Algernon Charles Swinburne Regarding the Attacks Made
      upon the Latter by Mortimer Collins and upon Both by Rob-
      ert Buchanan. Ed. Thomas J. Wise. London: Clay, 1921.
      Another one of Wise's productions. Rare.

1449 Williamson, George Charles. "Swinburne." Behind My Li-
      brary Door: Some Chapters on Authors, Books and Minia-
      tures. New York: Dutton, 1921. pp. 201-208.

1450 Woodberry, George Edward. "Late Victorian Verse: Brown-
      ing, Swinburne, Tennyson." Studies of a Litérateur. New
      York: Harcourt, Brace, 1921. pp. 37-60.

Dissertations

1451 Hoffman, Karl. Die Stuart-Trilogie Swinburnes: Eine
      kritische Untersuchung der drei Stuart-Dramen Algernon
      Charles Swinburnes, Chastelard, Bothwell, und Mary
      Stuart in Prison mit besonderer Berücksichtigung der
      Quellen. Munich, 1921.

1452 Hoser, Josef. Swinburnes Klassizismus im Lichte der
      freimaurerischen Weltanschauung. Munich, 1921.

Periodicals

1453 Catholic World, 112 (Feb. 1921), 696.
      Review of Selections from A. C. Swinburne, ed. E. Gosse
      and T. J. Wise.

1454 Figgis, Darrell. "On Not Seeing Swinburne." London Mer-
      cury, 4 (July 1921), 254-258.

1455 Pallis, Elisabeth Hude. "Tennysons og Swinburnes Arthur-
      digte." Edda, 15 (1921), 44-74.

1456 Partington, Wilfred George. Bookman's Journal, 4 (April 29,
      1921), 6.
      Review of T. J. Wise's A Bibliography of the Writings in
      Prose and Verse of Algernon Charles Swinburne (entry
      1412).

1457 Praz, Mario. "La triligia di Maria Stuarda di A. C. Swin-
      burne." Rivista di Cultura, 1921.

1458   Ralli, Augustus John. "The Soul of Swinburne." North
       American Review, 214 (Nov. 1921), 679-689.
       Reprinted: Critiques (entry 1601).

1459   Watts-Dunton, Clara Jane. "My Recollections of Swinburne."
       Nineteenth Century and After, 90 (Aug. 1921), 219-229; and
       90 (Sept. 1921), 438-447.

1460   _____. "Christmas with Swinburne." Nineteenth Century
       and After, 90 (Dec. 1921), 1007-1017.

1461   Wise, Thomas James. "Privately Printed Works of Swin-
       burne." Bookman's Journal, 4 (Aug. 5, 1921), 244-245.
       Wise had been "privately printing" bits of Swinburne's work
       for over a decade.

1922

Books

1462   Beerbohm, Max. Rossetti and His Circle. London:
       Heinemann, 1922.
       Swinburne on plates 11 and 17.

1463   Gosse, Edmund. "The First Draft of Swinburne's 'Anactor-
       ia.'" Aspects and Impressions. London: Cassell, 1922.
       pp. 87-95.
       Reprinted from Modern Language Review, July 1919 (entry
       1377).

1464   Hearn, Lafcadio. "Studies in Swinburne." Pre-Raphaelite
       and Other Poets: Lectures. Ed. John Erskine. New
       York: Dodd, Mead, 1922. pp. 122-179.

1465   Hoser, Josef. Freimaurerei, Neuheidentum und Umsturz,
       im Hinblick auf Ursprung und Ziel der Freimaurerei
       dargestellt an Swinburnes Neuklassizismus. Regensburg:
       Manz, 1922.

1466   Mallarmé, Stéphane. Five Letters from Stéphane Mallarmé
       to Algernon Charles Swinburne: With a Note by de V.
       Payrn-Payne. privately printed, 1922.

1467   Meredith, George. Letters from George Meredith to Alger-
       non Charles Swinburne and Theodore Watts-Dunton.
       Pretoria: privately printed, 1922.
       Rare.

1468 Reul, Paul de. L'Oeuvre de Swinburne. Brussels: Robert
      Sand, 1922. London: Oxford University Press (Humphrey
      Milford), 1922. Paris: Agence Générale de Libraire, 1922.
      This study is valuable primarily for its discussion of Swin-
      burne's criticism and of the relationship between Victor
      Hugo and Swinburne.
      Reviewed: J. F. C. Gutteling in Neophilologus (entry 1511);
      G. Lafourcade in Revue Anglo-Américaine (entry 1513);
      Times Literary Supplement (entry 1488); and W. van Doorn
      in English Studies (entry 1518).

1469 Rhys, Ernest. "Death of Swinburne." Modern English Es-
      says. Ed. Ernest Rhys. New York: Dutton, 1922. Vol.
      IV. pp. 178-195.

1470 [Squire, John Collings, writing as "Solomon Eagle"]. "Deli-
      cate Details." Books Reviewed. London: Heinemann,
      1922. pp. 276-283.

1471 Watts-Dunton, Clara. The Home Life of Algernon Charles
      Swinburne. London: Philpot, 1922.
      This book, describing the life of Swinburne while living
      with Theodore Watts-Dunton, was written by the wife of
      Theodore Watts-Dunton. Hereafter referred to as The
      Home Life of ACS.
      Reviewed: The Bookman (New York) (entry 1472); Book-
      man's Journal (entry 1473); E. F. Edgett in Boston Even-
      ing Transcript (entry 1474); H. S. Gorman in Outlook
      (entry 1475); L. R. Morris in New York Times Book Re-
      view (entry 1477); Nation and Athenaeum (entry 1478); New
      Statesman (entry 1479); Saturday Review (entry 1485); The
      Spectator (entry 1486); and Times Literary Supplement
      (entry 1487).

Periodicals

1472 The Bookman (New York), 56 (Oct. 22, 1922), 215.
      Review of C. Watts-Dunton's The Home Life of ACS (entry
      1471).

1473 Bookman's Journal, 6 (May 1922), 54.
      Review of C. Watts-Dunton's The Home Life of ACS (entry
      1471).

1474 Edgett, E. F. Boston Evening Transcript, April 5, 1922,
      p. 4.
      Review of C. Watts-Dunton's The Home Life of ACS (entry
      1471).

1475 Gorman, H. S. Outlook, 132 (Sept. 27, 1922), 158-159.
      Review of C. Watts-Dunton's The Home Life of ACS (entry
      1471).

1476   Mercure de France, 157 (July 15, 1922), 514-515.

1477   Morris, L. R.   New York Times Book Review, Aug. 20,
       1922, p. 5.
       Review of C. Watts-Dunton's The Home Life of ACS (entry
       1471).

1478   Nation and Athenaeum, 31 (April 1, 1922), 24.
       Review of C. Watts-Dunton's The Home Life of ACS (entry
       1471).

1479   New Statesman, 18 (April 1, 1922), 732.
       Review of C. Watts-Dunton's The Home Life of ACS (entry
       1471).

1480   Praz, Mario. "Le tragedie 'Greche' di A. C. Swinburne e
       le font: dell' 'Atalanta in Calydon.'"   Atene e Roma, n. s.
       I 3 (July-Sept. 1922), 157-189.

1481   _____. "Swinburne." La Cultura, 1 (Sept. 15, 1922),
       536-553.

1482   Reul, Paul de. "Swinburne and Contemporary England."
       Living Age, 314 (Sept. 2, 1922), 593-599.

1483   Rummons, Constance.   "The Ballad Imitations of Swinburne."
       Poet Lore, 33 (Jan. 1922), 58-84.

1484   "The Saturday and Swinburne." Saturday Review (London),
       134 (Nov. 18, 1922), 749-750.

1485   Saturday Review (London), 133 (April 1, 1922), 344.
       Review of C. Watts-Dunton's The Home Life of ACS (entry
       1471).

1486   The Spectator, 128 (April 15, 1922), 469.
       Review of C. Watts-Dunton's The Home Life of ACS (entry
       1471).

1487   "'Time with a Gift of Tears.'" Notes and Queries, 12th
       ser., 10 (March 18, 1922), 219.

1488   Times Literary Supplement, March 23, 1922, p. 189.
       Review of C. Watts-Dunton's The Home Life of ACS (entry
       1471).

1489   Times Literary Supplement, May 4, 1922, p. 288.
       Review of P. de Reul's L'Oeuvre de Swinburne (entry 1468).

1923

Books

1490   Brandes, Georg Morris Chen. "Algernon Charles Swinburne."
       Creative Spirits of the Nineteenth Century. Trans. Rasmus
       B. Anderson. New York: Crowell, [1923]. pp. 397-419.

1491   Broers, Bernarda Conradina. "Algernon Swinburne: 1837-
       1909. " Mysticism in the Neo-Romanticists. Amsterdam:
       H. J. Paris, 1923. pp. 123-134.
       Taken from a dissertation (entry 1500).

1492   Drinkwater, John. Victorian Poetry. London: Hodder and
       Stoughton, 1923.
       Hodder and Stoughton's People's Library.
       Swinburne on pages 107-113.
       Drinkwater remarks that "with a poetic scholarship as lib-
       eral as and more widely read than Arnold's, an ear as
       sensitive to the harmonics of words as Tennyson's, a gift
       of incantation as befumed as Rossetti's, a sense of roman-
       tic story as poignant and sparkling as was Morris's, and a
       metrical virtuosity that was unknown to any of them, or,
       indeed, to any other English poet, Swinburne was, technical-
       ly, at once the most unoriginal and the most accomplished
       of the great men of his age" (page 107).

1493   Gorman, Herbert Sherman. "Swinburne's Home Life. " The
       Procession of Masks. Boston: Brimmer, 1923. pp. 91-
       103.

1494   Gosse, Edmund. "Snapshots at Swinburne. " More Books on
       the Table. New York: Scribner, 1923. London: Heine-
       mann, 1923. pp. 105-112.

1495   Hardman, William. A Mid-Victorian Pepys: The Letters and
       Memoirs of Sir William Hardman. Ed. Stewart Marsh El-
       lis. London: Palmer, 1923. New York: Doran, 1923.
       Swinburne on pages 78-80.
       Publisher's memories of Swinburne.

1496   Lang, Andrew. "Ode of Jubilee, by A. C. S. " The Poetical
       Works. Ed. Mrs. Lang. London: Longmans, Green,
       1923. Vol. III. pp. 224-225.

1497   Saintsbury, George. "Mr. Swinburne. " Collected Essays
       and Papers of George Saintsbury, 1875-1923. 4 volumes.
       New York: Dutton, 1923-1924. Vol. II. pp. 220-230.
       Reprinted from Corrected Impressions, 1895 (entry 598).

1498   Sichel, Walter. The Sands of Time. London: 1923.
       Swinburne on page 109.

1499 Symonds, John Addington. "A. C. Swinburne." Letters and
      Papers of John Addington Symonds. Ed. Horatio F. Brown.
      New York: Scribner, 1923. pp. 51-52.

Dissertations

1500 Broers, Bernarda Conradina. University of Amsterdam,
      1923.
      Not examined.
      Published: entry 1491.

1501 Schaefer, Emma. Swinburnes Tristram of Lyonesse: Eine
      Quellenuntersuchung. Halle, 1923.

Periodicals

1502 Gosse, Edmund. "The Attack on 'Poems and Ballads' in
      1866." Times Literary Supplement, Dec. 20, 1923, p.
      896.

1503 Nash, J. V. "The Religion of Swinburne." Open Court,
      37 (Feb. 1923), 65-77.

1504 Ratchford, Fannie E. "Swinburne at Work." Sewanee Re-
      view, 31 (July 1923), 353-362.

1505 _____. "Swinburne's Projected Triameron." Texas Re-
      view, 9 (Oct. 1923), 64-74.

1924

In 1924, Heinemann published the Collected Poetical Works of Swinburne in two volumes.

Books

1506 Furniss, Harry. Some Victorian Men. London: Lane,
      [1924].
      Swinburne on pages 81-82.

1507 Noyes, Alfred. "Swinburne's Tragedies." Some Aspects of
      Modern Poetry. London: Hodder and Stoughton, 1924.
      pp. 261-272.

1508 Quinn, John. The Library of John Quinn. New York:
      Anderson Galleries, 1924.
      Swinburne on pages 926-960.

Periodicals

1509   Arvin, Newton. "Swinburne as a Critic." Sewanee Review,
       32 (Oct. 1924), 405-412.
       Discusses Swinburne's critical insight and skill.

1510   Freeman, John. "Swinburne." The Spectator, 133 (Nov. 8,
       1924), 686-688.
       Review of Collected Poetical Works.

1511   Gutteling, J. F. C. Neophilologus, 9 (Jan. 1924), 145-150.
       Review of P. de Reul's L'Oeuvre de Swinburne (entry 1468).

1512   Lafourcade, Georges. "Swinburne et Baudelaire: Etude sur
       'Ave atque Vale' suivie d'une traduction en vers." Revue
       Anglo-Américaine, 1 (Feb. 1924), 183-196.

1513   _____. Revue Anglo-Américaine, 1 (Aug. 1924), 542-548.
       Review of P. de Reul's L'Oeuvre de Swinburne (entry 1468).

1514   MacCarthy, Desmond. "The Silent Woman." New Statesman,
       24 (Nov. 22, 1924), 203.

1515   Mandin, Louis. Mercure de France, 176 (Nov. 15, 1924),
       260-261.

1516   "Men and Matters: Swinburne and His Contemporaries."
       Bookman's Journal, 9 (Jan. 1924), 151.

1517   Ratchford, Fannie E. "The First Draft of Swinburne's
       Hertha." Modern Language Notes, 39 (Jan. 1924), 22-26.

1518   Van Doorn, Willem. English Studies, 6 (June-Aug. 1924),
       122-125.
       Review of P. de Reul's L'Oeuvre de Swinburne (entry 1468).

1519   _____. "An Enquiry into the Causes of Swinburne's Fail-
       ure as a Narrative Poet: With Special Reference to the
       'Tale of Balen.'" Neophilologus, 10 (Oct. 1924 through
       July 1925), 36-42, 120-125, 199-213, and 273-286.

1925

Heinemann of London and Wells of New York began publishing The
Complete Works of Algernon Charles Swinburne in 1925. Custom-
arily known as the Bonchurch Edition, The Complete Works would
extend to twenty volumes and be completed in 1927. It was edited

by Edmund Gosse and Thomas James Wise, with Gosse's biography
of Swinburne comprising the nineteenth volume and Wise's bibliography the twentieth. Unfortunately, The Complete Works was not
complete, even for its day. Gosse and Wise omitted works that
might have been in poor taste, and they apparently missed some of
Swinburne's early works. The texts of the poems are not as reli-
able as they should be for scholarly reference, yet The Complete
Works remains a standard source--primarily because of its con-
venience. In his essay in the 1968 edition of The Victorian Poets
(entry 2054), C. K. Hyder remarks, "Without explanation Gosse and
Wise capriciously changed the order of some poems and omitted
others, as well as extensive prose passages. While the Bonchurch
Edition is convenient for reference, one should be wary of quoting
from it on the assumption that one is quoting accurately. The text
of the first collected edition of the poems and dramatic works,
brought out in the poet's lifetime, is far more dependable." Hyder
here refers to the 1904 edition, The Poems of Algernon Charles
Swinburne (London: Chatto and Windus; New York: Harper), and
to the 1905 edition, The Tragedies of Algernon Charles Swinburne
(London: Chatto and Windus). Although these editions have their
own problems, the present bibliographer agrees with Hyder's sug-
gestion.

        Samuel Claggett Chew documents some of the errors in The
Complete Works in his Swinburne (entry 1629). Neither he nor any
other scholar has been able to explain why Gosse and Wise created
such an unreliable edition. Wise states in his bibliography that
there are works of Swinburne that should not be published--thus
one can easily blame him for many of the omissions. However,
Gosse's own carelessness as a researcher shows in his biography
of Swinburne (entry 1240). One may naturally be reluctant to con-
nect Gosse with Wise, who is notorious for his forgeries and un-
pleasant personality. Gosse, in most accounts, is a likable, though
not intellectually gifted, man. Nonetheless, he collaborated with
Wise for nearly two decades in the exploitation of Swinburne's name
and reputation for the sake of producing artificially rare first editions of Swinburne's works; he helped Wise produce a host of small
publications of dubious scholarly value, which--because of their
small numbers (usually only twenty-five or thirty copies)--could not
truly have been intended to enhance the world's knowledge of Swinburne.

        Also published in 1925 was Ballads of the English Border,
edited by W. A. MacInnes.

Books

1520   Barrus, Clara. The Life and Letters of John Burroughs.
            Vol. I. Boston: Houghton Mifflin, 1925.
            Swinburne on pages 288-289.

1521   Braybrooke, Patrick. "On Swinburne." Considerations on
            Edmund Gosse. London: Drane's, [1925]. pp. 9-26.

Braybrooke praises Gosse's biography of Swinburne (entry 1240).

1522   Dicey, Albert Venn. Memorials of Albert Venn Dicey: Being Chiefly Letters and Diaries. Ed. Robert S. Rait. London: Macmillan, 1925. Swinburne on pages 27-30.

1523   Forbes-Robertson, Johnston. A Player Under Three Reigns. London: Unwin, 1925. Boston: Little, Brown, 1925. Swinburne on pages 43-45. Firsthand account of Swinburne as a young man that portrays the writer as a charming eccentric.

1524   Galimberti, Alice. L'Aedo d'Italia: Algernon Charles Swinburne: Con versioni originali, ritratti e facsimile une lettera del Senatore Prof. Cippico. Palermo: Remo Sandron, 1925. Biblioteca 'Sandron, di Scienze e Lettere, No. 108. This is possibly the best work on Swinburne in Italian for Italians. Its greatest usefulness for researchers may be its extensive bibliography of Continental publications on Swinburne, many of which the present bibliographer was unable to locate and therefore does not list.

1525   Gosse, Edmund. Swinburne: An Essay Written in 1875: And Now First Printed. London: privately printed, 1925. This private printing encompassed a hundred and twenty-five copies. Reviewed: Times Literary Supplement (entry 1591).

1526   Hellman, George Sidney. The True Stevenson: A Study in Clarification. Boston: Little, Brown, 1925. Swinburne on page 120.

1527   Ionides, Luke. Mémoires. Paris: 1925.

1528   Knickerbocker, William Skinkle. Creative Oxford: Its Influence in Victorian Literature. Syracuse: State University of New York Press, [1925].

1529   Le Gallienne, Richard. The Romantic '90s. New York: Doubleday, Page, 1925. Swinburne on pages 20-34.

1530   Löhrer, Alfred. Swinburne als Kritiker der Literatur: Mit besonderer Berücksichtigung seiner unveröffentlichten Schriften. Weida: Thomas and Hubert, 1925. Publication of a dissertation (entry 1534). Presents the opinions of Swinburne about literature. Reviewed: K. Horn in Zeitschriften für Französischen und Englischen Unterricht (entry 1608); and S. B. Liljegren in Beiblatt zur Anglia (entry 1572).

1531   Marks, Jeannette. "Stigmata." Genius and Disaster: Stud-
       ies in Drugs and Genius. New York: Adelphi, 1925. pp.
       129-152.

1532   Northrup, Clark Sutherland. A Register of Bibliographies of
       the English Language and Literature. New Haven, Conn.:
       Yale University Press, 1925.
       Swinburne on pages 369-371.

1533   Wise, T. J. A Swinburne Library: A Catalogue of Printed
       Books, Manuscripts and Autograph Letters, by Algernon
       Charles Swinburne. London: privately printed, 1925.
       Listing of T. J. Wise's private collection.
       Reviewed: Times Literary Supplement (entry 1595).

Dissertation

1534   Löhrer, Alfred. Swinburne als Kritiker der Literatur: mit
       besonerer Berücksichtung seiner unveröffentlichten Schriften.
       University of Zurich, 1925.
       Published: entry 1530.

Periodicals

1535   Bensly, Edward. "Swinburne: T. Hayman." Notes and
       Queries, 148 (Feb. 14, 1925), 122.

1536   Dottin, Paul. "Swinburne: Poète Grec et Latin." Revue
       Anglo-Américaine, 2 (April 1925), 328-330.

1537   _____. "Swinburne et Les Dieux." Revue Anglo-
       Américaine, 2 (June 1925), 419-427.

1538   _____. "La Littérature et l'Histoire anciennes dans les
       Poèmes de Swinburne." Revue de l'Enseignement des
       Langues Vivantes, 52 (April 1925), 145-154.

1539   _____. "Les Poèmes de Swinburne et les Légendes
       héroïques de la Grèce." Revue de l'Enseignement des
       Langues Vivantes, 52 (Jan. 1925), 9-15.

1540   "A French Critic." Times Literary Supplement, Jan. 1,
       1925, p. 9.

1541   Lafourcade, Georges. "Atalanta in Calydon: Le Manuscrit,
       Les Sources." Revue Anglo-Américaine, 3 (Oct. 1925),
       34-47; and 3 (Dec. 1925), 128-133.

1542   Leaf, K. S. "Swinburne and the 'Spectator.'" The Specta-
       tor, 134 (April 4, 1925), 531-532.

1543   Lucas, Frank Laurence. "Enfant Terrible: Enfant Gâté."
       New Statesman, 24 (Jan. 17, 1925), 420-421.
       Review of the Collected Poetical Works.

1544   Noyes, Alfred. "Swinburne and Conventional Criticism."
       The Bookman (London), 67 (Jan. 1925), 195-200.
       Discusses Collected Poetical Works.
       Reprinted: Living Age, 325 (May 2, 1925), 265-272.

1545   "Swinburne and Morley." Living Age, 327 (Nov. 14, 1925),
       378.

1546   Torossian, Aram. "Stevenson as a Literary Critic." Uni-
       versity of California Chronicle, 27 (Jan. 1925), 43-60.

1547   Viereck, George Sylvester. "Freudian Glimpses of Swin-
       burne." Stratford Monthly, 4 (Jan. 1925), 3-10.

1548   Welby, Thomas Earle. "A Swinburne Library." Saturday
       Review (London), 140 (Sept. 19, 1925), 306-307.

1926

Books

1549   Calverton, V. F. Sex Expressions in Literature. New York:
       Boni and Liveright, 1926.
       Swinburne on pages 252-253.

1550   Grierson, Herbert. "Byron, Arnold and Swinburne." The
       Background of English Literature. New York: Holt, 1926.
       pp. 68-114.
       Reprinted from British Academy (entry 1378).
       See entry 1378 for other reprinting.

1551   Gwynn, Stephen. Experiences of a Literary Man. London:
       Butterworth, [1926].
       Swinburne on pages 174-175.

1552   Lucas, Frank Laurence. "Enfant terrible: enfant gâté."
       Authors Dead and Living. New York: Macmillan, 1926.
       pp. 115-123.

1553   Mackail, J. W. "Swinburne." Studies in English Poets.
       London: Longmans, Green, 1926. pp. 201-205.
       Reprinted from Swinburne: A Lecture (entry 972).
       Reviewed: F. Bickley in The Bookman (New York) (entry
       1560), Nation and Athenaeum (entry 1579), J. St. L.
       Strachey in The Spectator (entry 1590), and Times Literary
       Supplement (entry 1593).

1554   Morley, J. M. "Mr. Swinburne's New Poems: Poems and

Ballads. " Notorious Literary Attacks.   Ed. Albert Mordell.
New York: Boni and Liveright, 1926.   pp. 171-184.
Reprinted from the Saturday Review, Aug. 1866 (entry 48).
See entry 48 for other reprinting.

1555   Nicolson, Harold.   "Swinburne and Baudelaire. "   Essays by
Divers Hands: Being the Transactions of the Royal Society
of Literature of the United Kingdom.   Ed. G. K. Chesterton.   London: Oxford University Press, 1926.   pp. 117-
137.
A comparative study of the two men's writings.
Reprinted: Swinburne and Baudelaire: A Lecture (entry
1675) (see this entry for list of reviews); and The English
Sense of Humor (entry 1925).

1556   _____ .   Swinburne.   London: Macmillan, 1926.   New
York: Macmillan, 1926.
English Men of Letters.
This book is more valuable for its criticism than its bio-
graphical information.
Reviewed: N. Arvin in New York Herald Tribune Books
(entry 1558); W. R. Benét in Saturday Review of Literature
(New York) (entry 1559); Booklist (entry 1561); S. C. Chew
in Yale Review (entry 1603); G. H. Clarke in Virginia Quarterly Review (entry 1604); Contemporary Review (entry 1605);
E. F. Edgett in Boston Evening Transcript (entry 1567);
H. B. Fuller in Literary Digest International Book Review
(entry 1568); W. Gibson in The Bookman (London) (entry
1569); G. Lafourcade in Revue Anglo-Américaine (entry
1571); L. Mumford in New Republic (entry 1577); New
Statesman (entry 1580); New York Times Book Review
(entry 1582); E. Pearson in Outlook (entry 1584); H. Read
in Nation and Athenaeum (entry 1585); E. Shanks in Saturday Review (London) (entry 1588); The Spectator (entries
1589 and 1574); Times Literary Supplement (entry 1594);
and W. Van Doorn in English Studies (entry 1612).

1557   Welby, T. Earle.   A Study of Swinburne.   New York: Doran,
1926.
Not to be confused with Welby's 1914 Swinburne: A Critical
Study (entry 1191).   Although its organization is a little confusing, this book is a valuable study of Swinburne's work.
Reviewed: S. C. Chew in Saturday Review of Literature
(New York) (entry 1564); N. H. D. in Boston Evening Transcript (entry 1565); E. Muir in Nation and Athenaeum
(entry 1576); New Statesman (entry 1610); I. Paterson in
New York Herald Tribune Books (entry 1583); Saturday Review (London) (entry 1587); and Times Literary Supplement
(entry 1597).

Periodicals

1558   Arvin, Newton.   New York Herald Tribune Books, May 30,

1926, 4.
Review of H. G. Nicolson's Swinburne (entry 1556).

1559 Benét, William Rose. "On Swinburne." Saturday Review of
Literature (New York), 2 (May 22, 1926), 801-802.
Review of H. G. Nicolson's Swinburne (entry 1556).

1560 Bickley, F. The Bookman (New York), 70 (July 1926), 226.
Review of J. W. Mackail's Studies in English (entry 1553).

1561 Booklist, 22 (July 1926), 418.
Review of H. G. Nicolson's Swinburne (entry 1556).

1562 Brockbank, James. "Swinburne." Papers of the Manchester
Literary Club, 52 (1926), 175-181.

1563 Buzzichini, M. "Swinburne o l'Italia." I Libri del Giorno,
9 (March 1926), 130-132.

1564 Chew, S. C. Saturday Review of Literature (New York), 3
(Dec. 4, 1926), 358.
Review of T. E. Welby's A Study of Swinburne (entry 1557).

1565 D., N. H. Boston Evening Transcript, Nov. 24, 1926, p. 6.
Review of T. E. Welby's A Study of Swinburne (entry 1557).

1566 Delattre, Floris. "Swinburne et la France." Revue des
Cours et Conférences, 27 (Feb. 28, 1926), 548-567.

1567 Edgett, E. F. Boston Evening Transcript, May 15, 1926,
p. 5.
Review of H. G. Nicolson's Swinburne (entry 1556).

1568 Fuller, H. B. Literary Digest International Book Review, 4
(Aug. 1926), 545-546.
Review of H. G. Nicolson's Swinburne (entry 1556).

1569 Gibson, Wilfrid. The Bookman (London), 70 (June 1926),
149-150.
Review of H. G. Nicolson's Swinburne (entry 1556).

1570 Lafourcade, Georges. "Swinburne and Lord Morley." Times
Literary Supplement, July 1, 1926, p. 448.

1571 _____. Revue Anglo-Américaine, 4 (Dec. 1926), 163-169.
Review of H. G. Nicolson's Swinburne (entry 1556).

1572 Liljegren, S. B. Beiblatt zur Anglia, 37 (May 1926), 137-
138.
Review of A. Löhrer's Swinburne als Kritiker der Literatur
(entry 1530).

1573 MacCarthy, Desmond. "Swinburne's Prose." Empire Review,
44 (Nov. 1926), 458-461.

1574 "The Mechanical Swinburne." The Spectator, 136 (April 24, 1926), 764.
      Review of H. G. Nicolson's Swinburne (entry 1556).

1575 Morley, J. Living Age, 329 (June 12, 1926), 587-592.
      Review of The Springtide of Life, ed. E. Gosse.

1576 Muir, Edwin. Nation and Athenaeum, 40 (Dec. 11, 1926), 390.
      Review of T. E. Welby's A Study of Swinburne (entry 1557).

1577 Mumford, L. New Republic, 48 (Sept. 29, 1926), 167.
      Review of H. G. Nicolson's Swinburne (entry 1556).

1578 Nairn, John Arbuthnot. "Mary Queen of Scots in Drama."
      Fortnightly Review, 126 (Aug. 1926), 185-198.

1579 Nation and Athenaeum, 39 (April 17, 1926), 78.
      Review of J. W. Mackail's Studies in English Poets (entry 1553).

1580 New Statesman, 27 (June 5, 1926), 198; and 27 (June 12, 1926), 232.
      Review of H. G. Nicolson's Swinburne (entry 1556).

1581 "A New Swinburne Letter." London Mercury, 14 (Aug. 1926), 367.

1582 New York Times Book Review, May 30, 1926, p. 11.
      Review of H. G. Nicolson's Swinburne (entry 1556).

1583 Paterson, Isabel. New York Herald Tribune Books, Dec. 19, 1926, p. 12.
      Review of T. E. Welby's A Study of Swinburne (entry 1557).

1584 Pearson, E. Outlook, 143 (July 21, 1926), 417-418.
      Review of H. G. Nicolson's Swinburne (entry 1556).

1585 Read, Herbert. Nation and Athenaeum, 39 (May 1, 1926), 131-132.
      Review of H. G. Nicolson's Swinburne (entry 1556) and
      Ballads of the English Border, ed. W. A. MacInnes.

1586 Saturday Review of Literature (New York), 3 (Oct. 23, 1926), 242.
      Review of The Springtide of Life, ed. E. Gosse.

1587 Saturday Review (London), 142 (Nov. 27, 1926), 649.
      Review of T. E. Welby's A Study of Swinburne (entry 1557).

1588 Shanks, E. Saturday Review (London), 141 (April 10, 1926), 478.
      Review of H. G. Nicolson's Swinburne (entry 1556).

1589   The Spectator, 136 (April 3, 1926), 640.
       Notice of H. G. Nicolson's Swinburne (entry 1556).

1590   Strachey, J. St. Loe.   The Spectator, 136 (June 26, 1926),
       1083.
       Review of T. E. Mackail's Studies in English Poets   (entry
       1553).

1591   Times Literary Supplement, Jan. 7, 1926, p. 9.
       Reviews of E. W. Gosse's Swinburne: An Essay Written in
       1875 (entry 1525) and The Complete Works.

1592   Times Literary Supplement, Nov. 25, 1926, p. 855.
       Further review of The Complete Works.

1593   Times Literary Supplement, March 11, 1926, p. 179.
       Review of J. W. Mackail's Studies in English Poets (entry
       1553).

1594   Times Literary Supplement, April 15, 1926, p. 279.
       Review of H. G. Nicolson's Swinburne (1556).

1595   Times Literary Supplement, April 29, 1926, p. 319.
       Review of T. J. Wise's A Swinburne Library (entry 1533).

1596   Times Literary Supplement, July 15, 1926, p. 476.
       Review of Ballads of the English Border, ed. W. A. Mac-
       Innes.

1597   Times Literary Supplement, Dec. 16, 1926, p. 931.
       Review of T. E. Welby's A Study of Swinburne (entry 1557).

1927

Books

1598   Braybrooke, Patrick.   "Max Beerbohm, Swinburne, and Other
       Things."   Peeps at the Mighty.   Philadelphia: Lippincott,
       [1927].   pp. 43-58.
       Although Braybrooke does not identify it by title, his quo-
       tations are from Beerbohm's "No. 2.   The Pines" (entry
       1437).   A clumsy discussion of Beerbohm's essay on Swin-
       burne.

1599   Hearn, Lafcadio.   "Swinburne."   A History of English Liter-
       ature: in a Series of Lectures.   Vol. II.   Tokyo: Hoku-
       seido, 1927.   pp. 675-686.

132 Swinburne: A Bibliography

1600 Lafourcade, Georges. Swinburne's "Hyperion" and Other
Poems: With an Essay on Swinburne and Keats. London:
Faber and Gwyer, 1927.
Lafourcade's comments and ideas remain of interest.
Reviewed: E. A. Baker in Modern Language Review (entry
1638); A. Koszul in Revue Anglo-Américaine (entry 1624);
P. Quennell in New Statesman (entry 1627); Times Literary
Supplement (entry 1665); and L. Woolf in Nation and Athe-
naeum (entry 1628).

1601 Ralli, Augustus John. "The Soul of Swinburne." Critiques.
London: Longmans, Green, 1927. pp. 51-65.
Reprinted from North American Review, Nov. 1921 (entry
1458).

1602 Ruhrmann, Friedrich G. Studien zur Geschichte und Charak-
teristik des Refrains in der englischen Literatur. Heidelberg: Winter, 1927.
Anglistische forschungen, 64.
Swinburne on pages 160-175.

Periodicals

1603 Chew, S. C. Yale Review, n.s. 16 (April 1927), 612-616.
Review of H. G. Nicolson's Swinburne (entry 1556).

1604 Clarke, G. H. Virginia Quarterly Review, 3 (Jan. 1927),
156-158.
Review of H. G. Nicolson's Swinburne (entry 1556).

1605 Contemporary Review, 131 (June 1927), 804-808.
Review of H. G. Nicolson's Swinburne (entry 1556).

1606 Fehr, Bernhard. "Swinburne und Theodor Opitz: Zwei
unveröffentlichte Swinburne-briefe." Englische Studien,
62 (Nov. 10, 1927), 243-249.
Includes two letters by Swinburne.

1607 Freeman, A. E. "The Psychological Basis of Swinburne's
Convictions." Poet Lore, 38 (Dec. 1927), 579-589.

1608 Horn, K. Zeitschriften für Französischen und Englischen
Unterricht, 26 (1927), 309-310.
Review of A. Löhrer's Swinburne als Kritiker der Literatur
(entry 1530).

1609 Lafourcade, Georges. "Swinburne and Walt Whitman."
Modern Language Review, 22 (Jan. 1927), 84-86.
Revised version: Revue Anglo-Américaine (entry 1710).

1610 New Statesman, 28 (Jan. 1, 1927), 365.
Review of T. E. Welby's A Study of Swinburne (entry 1557).

1611   Times Literary Supplement, Aug. 25, 1927, p. 579.
       Review of A Golden Book of Swinburne's Lyrics, ed. Ed-
       ward Henry Blakeney (London: Hopkinson, 1927).

1612   Van Doorn, Willem.   English Studies, 9 (April 1927),   54-55.
       Review of H. G. Nicolson's Swinburne (entry 1556).

1928

Books

1613   Brie, Friedrich.   Imperialistische Strömungen in der
       englischen Literatur.   Halle an der Saale: Niemeyer,
       1928.
       Swinburne on pages 197-204.

1614   Dobson, Alban.   Austin Dobson: Some Notes.   London: Ox-
       ford University Press (Humphrey Milford), 1928.

1615   Fehr, Bernhard.   Die englische Literatur des 19. und 20.
       Jahrhunderts: mit einer Einführung in die englische
       Frühromantik.   Berlin-Neubabelsberg: Akademische
       Verlagsgesellschaft, [1928].
       Swinburne on pages 182-183 and 230-240.

1616   Kellett, Ernest Edward.   "Swinburne."   Reconsiderations:
       Literary Essays.   Cambridge: Cambridge University Press,
       1928.   pp. 219-242.
       Reprinted from London Quarterly Review, July 1909 (entry
       1029).

1617   Lafourcade, Georges.   La Jeunesse de Swinburne (1837-1867).
       2 volumes.   Paris: Université de Strasbourg, 1928.   Lon-
       don: Oxford University Press (Humphrey Milford), 1928.
       New York: Oxford University Press, 1928.
       Publications de la Faculté des Lettres de l'Université de
       Strasbourg, 44-45.
       Volume I is devoted to Swinburne's life; Volume II to his
       work.
       This is one of the truly excellent works on Swinburne.
       Lafourcade provides a good account of Swinburne's youth and
       presents a record of his early (especially unpublished) work
       superior to that in T. J. Wise's bibliography (entry 1412).
       The book's organization is a little confusing, partly because
       the time span of 1837 to 1867 seems chosen only for conven-
       ience, and partly because Lafourcade devotes unequal amounts

of space to works that seem to be of equal importance. Never-
theless, Lafourcade brings keen thinking and superior research
to his study of Swinburne.
Publication of a dissertation (entry 1622).
Reviewed: E. A. Baker in Modern Language Review (entry
1638); B. Fehr in Beiblatt zur Anglia (entry 1642); R. Galland in Revue Anglo-Américaine (entry 1645); H. J. C.
Grierson in Review of English Studies (entry 1683); C. K.
Hyder in Modern Language Notes (entry 1684) and Saturday
Review of Literature (New York) (entry 1648); H. M. Jones
in Modern Philology (entry 1709); S. B. Liljegren in
Englische Studien (entry 1711); P. Quennell in New States-
man (entry 1627); P. de Reul in Revue Belge (entry 1657);
and D. Saurat in Litteris (entry 1660).

1618 Lee, E. D. The Papers of an Oxford Man. London: Ingpen
and Grant, [1928].
Swinburne on pages 166-172.

1619 Tabb, John Bannister. "Swinburne." The Poetry of Father
Tabb. By Francis A. Litz. London: 1928. p. 411.
Poem.

1620 Waugh, Evelyn. Rossetti: His Life and Works. New York:
Dodd, Mead, 1928.

Dissertations

1621 Höcht, August. Swinburnes Stil in seinen epischen Dichtungen.
Vienna, 1928.

1622 Lafourcade, Georges. La Jeunesse de Swinburne (1837-1867).
University of Strasbourg.
Published: entry 1617.

Periodicals

1623 Galland, René. "Emerson, Swinburne et Meredith." Revue
Anglo-Américaine, 6 (Oct. 1928), 37-43.

1624 Koszul, A. Revue Anglo-Américaine, 6 (Dec. 1928), 175-177.
Review of G. Lafourcade's Swinburne's "Hyperion" (entry
1600).

1625 Lafourcade, Georges. "Swinburne's 'Death of Sir John Franklin.'" Times Literary Supplement, Feb. 9, 1928, p. 9.

1626 "The Literary Pages of the 'Spectator.'" The Spectator, 141
(Nov. 3, 1928), 645; and 141 (Nov. 10, 1928), 691.

1627 Quennell, Peter. "Swinburne." New Statesman, 31 (Sept.
22, 1928), 732.
Review of G. Lafourcade's Swinburne's "Hyperion" (entry
1600) and La Jeunesse de Swinburne (1617).

1628   Woolf, L.   Nation and Athenaeum, 43 (Sept. 8, 1928), 734.
       Review of G. Lafourcade's Swinburne's "Hyperion" (entry
       1600).

1929

Books

1629   Chew, Samuel C.   Swinburne.   Boston: Little,   Brown,
       1929.   London: Murray, 1931.
       This is a fine study of Swinburne, valuable for its insights
       and carefully researched background.   Chew's knowledge of
       Victorian England gives this book a depth and sense of
       place that is absent in many studies of Swinburne.   Chew's
       Swinburne remains a standard reference for scholars.
       Reviewed: Booklist (entry 1639); V. W. Brooks in New
       York Herald Tribune (entry 1640); O. Burdett in Saturday
       Review (London) (entry 1703); Christian Science Monitor
       (entry 1641); H. B. Fuller in Poetry (entry 1644); C. K.
       Hyder in Saturday Review of Literature (entry 1648); G.
       Lafourcade in Litteris (entry 1685); H. Leffert in The
       Bookman (New York) (entry 1651); R. M. Lovett in New
       Republic (entry 1652); D. L. M. in Boston Evening Tran-
       script (entry 1653); New York Times Book Review (entry
       1654); F. E. Pierce in Yale Review (entry 1655); E.
       Ritchie in Dalhousie Review (entry 1658); G. W. Stonier
       in New Statesman and Nation (entry 1720); L. Trilling in
       New York Evening Post (entry 1667); M. D. Zabel in
       Nation (entry 1668); and Times Literary Supplement (entry
       1721).

1630   Chilton, Eleanor Carroll, and Herbert Agar.   The Garment
       of Praise: The Necessity for Poetry.   Garden City, N. Y.:
       Doubleday, Doran, 1929.
       Swinburne on pages 303-311.

1631   Granville-Barker, Harley Granville.   "Tennyson, Swinburne,
       Meredith and the Theatre."   The Eighteen-Seventies: Es-
       says by Fellows of the Royal Society of Literature.   Cam-
       bridge: Cambridge University Press, 1929.   pp. 161-191.
       Also published in Fortnightly Review (entry 1646).

1632   Oursler, Fulton.   The World's Delight.   New York: Harper,
       1929.

1633   Payne, William Morton.   "Algernon Charles Swinburne."
       The Columbia University Course in Literature.   New York:
       Columbia University Press, 1929.   Vol. XV.   pp. 105-108.

1634   Symons, Arthur. "Algernon Charles Swinburne." Studies in
       Strange Souls. London: Sawyer, 1929. pp. 50-83.
       Reviewed: Times Literary Supplement (entry 1664).

1635   Weatherhead, Leslie D. "Swinburne." The After-World of
       the Poets. London: Epworth, [1929]. pp. 153-170.

1636   Welby, Thomas Earle. The Victorian Romantics, 1850-1870:
       The Early Work of Dante Gabriel Rossetti, William Morris,
       Burne-Jones, Swinburne, Simeon Solomon, and Their Asso-
       ciates. London: Howe, 1929.
       Primarily a historical work.
       Reviewed: Times Literary Supplement (entry 1666).

Dissertation

1637   App, August J. Lancelot in English Literature: His Role
       and Character. Catholic University, 1929.

Periodicals

1638   Baker, E. A. Modern Language Review, 24 (Oct. 1929),
       485-488.
       Review of G. Lafourcade's Swinburne's "Hyperion" (entry
       1600) and his La Jeunesse de Swinburne (entry 1617).

1639   Booklist, 25 (June 1929), 357.
       Review of S. C. Chew's Swinburne (entry 1629).

1640   Brooks, Van Wyck. New York Herald Tribune Books, April
       14, 1929, p. 2.
       Review of S. C. Chew's Swinburne (entry 1629).

1641   Christian Science Monitor, May 8, 1929, p. 10.
       Review of S. C. Chew's Swinburne (entry 1629).

1642   Fehr, B. Beiblatt zur Anglia, 40 (Jan. 1929), 1-4.
       Review of G. Lafourcade's La Jeunesse de Swinburne
       (entry 1617).

1643   Fitzgerald, Maurice H. "Swinburne on Emerson." Notes
       and Queries, 157 (Nov. 2, 1929), 315.

1644   Fuller, H. B. Poetry, 34 (Aug. 1929), 294-296.
       Review of S. C. Chew's Swinburne (entry 1629).

1645   Galland, R. Revue Anglo-Américaine, 6 (Aug. 1929), 508-
       515.
       Review of G. Lafouracde's La Jeunesse de Swinburne
       (entry 1617).

1646   Granville-Barker, Harley Granville. "Tennyson, Swinburne,
       Meredith and the Theatre." Fortnightly Review, 131 (May

1929), 655-672.
Also published in The Eighteen-Seventies (entry 1631).

1647 _____. "Some Victorians Afield, II: The Poet as Dramatist." Theatre Arts Monthly, 13 (May 1929), 361-372.

1648 Hyder, C. K. Saturday Review of Literature (New York), 5
(June 8, 1929), 1087 and 1091.
Reviews of S. C. Chew's Swinburne (entry 1629) and G.
Lafourcade's La Jeunesse de Swinburne (entry 1617).

1649 Kernahan, Coulson. "Swinburne and Emerson: Reminiscences of a Famous Literary Quarrel." Living Age, 336
(June 1929), 257-262.

1650 _____. "Swinburne and Emerson: The Story of, and a
Sequel to, an Ancient Enmity." National Review, 93
(April 1929), 229-241.

1651 Leffert, H. The Bookman (New York), 69 (May 1929), 318-
319.
Review of S. C. Chew's Swinburne (entry 1629).

1652 Lovett, R. M. New Republic, 59 (June 12, 1929), 103-104.
Review of S. C. Chew's Swinburne (entry 1629).

1653 M., D. L. Boston Evening Transcript, April 6, 1929, p. 7.
Review of S. C. Chew's Swinburne (entry 1629).

1654 New York Times Book Review, March 24, 1929, p. 2.
Review of S. C. Chew's Swinburne (entry 1629).

1655 Pierce, F. E. Yale Review, n. s. 19 (Sept. 1929), 203-204.
Review of S. C. Chew's Swinburne (entry 1629).

1656 Praz, Mario. "Il manoscritto dell' 'Atalanta in Calydon.'"
La Cultura, 8 (July 1929), 405-415.

1657 Reul, P. de. Revue Belge, 8 (Jan.-March 1929), 222-230.
Review of G. Lafourcade's La Jeunesse de Swinburne
(entry 1617).

1658 Ritchie, E. Dalhousie Review, 9 (1929), 405-406.
Review of S. C. Chew's Swinburne (entry 1629).

1659 Rutland, William. "Swinburne the Hellene." Times Literary
Supplement, Aug. 8, 1929, p. 624.

1660 Saurat, D. Litteris, 6 (April 1929), 39-42.
Review of G. Lafourcade's La Jeunesse de Swinburne
(entry 1617).

1661 Schücking, L. L. "Besuch bei Swinburne." Die Leipziger
Neunundneunzig, 25 (1929), 193-199.

1662   "Swinburne on Emerson. " Notes and Queries, 157 (Dec. 7,
        1929), 411.

1663   "Swinburne on Emerson: Philosophaster. " Notes and Que-
        ries, 157 (Dec. 28, 1929), 463.

1664   Times Literary Supplement, June 13, 1929, 471.
        Review of A. Symons's Studies in Strange Souls (entry 1634).

1665   Times Literary Supplement, Sept. 20, 1929, p. 663.
        Review of G. Lafourcade's Swinburne's "Hyperion" (entry
        1600).

1666   Times Literary Supplement, Nov. 14, 1929, p. 919.
        Review of T. E. Welby's The Victorian Romantics (entry
        1636).

1667   Trilling, Lionel. New York Evening Post, May 18, 1929,
        p. 8.
        Review of S. C. Chew's Swinburne (entry 1629).

1668   Zabel, M. D. Nation (New York), 128 (May 1, 1929), 536.
        Review of S. C. Chew's Swinburne (entry 1629).

1930

Books

1669   Auslander, Joseph, and Frank Ernest Hill.   The Winged
        Horse.   Garden City, N. Y.: Doubleday, Doran, 1930.
        Swinburne on pages 379-388.

1670   Benson, Edward Frederic.   As We Were: A Victorian Peep-
        Show. New York: Longmans, Green, 1930.

1671   Delattre, Floris.   Charles Baudelaire et le jeune Swinburne.
        Paris: Champion, 1930.
        Delattre claims too much, perhaps, for the influence of
        Baudelaire on Swinburne.
        Reviewed: G. Lafourcade in Litteris (entry 1685).

1672   Graham, Stephen.   "The Island of Hugo and Swinburne" and
        "No One's Island: Sark. " The Death of Yesterday. Lon-
        don: Benn, [1930]. pp. 20-27.

1673   Hardman, William.   The Hardman Papers: A Further Selec-
        tion, 1865-1868.   Ed. Stewart Marsh Ellis. London:

Palmer, 1930.
Swinburne on pages 164-167, 191-192, 209-210, 291-292,
and 326-330.

1674 Lucas, Frank Laurence. "Swinburne." Eight Victorian
Poets. Cambridge: Cambridge University Press, 1930.
New York: Macmillan, 1930. pp. 115-131.
Reprinted: Ten Victorian Poets (entry 1836).
Reviewed: Times Literary Supplement (entry 1688).

1675 Nicolson, Harold. Swinburne and Baudelaire: A Lecture.
London: Oxford University Press (Clarendon Press), 1930.
Reprinted from Essays by Divers Hands (entry 1555).
See entry 1555 for other reprinting.
Reviewed: G. Lafourcade in Litteris (entry 1685); P.
Meisner in Beiblatt zur Anglia (entry 1746); and J. O'Brien
in The Bookman (New York) (entry 1715).

1676 Page, Curtis Hidden, and Stith Thompson. "Swinburne: List
of References." British Poets of the Nineteenth Century.
New York: Sanborn, 1930. pp. 894-895.

1677 Quiller-Couch, Arthur Thomas. "Unity Put Quarterly."
Green Bays: Verses and Parodies. London: Oxford University Press, 1930. pp. 76-77.

1678 Steegmuller, Francis. Maupassant. London: Collins, 1930.

1679 Woods, George Benjamin. Poetry of the Victorian Period.
New York: Scott, Foresman, [1930].

1680 Woods, Margaret L. "Poets of the 'Eighties." The
Eighteen-Eighties: Essays by Fellows of the Royal Society
of Literature. Ed. Walter de la Mare. Cambridge: Cambridge University Press, 1930. pp. 3-4.

Periodicals

1681 Bradi, Lorenzi de. "Swinburne--est-il obscur et sans
pensée?" Revue Bleue, 68 (March 15, 1930), 184-187.

1682 Gosse, Edmund. "Matthew Arnold and Swinburne." Times
Literary Supplement, Aug. 12, 1930, p. 517.

1683 Grierson, Herbert. Review of English Studies, 6 (Jan.
1930), 77-87.
Review of G. Lafourcade's La Jeunesse de Swinburne
(entry 1617).
Reprinted: Essays and Addresses (entry 1826).

1684 Hyder, C. K. Modern Language Notes, 45 (Feb. 1930),
133-135.
Review of G. Lafourcade's La Jeunesse de Swinburne
(entry 1617).

1685 Lafourcade, Georges. Litteris, 7 (Dec. 1930), 165-175.
      Review of S. C. Chew's Swinburne (entry 1629), F.
      Delattre's Charles Baudelaire et le jeune Swinburne (entry
      1671), and H. G. Nicolson's Swinburne and Baudelaire
      (entry 1675).

1686 Macy, John. "Swinburne: Thaumaturgist." The Bookman
      (New York), 72 (Sept. 1930), 45-55.

1687 Praz, Mario. "Swinburniana (con una nota sul tipo
      letterario dell' inglese sadico)." La Cultura, 9 (Jan.
      1930), 11-23.

1688 Times Literary Supplement, Nov. 13, 1930, 936.
      Review of F. L. Lucas's Eight Victorian Poets (entry
      1674).

1689 Times Literary Supplement, Dec. 11, 1930, p. 1060.
      Review of Atalanta in Calydon, ed. John Haldone Blackie
      (London: Oxford University Press, 1930; facsimile of
      1865 edition).

1931

Books

1690 Charteris, Evan. The Life and Letters of Sir Edmund Gosse.
      London: Heinemann, 1931. New York: Harper, 1931.

1691 Farmer, Albert J. Le Mouvement aesthétique et "décadent"
      en Angleterre (1873-1900). Paris: Champion, 1931.
      Bibliothèque de la Revue de littérature comparée, 75.
      Swinburne on pages 22-27.

1692 Halperin, Maurice. "Le triomphe de l'amour--Le 'Tristram
      of Lyonesse' d'Algernon Swinburne." Le roman de Tristan
      et Iseut dans la littérature anglo-américaine au XIXe et au
      XXe siècles. Paris: Jouve, 1931. pp. 40-53.
      Publication of a dissertation (entry 1700).

1693 Hardy, Thomas. "A Singer Asleep (Algernon Charles Swin-
      burne, 1837-1909)." Collected Poems of Thomas Hardy.
      London: Macmillan, 1931. pp. 304-305.
      Reprinted from English Review (entry 1110).

1694 Hengelhaupt, Margrit. Die Personification bei George Mere-
      dith. Hannover: Künster, 1931.

Swinburne on pages 5-8 and 22-24.
Publication of a dissertation (entry 1701).

1695   Kitchin, George. A Survey of Burlesque and Parody in English. Edinburgh: Oliver and Boyd, 1931.
       Swinburne on pages 305-311.

1696   Rothenstein, William. Men and Memoirs: Recollections of William Rothstein, 1872-1900. London: Faber and Faber, [1931].

1697   Rutland, William R. Swinburne: A Nineteenth Century Hellene: With Some Reflections on the Hellenism of Modern Poets. London: Oxford University Press, 1931.
       Reviewed: D. Bush in Philological Quarterly (entry 1704); C. K. Hyder in Modern Language Notes (entry 1741); G. Lafourcade in Revue de Littérature Comparée (entry 1743); S. B. Liljegren in Beiblatt zur Anglia (entry 1745); Oxford Magazine (entry 1748); M. Praz in Review of English Studies (entry 1750); G. W. Stonier in New Statesman and Nation (entry 1720); and Times Literary Supplement (entry 1721).

1698   Stewart, Jean. Poetry in France and England. London: Hogarth, 1931.

Dissertations

1699   Clapp, Edwin Roosa. English Literary Criticism, 1830-1890. Harvard, 1931.

1700   Halperin, Maurice. Le roman de Tristan et Iseut dans la littérature anglo-américaine au XIXe et au XXe siècles. Paris, 1931.
       Published: entry 1692.

1701   Hengelhaupt, Margrit. Die Personification bei George Meredith. Freiburg, 1931.
       Published: entry 1694.

1702   Kuffner, Erich. Die Verwendung des Adjektivs bei Swinburne. Vienna, 1931.

Periodicals

1703   Burdett, Osbert. "How to Read Swinburne." Saturday Review (London), 151 (April 18, 1931), 576-577.
       Review of S. C. Chew's Swinburne (entry 1629).

1704   Bush, D. Philological Quarterly, 10 (Oct. 1931), 413-414.
       Review of W. R. Rutland's Swinburne (entry 1697).

1705   Cairns, William Bateman. "Swinburne's Opinion of Whitman." American Literature, 3 (May 1931), 125-135.

1706 Duffy, James. "The First American 'Atalanta.'" Times
      Literary Supplement, Feb. 5, 1931, p. 99.

1707 Galimberti, Alice. "Swinburne and Saffi." Times Literary
      Supplement, Nov. 5, 1931, p. 866.

1708 Hyder, Clyde Kenneth. "The Medieval Background of Swin-
      burne's The Leper." PMLA, 46 (Dec. 1931), 1280-1288.

1709 Jones, H. M. Modern Philology, 28 (May 1931), 493-497.
      Review of G. Lafourcade's Le Jeunesse de Swinburne
      (entry 1617).

1710 Lafourcade, Georges. "Swinburne et Walt Whitman."
      Revue Anglo-Américaine, 9 (Oct. 1931), 49-50.
      Revised version of essay that appeared in the Modern
      Language Review, Jan. 1927 (entry 1609).

1711 Liljegren, S. B. Englische Studien, 65 (1931), 415-418.
      Review of G. Lafourcade's La Jeunesse de Swinburne
      (entry 1617).

1712 Macdonnell, A. E. "Swinburne's Methods." Times Liter-
      ary Supplement, Jan. 8, 1931, p. 28.

1713 Modern Language Review, 26 (July 1931), 373.
      Review of Atalanta in Calydon, ed. John Haldone Blackie
      (London: Oxford University Press, 1931; facsimile of
      1865 edition).

1714 Monroe, Will Seymore. "Swinburne's Recantation of Walt
      Whitman." Revue Anglo-Américaine, 8 (April 1931), 347-
      351.

1715 O'Brien, J. The Bookman (New York), 73 (April 1931), 211.
      Review of H. G. Nicolson's Swinburne and Baudelaire
      (entry 1675).

1716 Praz, Mario. English Studies, 13 (Feb. 1931), 34.
      Review of Atalanta in Calydon, reprint of 1865 version.

1717 Purves, John. "Swinburne and Aurelio Saffi." Times Liter-
      ary Supplement, Sept. 24, 1931, pp. 729-730.

1718 _____. "Swinburne and Saffi." Times Literary Supple-
      ment, Nov. 26, 1931, p. 960.

1719 Rutland, W. R. Times Literary Supplement, Aug. 6, 1931,
      p. 609; and Aug. 20, 1931, p. 633.
      Rutland discusses his book on Swinburne (entry 1697).
      See entry 1721 for the Times Literary Supplement review.

1720 Stonier, G. W. New Statesman and Nation, 1 (June 27,

1931), 658-660.
Review of S. C. Chew's Swinburne (entry 1629) and W. R.
Rutland's Swinburne (entry 1697).

1721   "Swinburne Revisited." Times Literary Review, July 23,
1931, p. 579.
Review of S. C. Chew's Swinburne (entry 1629) and W. R.
Rutland's Swinburne (entry 1697).

1932

Books

1722   Brooks, Van Wyck. "Swinburne in the Flesh." Sketches in
Criticism. New York: Dutton, 1932. pp. 270-273.

1723   Carroll, Lewis [pseudonym of Charles Lutwidge Dodgson].
"Atalanta in Camden-town" and "The Little Man That Had a
Little Gun." The Collected Verse of Lewis Carroll. Lon-
don: Macmillan, 1932. pp. 210-212 and 385, respectively.
"Atalanta in Camden-town" reprinted from Punch, July 27,
1867 (entry 77).
"The Little Man That Had a Little Gun" reprinted in The
Humorous Verse of Lewis Carroll (entry 1955).

1724   Chesterton, Gilbert Keith. "On Algernon Charles Swinburne."
All Is Grist: A Book of Essays. New York: Dodd, Mead,
1932. pp. 243-262.
A stinging attack on Swinburne's inconsistent ethos and on
Swinburne's contemporary critics. Remarks Chesterton:
"The critics were wrong in the worst way in which a critic
can be wrong about a poem: in being wrong about the point
of it" (page 251). Also, "We must understand what the
man has really said, and not hang him as a heretic for say-
ing something he never said" (page 252).

1725   Chudoba, F. "Na Skok U Swinburna." Pod Listnatým
Stromen: Essaye. [Prague]: Melantrich A. S. Praha,
1932. pp. 201-218.
A general discussion of Swinburne's works, emphasizing
influences on his work.

1726   Glücksmann, Hedwig Luise. "Algernon Charles Swinburne."
Die Gegenüberstellung von Antike-Christentum in der
englischen Literatur des neunzehnten Jahrhunderts. Han-
nover: Küster, 1932. pp. 8-41.
Publication of a dissertation (entry 1733).

1727 Gutbier, Elisabeth. Psychologisch-ästhetische Studien zu
      Tristan-Dichtungen der neueren englischen Literatur.
      Erlangen: Döres, 1932.
      Publication of a dissertation (entry 1734).

1728 Lafourcade, Georges. Swinburne: A Literary Biography.
      London: Oxford University Press, 1932.
      This biography of Swinburne has been long the standard
      reference for the poet's life. It is now outdated by four
      decades of research, but has not been fully supplanted by
      another biography--although good ones have been written
      since 1932. (See, however, entry 2166.)
      Reviewed: Booklist (entry 1735); Boston Evening Transcript
      (entry 1736); Christian Science Monitor (entry 1737); George
      Dangerfield in The Bookman (New York) (entry 1738); W. C.
      De Vane in Yale Review (entry 1771); G. Grigson in Satur-
      day Review (London) (entry 1740); C. K. Hyder in Saturday
      Review of Literature (entry 1742); S. B. Liljegren in
      Beiblatt zur Anglia (entry 1775); New York Times Book Re-
      view (entry 1747); M. Praz in Review of English Studies
      (entry 1777); J. Sparrow in The Spectator (entry 1751);
      Richard Sunne in New Statesman and Nation (entry 1752);
      Times Literary Supplement (entry 1754); L. Trilling in
      Nation (New York) (entry 1755); E. L. Walton in New York
      Herald Tribune (entry 1756); and A. Waugh in The Bookman
      (London) (entry 1757).

1729 Lucas, Edward Verrall. Reading, Writing and Remembering:
      A Literary Record. New York: Harper, 1932. London:
      Methuen, 1932.
      Swinburne on pages 140-144.

1730 Sherman, Stuart Pratt. "Core of Swinburne. " Emotional
      Discovery of America: and Other Essays. New York:
      Farrar, 1932. pp. 103-114.

1731 Turner, W. J. "Algernon Charles Swinburne. " The Great
      Victorians. Ed. H. J. Massingham and H. Massingham.
      London: Nicholson and Watson, [1932]. pp. 489-502.

1732 Van Doorn, Willem. Theory and Practice of English Narra-
      tive Verse Since 1833: An Enquiry. Amsterdam: De
      Arbeitersperst, [1932].
      Swinburne on pages 143-155 and 179-196.

Dissertations

1733 Glücksmann, Hedwig Luise. Die Gegenüberstellung von
      Antike-Christentum in der englischen Literatur des
      neunzehnten Jahrhunderts. Freiburg, 1932.
      Published: entry 1726.

1734 Gutbier, Elisabeth. Psychologisch-ästhetische Studien zu

Tristan-Dichtungen der neueren englischen Literatur.
Erlangen, 1932.
Published: entry 1727.

Periodicals

1735 Booklist, 29 (Dec. 1932), 112.
      Review of G. Lafourcade's Swinburne (entry 1728).

1736 Boston Evening Transcript, Oct. 22, 1932, p. 1.
      Review of G. Lafourcade's Swinburne (entry 1728).

1737 Christian Science Monitor, Sept. 10, 1932, p. 12.
      Review of G. Lafourcade's Swinburne (entry 1728).

1738 Dangerfield, George. The Bookman (New York), 75 (Oct.
      1932), 628.
      Review of G. Lafourcade's Swinburne (entry 1728).

1739 Griggs, Earl L. "Swinburne on Coleridge." Modern Phi-
      lology, 30 (Nov. 1932), 215-216.

1740 Grigson, Geoffrey. Saturday Review (London), 153 (May 28,
      1932), 545.
      Review of G. Lafourcade's Swinburne (entry 1728).

1741 Hyder, C. K. Modern Language Notes, 47 (Feb. 1932),
      134-135.
      Review of W. R. Rutland's Swinburne (entry 1697).

1742 _____. Saturday Review of Literature (New York), 9
      (Sept. 24, 1932), 122.
      Review of G. Lafourcade's Swinburne (entry 1728).

1743 Lafourcade, Georges. Revue de Littérature Comparée, 12
      (April 1932), 464-467.
      Review of W. R. Rutland's Swinburne (entry 1697).

1744 _____. Times Literary Supplement, June 9, 1932,
      p. 427.
      A reply to a review of Lafourcade's Swinburne, which
      appeared in the June 2nd Times Literary Supplement
      (entry 1754).

1745 Liljegren, S. B. Beiblatt zur Anglia, 43 (Feb. 1932), 33-39.
      Review of W. R. Rutland's Swinburne (entry 1697).

1746 Meissner, P. Beiblatt zur Anglia, 43 (Jan. 1932), 25-26.
      Review of H. G. Nicolson's Swinburne and Baudelaire
      (entry 1675).

1747 New York Times Book Review, Oct. 2, 1932, p. 4.
      Review of G. Lafourcade's Swinburne (entry 1728).

1748   Oxford Magazine, April 28, 1932, p. 606.
       Review of W. R. Rutland's Swinburne (entry 1697).

1749   Partington, Wilfred George. "Swinburne, Dickens, and the
       Lovely Circus-Rider." The Bookman (New York), 75 (June
       1932), 292-294.

1750   Praz, Mario. Review of English Studies, 8 (July 1932),
       354-357.
       Review of W. R. Rutland's Swinburne (entry 1697).

1751   Sparrow, John. The Spectator, 148 (June 4, 1932), 804.
       Review of G. Lafourcade's Swinburne (entry 1728).

1752   Sunne, Richard. New Statesman and Nation, 3 (May 14,
       1932), 620.
       Review of G. Lafourcade's Swinburne (entry 1728).

1753   Symons, Arthur. "Notes on Two Manuscripts." English
       Review, 54 (May 1932), 514-520.

1754   Times Literary Supplement, June 2, 1932, p. 404.
       Review of G. Lafourcade's Swinburne (entry 1728).
       Lafourcade replied in the June 9th Times Literary Supple-
       ment (entry 1744).

1755   Trilling, Lionel. Nation (New York), 135 (Dec. 14, 1932),
       594.
       Review of G. Lafourcade's Swinburne (entry 1728).

1756   Walton, E. L. New York Herald Tribune Books, Oct. 2,
       1932, p. 6.
       Review of G. Lafourcade's Swinburne (entry 1728).

1757   Waugh, A. The Bookman (London), 82 (June 1932), 154.
       Review of G. Lafourcade's Swinburne (entry 1728).

1933

Books

1758   Compton-Rickett, Arthur. "Swinburne and Watts-Dunton."
       I Look Back: Memories of Fifty Years. London: Jen-
       kins, 1933. pp. 143-157.
       Borrows an anecdote from V. W. Brooks's "Swinburne in
       the Flesh" (in Sketches in Criticism) (entry 1722).
       Compton-Rickett remarks, "Swinburne, however, was,

from the sex point of view, as chaste as the driven snow.
All his 'sins' were literary sins. His life was blameless"
(page 150). One cannot be certain that Compton-Rickett
was as well acquainted with Swinburne as he implies.

1759 Evans, Ifor. "Algernon Charles Swinburne." English Poetry
in the Later Nineteenth Century. London: Methuen, 1933.
pp. 26-64.
Second edition, revised: New York: Barnes and Noble,
1966. pp. 45-86.
This excellent and well-written chapter is a good introduction to Swinburne's life and work. Evans outlines Swinburne's development as an artist and presents some criticism. He remarks, "The study of Swinburne's work may
impress with the massiveness of his talent, though for
decades now there is no indication that it is doing so; the
return to his lyrical poetry reveals his genius" (page 71,
2nd edition).

1760 Hamilton, Cosmo. "Algernon Charles Swinburne." People Worth
Talking About. New York: McBride, 1933. pp. 227-234.

1761 Hyder, Clyde Kenneth. Swinburne's Literary Career and
Fame. Durham, N.C.: Duke University Press, 1933.
Reprinted: New York: Russell and Russell, 1963.
Publication of a dissertation (entry 1767).
Hereafter referred to as C. K. Hyder's Swinburne's L. C.
and F.
This fine study has never been supplanted. Its discussion
of Swinburne's reputation remains the best one. The book
is one of the standard references for students of Swinburne.
Reviewed: C. S. C. in Christian Science Monitor (entry
1770); S. Chew in Modern Language Notes (entry 1797);
M. Colby in Harvard Graduate Magazine (entry 1786); W.
S. Knickerbocker in Sewanee Review (entry 1789); C. Still-
man in New York Herald Tribune Books (entry 1778); R. D.
Waller in Modern Language Review (entry 1790); and E.
Walton in New York Times Book Review (entry 1780).

1762 Praz, Mario. The Romantic Agony. London and New York:
Oxford University Press, 1933. Second edition, 1951.
Reprinted, paperbound, 1970.
Swinburne mentioned frequently throughout.

1763 Stonier, George Walter. "Swinburne." Gog Magog: and
Other Critical Essays. London: Dent, 1933. pp. 64-69.

1764 Strong, Archibald Thomas. "Swinburne's Mary Stuart Trilogy." Four Studies. Adelaide: Preece, 1933.
Reviewed: Times Literary Supplement (entry 1779).

1765 Winwar, Frances [pseudonym of Frances Grebanier]. Poor
Splendid Wings. Boston: Little, Brown, 1933.

Dissertations

1766 Baxter, Frank C. Criticism and Appreciation of the Eliza-
      bethan Drama: Dryden to Swinburne. Cambridge, 1933.

1767 Hyder, Clyde Kenneth. Swinburne's Literary Career and
      Fame. Harvard, 1933.
      Published: entry 1761.

1768 Tilgham, Tench Francis. The Literary Ballad in English
      Poetry of the Nineteenth Century. University of Virginia,
      1933.

Periodicals

1769 Benson, Arthur Christopher. "Swinburne and Watts-Dunton."
      Living Age, 343 (Feb. 1933), 531-538.

1770 C., S. C. [Samuel Chew?]. Christian Science Monitor, Sept.
      30, 1933, p. 9.
      Review of C. K. Hyder's Swinburne's L. C. and F. (entry
      1761).

1771 De Vane, W. C. Yale Review, n. s. 22 (March 1933), 633-
      634.
      Review of G. Lafourcade's Swinburne (entry 1728).

1772 Dingle, Herbert. "Swinburne's 'Internal Centre.'" Queen's
      Quarterly, 40 (May 1933), 212-228.

1773 Hyder, Clyde Kenneth. "Emerson on Swinburne: A Sensa-
      tional Interview." Modern Language Notes, 48 (March
      1933), 180-182.
      See "Emerson: A Literary Interview" in Frank Leslie's
      Illustrated Newspaper (entry 166).

1774 Knickerbocker, Kenneth Leslie. "The Source of Swinburne's
      'Les Noyades.'" Philological Quarterly, 12 (Jan. 1933),
      82-83.
      Proposes Carlyle as the source of the legend used by
      Swinburne.

1775 Liljegren, S. B. Beiblatt zur Anglia, 44 (1933), 211-212.
      Review of G. Lafourcade's Swinburne (entry 1728).

1776 Motter, T. H. Vail. "A New Arnold Letter and an Old
      Swinburne Quarrel." Times Literary Supplement, Aug.
      31, 1933, p. 576.

1777 Praz, Mario. Review of English Studies, 9 (July 1933),
      351-353.
      Review of G. Lafourcade's Swinburne (entry 1728).

1778 Stillman, C. G. New York Herald Tribune Books, Oct. 1,
      1933, p. 21.
      Review of C. K. Hyder's Swinburne's L. C. and F. (entry
      1761).

1779 Times Literary Supplement, April 27, 1933, p. 291.
      Review of A. T. Strong's Four Studies (entry 1764).

1780 Walton, E. L. New York Times Book Review, Oct. 15,
      1933, p. 2.
      Review of C. K. Hyder's Swinburne's L. C. and F. (entry
      1761).

1934

Books

1781 Carter, John, and Graham Pollard. "Algernon Charles Swin-
      burne." An Enquiry into the Nature of Certain Nineteenth
      Century Pamphlets. London: Constable, 1934. pp. 267-
      292.
      Reprinted: Haskell House, 1971.
      This book is fundamentally important for bibliographers
      specializing in nineteenth-century British authors. It lists
      several forgeries, probable forgeries, and suspicious pub-
      lications of Swinburne "first editions." It identifies the
      T. J. Wise forgeries.

1782 Cunliffe, John W. "Mid-Victorian Poets." Leaders of the
      Victorian Revolution. New York: Appleton-Century,
      [1934]. pp. 241-248.

1783 Falk, Bernard. The Naked Lady: or Storm over Adah: A
      Biography of Adah Isaacs Menken. London: Hutchinson,
      1934.
      Revised edition: 1952.
      Poor documentation makes this book difficult to work with.
      The contention that Menken inspired Swinburne's "Dolores"
      is dubious at best.
      Reviewed: C. Wilkinson in London Mercury (entry 1791).

Periodicals

1784 Beatty, Richmond Croom. "Swinburne and Bayard Taylor."
      Philological Quarterly, 13 (July 1934), 297-299.

1785 Bragman, Louis J. "The Case of Algernon Charles Swinburne: A Study in Sadism. " Psychoanalytic Review, 21 (Jan. 1934), 59-74.

1786 Colby, M. Harvard Graduates Magazine, 42 (1934), 246-247. Review of C. K. Hyder's Swinburne's L. C. and F. (entry 1761).

1787 Hughes, Randolph. "Mallarmé: A Study in Esoteric Symbol- ism. " Nineteenth Century and After, 116 (1934), 114-128.

1788 Hyder, Clyde Kenneth. "Swinburne and the Popular Ballad. " PMLA, 49 (March 1934), 295-309.

1789 Knickerbocker, W. S. Sewanee Review, 42 (1934), 359-361. Review of C. K. Hyder's Swinburne's L. C. and F. (entry 1761).

1790 Waller, R. D. Modern Language Review, 29 (1934), 353-354. Review of C. K. Hyder's Swinburne's L. C. and F. (entry 1761).

1791 Wilkinson, C. London Mercury, 30 (1934), 183-185. Review of B. Falk's The Naked Lady (entry 1783).

1792 Wright, Herbert G. "Unpublished Letters from Theodore Watts-Dunton to Swinburne. " Review of English Studies, 10 (April 1934), 129-155.

1935

Books

1793 Leathes, Stanley. Rhythm in English Poetry. London: Heinemann, 1935. Swinburne on pages 71-73 and 133-143.

1794 Orage, Alfred Richard. "Swinburne: Changeling. " Selected Essays and Critical Writings. Ed. H. Read and D. Saurat. London: Allen, 1935. pp. 73-77.

Dissertations

1795 Chandler, Josephine. The So-Called Elizabethan Tragedies of Swinburne: A Study in Literary Assimilation. University of California, 1935.

1796 Probst, Elfriede. Der Einfluss Shakespeares auf die Stuart- Trilogie Swinburnes. Munich, 1935.

Periodicals

1797 Chew, Samuel. Modern Language Notes, 50 (1935), 59-60.
      Review of C. K. Hyder's Swinburne's L. C. and F. (entry
      1761).

1798 Lafourcade, Georges. "L'Algolagnie de Swinburne."
      Hippocrate, March-April 1935.

1936

Books

1799 Beach, Joseph Warren. "Swinburne." The Concept of Nature
      in Nineteenth-Century English Poetry. New York: Macmil-
      lan, 1936. pp. 455-469.
      Reprinted: New York: Pageant, 1956; and New York:
      Russell and Russell, 1966.
      Beach discusses Swinburne's Songs Before Sunrise and what
      the collection of poems reveals about Swinburne's ethos.
      Beach remarks, "With Swinburne we come at length to an
      English poet in whom the evolutionary ideas have borne
      fruit in a nature-poetry militantly 'naturalistic'" (page 455).

1800 Chesterton, G. K. The Autobiography of G. K. Chesterton.
      New York: Sheed and Ward, 1936.
      Swinburne on pages 60, 96, 290-291, and 292.

1801 Ehrsam, Theodore G.; Robert H. Deily; and Robert M.
      Smith. "Algernon Charles Swinburne." Bibliographies of
      Twelve Victorian Authors. New York: H. W. Wilson,
      1936. pp. 263-297.
      Reprinted: New York: Octagon, 1968.
      This book is an extraordinary achievement in enumerative
      bibliography. Its authors uncovered tens of thousands of
      secondary sources for twelve authors. The Swinburne sec-
      tion is useful primarily for its listing of nineteenth-century
      references. There are gaps in the section's listings, es-
      pecially for later works. There are also many errors and
      inexplicable multiple listings for single works. The sec-
      tion's greatest weakness may be its confusing alphabetical
      arrangement. It was nonetheless a great help to the present
      bibliographer, who figures that the efforts of Ehrsam, Deily,
      and Smith saved him a year's work.

1802 Leavis, F. R. Revaluation. London: Chatto and Windus,
      1936.

1803   Reynolds, Ernest. Early Victorian Drama. Cambridge,
       England: Heffer, 1936.

1804   Weygandt, Cornelius. "Algernon Charles Swinburne." The
       Times of Tennyson: English Victorian Poetry as It Affected
       America. New York: Appleton-Century, 1936. pp. 226-
       242.

Dissertation

1805   Hesse, Gerhard. Das politische Element in der Lyrik Swin-
       burnes und Tennysons. Greifswald, 1936.

Periodicals

1806   Aubry, G. Jean. "Victor Hugo et Swinburne." Revue Bleue,
       74 (March 7, 1936).

1937

Books

1807   Bush, Douglas. "Swinburne." Mythology and the Romantic
       Tradition in English Poetry. Cambridge, Mass.: Harvard
       University Press, 1937.
       Harvard Studies in English, Vol. 18.
       Reprinted: New York: Pageant, 1957.

1808   Compton-Rickett, Arthur. "The Swinburne Legend" and
       "Rossetti-Swinburne Letters." Portraits and Personalities.
       London: Selwyn and Blount, 1937. pp. 99-116 and 311-320,
       respectively.
       "Rossetti-Swinburne Letters" reprinted from "Rossetti and
       Swinburne" in Times Literary Supplement, Oct. 16, 1919
       (entry 1374).
       "The Swinburne Legend" is primarily a defense of Theodore
       Watts-Dunton's influence on Swinburne.

1809   Ford, Ford Madox. "Swinburne." Portraits from Life.
       New York: Houghton Mifflin, 1937. pp. 183-203.

1810   Kipling, Rudyard. Something of Myself. Garden City, N. Y.:
       Doubleday, Doran, 1937.

Dissertation

1811   Mulhauser, Frederick L., Jr. Mazzini, Carlyle, Meredith,

and Swinburne: A Study in Literary Relationships. Yale,
1937.

Periodicals

1812   Brown, E. K. "Swinburne: A Centenary Estimate." Uni-
       versity of Toronto Quarterly, 6 (Jan. 1937), 215-235.
       Reprinted: Victorian Literature, ed. Austin Wright (entry
       1975).

1813   Child, Ruth C. "Swinburne's Mature Standards of Criticism."
       PMLA, 52 (1937), 870-879.
       Child presents evidence of Swinburne's concern for ideas.

1814   Hopkinson, Alfred. "The Centenary of Algernon Charles Swin-
       burne." Contemporary Review, 152 (Oct. 1937), 447-452.

1815   Hughes, Randolph. "Algernon Charles Swinburne: A Centen-
       ary Survey." Nineteenth Century and After, 121 (June 1937),
       721-763.

1816   Knaplund, P. University of Toronto Quarterly, 6 (1937).
       Mentioned in C. K. Hyder's article in The Victorian Poets,
       ed. F. E. Faverty (entry 1924). Not examined.

1817   Lafourcade, Georges. "Le triomphe du temps: ou la
       réputation de Swinburne." Etudes Anglaises, 1 (March
       1937).

1818   "The Voice of Swinburne: A Singer's Conquest and After."
       Times Literary Supplement, April 10, 1937, 261-262.

1938

Books

1819   Batho, Edith. "The Victorians and After, 1830-1914."
       Introduction to English Literature. Ed. Bonamy Dobrée.
       London: Cresset, 1938.

1820   [Russell, George William]. "Swinburne." Living Torch.
       Ed. M. Gibbon. New York: Macmillan, 1938.

Dissertation

1821   Muller, Anne-Marie. Die Auffassung von Liebe und Tod in
       Swinburnes Tristram of Lyonesse. Zurich, 1938.

Periodicals

1822   Lafourcade, Georges.   "Swinburne Vindicated. "   London
       Mercury, 34 (1938).
       Defense of Swinburne's expressions of love.

1939

Book

1823   Partington, W.   Forging Ahead.   New York: 1939.
       Revised edition: Thomas J. Wise in the Original Cloth
       (entry 1847).
       Discusses the Wise forgeries.

Periodicals

1824   Fucilla, Joseph G.   "Bibliographies of Twelve Victorian Au-
       thors: A Supplement. "   Modern Philology, 37 (Aug. 1939),
       89-96.

1940

Books

1825   Evans, B. Ifor.   Tradition and Romanticism: Studies in
       English Poetry from Chaucer to W. B. Yeats.   New York:
       Longmans, Green, 1940.
       Evans remarks, "Poems and Ballads (1866) carried verse
       to the limits of verbal music and stanzaic ingenuity.   All
       that followed would have to be imitative or dim, unless
       verse could work out its own salvation in some other way"
       (page 180).   Evans adds, "Compared with Baudelaire the
       verse of Swinburne seems amateurish in its exploration of
       evil, half-serious, despite the maze of words" (page 181).

1826   Grierson, H. J. C.   "Review of La Jeunesse de Swinburne,
       by Georges Lafourcade. "   Essays and Addresses.   Toronto:
       Macmillan, 1940.   pp. ˆ45-259.
       Reprinted from Review of English Studies, Jan. 1930 (entry
       1683).

1827 Noyes, Alfred. "Swinburne." Pageant of Letters. New
      York: Sheed, 1940. pp. 297-317.

1828 Rudman, H. W. Italian Nationalism and English Letters.
      1940.
      Mentioned by C. K. Hyder in his article in The Victorian
      Poets, ed. F. E. Faverty (entry 2054). Not examined.

1829 Shuster, G. N. English Ode from Milton to Keats. New
      York: Columbia University Press, 1940.
      Columbia University Studies in English and Comparative
      Literature, no. 150.

Periodical

1830 Brown, Calvin S., Jr. "More Swinburne-D'Annunzio Paral-
      lels." PMLA, 55 (1940), 559-567.
      Discusses D'Annunzio's use in his own writings of Swin-
      burne's work.

1941

Books

1831 Bateson, F. W. The Cambridge Bibliography of English Lit-
      erature. Vol. III. New York: Macmillan, 1941. pp.
      317-322.

1832 Bevington, Merle M. The Saturday Review. New York:
      Columbia University Press, 1941.

1833 Sampson, George. The Concise Cambridge History of English
      Literature. Cambridge: Cambridge University Press,
      1941.

1834 Thomas, Henry, and Dana Lee Thomas [pseudonyms of H. T.
      Schnittkind and D. A. Schnittkind, respectively]. "Alger-
      non Charles Swinburne." Living Biographies of Great Poets.
      New York: Garden City, 1941. pp. 199-213.

1942

Books

1835 Gaunt, William. The Pre-Raphaelite Tragedy. London:
          Cape, 1942.
          Biographical study.

1836 Lucas, F. L. "Swinburne." Ten Victorian Poets. Cam-
          bridge: Cambridge University Press, 1942. pp. 161-179.
          Reprinted from Eight Victorian Poets (entry 1674).

1943

Dissertation

1837 Ziegler, William H. The Literary Criticism of Algernon
          Charles Swinburne. Princeton, 1943.

Periodical

1838 Hyder, Clyde K. "Swinburne: Changes of Aspect and Short
          Notes." PMLA, 58 (1943), 223-244.
          Texts with notes.
          See C. K. Hyder's "A Swinburne Allusion to Blake" in the
          PMLA (entry 1845).

1944

Books

1839 Ford, George H. "Morris, Swinburne, and Some Others."
          Keats and the Victorians: A Study of His Influence and
          Rise to Fame, 1821-1895. New Haven, Conn.: Yale Uni-
          versity Press, 1944. pp. 164-169.
          Yale Studies in English, Vol. 101.
          Reprinted: Hamden, Conn.: Archon, 1962.

Dissertation

1840   Eidenbenz, Alfred.   Das starre Wortmuster und die Zeit in
       Swinburnes Poems and Ballads.   Zurich, 1944.

Periodical

1841   Spivey, Gaynell C.   "Swinburne's Use of Elizabethan Drama."
       Studies in Philology, 41 (1944), 250-263.

1945

Books

1842   Forman, H. Buxton, and Thomas J. Wise.   Between the
       Lines: Letters and Memoranda Interchanged by H. Buxton
       Forman and T. J. Wise.   Ed. Fannie E. Ratchford.   Aus-
       tin: University of Texas Press, 1945.
       Indicates Forman's complicity with Wise in at least one
       forgery.   Swinburne mentioned in Ratchford's introduction.

1843   Gaunt, William.   "Poet in Frenzy."   The Aesthetic Adven-
       ture.   London: Cape, 1945.   New York: Harcourt, 1945.
       pp. 45-54.

Dissertation

1844   Dahl, Curtis.   Mary Queen of Scots in the Literature of the
       Romantic Period and the Later Nineteenth Century.   Yale,
       1945.

Periodical

1845   Hyder, Clyde K.   "A Swinburne Allusion to Blake."   PMLA,
       60 (1945), 618.
       Refers to C. K. Hyder's "Swinburne" in PMLA, 1943
       (entry 1838).

1946

Books

1846   Grierson, H. J. C., and J. C. Smith.   "Mid-Victorian
       Poetry: the Pre-Raphaelite Group."   Critical History of
       English Poetry.   New York: Oxford University Press,
       1946.   pp. 484-495.

1847   Partington, Wilfred.   Thomas J. Wise in the Original Cloth.
       London: Hale, 1946.
       Revised version of Forging Ahead (entry 1823).

Periodicals

1848   Carter, John, and Graham Pollard.   Times Literary Supple-
       ment, June 1, 1946.
       Carter and Pollard discuss the forgeries imprinted "Charles
       Ottley, Landon & Co."

1849   Grantham, Evelyn.   "Letters from Symonds to Swinburne."
       More Books, 21 (1946), 212-221.

1947

Books

1850   Empson, William.   Seven Types of Ambiguity.   London:
       Chatto and Windus, 1947.
       Second edition: 1949.
       Third edition: 1953.
       Reprinted: New York: Noonday, 1955; and London:
       Penguin, 1961.

1851   Meynell, A. C. T.   "Swinburne."   Prose and Poetry: Cen-
       tenary Volume.   Ed. F. P. [Frederick Page].   London:
       Cape, 1947.   pp. 148-160.

Periodicals

1852   Hare, Humphrey.   "Swinburne and 'Le vice anglais.' "
       Horizon, 1947.

1853   Knickerbocker, Kenneth L.   "Browning and Swinburne: An
       Episode."   Modern Language Notes, 62 (1947), 240-244.

Discusses Browning's efforts to persuade Chapman not to publish Swinburne's poetry.

1948

Books

1854   Carter, John, and Graham Pollard.   The Firm of Charles
         Ottley, Landon & Co.:   Footnote to An Enquiry.   London:
         Hart-Davis, 1948.   New York: Scribner, 1948.
         This book is devoted to the problems involved in T. J.
         Wise's forgeries of pamphlets of Swinburne's works.   Wise's
         efforts to preserve first-edition status for his forgeries are
         examined.
         Reviewed: P. Brooks in New York Times Book Review
         (entry 1870); and Times Literary Supplement (entry 1861).

1855   Chew, S. C. in A Literary History of England.   Ed. Albert
         C. Baugh.   New York: Appleton-Century-Crofts, 1948.
         Reprinted: 1967.

1856   Thompson, Francis.   "Mrs. Boythorn and Her Canary."
         Literary Criticisms: Newly Discovered and Collected.
         Ed. Terence L. Connolly.   New York: Dutton, 1948.

1857   Thomson, James A. K.   The Classical Background of Eng-
         lish Literature.   London: Allen and Unwin, 1948.

1858   Tillyard, E. M. W.   "Swinburne: Hertha, 1870."   Five
         Poems, 1470-1870.   London: Chatto and Windus, 1948.
         pp. 87-103.
         This essay reads more like social criticism than literary
         criticism.
         Book reprinted as Poetry and Its Background: Illustrated
         by Five Poems, 1470-1870 (New York: Barnes and Noble,
         1970).

Periodicals

1859   Lang, Cecil.   "Swinburne and American Literature: With
         Six Hitherto Unpublished Letters."   American Literature,
         19 (1948), 336-350.
         Texts with commentary.

1860   "From Sunrise to Sunset."   Times Literary Supplement,
         Aug. 28, 1948, p. 484.

1861   Times Literary Supplement, Dec. 11, 1948, p. 698.
       Review of J. Carter and G. Pollard's The Firm of Charles
       Ottley (entry 1854).

1949

Books

1862   Angeli, Helen Rossetti. "Algernon Charles Swinburne."
       Dante Gabriel Rossetti: His Friends and Enemies.   Lon-
       don: Hamilton, 1949. pp. 97-109.
       Swinburne examined from the point of view of D. G. and
       Lizzie Rossetti.
       Reprinted: New York: Blom, 1972.

1863   Bowra, Cecil Maurice. "Atalanta in Calydon." The Roman-
       tic Imagination. Cambridge, Mass.: Harvard University
       Press, 1949. London: Oxford University Press, 1949.
       A good, sensible study, by someone well versed in Greek
       literature.

1864   Dingle, Herbert. Science and Literary Criticism. London
       and New York: Nelson, 1949.

1865   Doughty, Oswald. Dante Gabriel Rossetti. New Haven,
       Conn.: Yale University Press, 1949.
       Reprinted: London and New York: Longmans, Green,
       1957.
       Reprinted as A Victorian Romantic: Dante Gabriel Rossetti
       (London: Oxford University Press, 1960).

1866   Hare, Humphrey. Swinburne: A Biographical Approach.
       London: Witherby, 1949.
       Minor biography.

1867   Hough, Graham. The Last Romantics. London: Duckworth,
       1949.
       New edition: London and New York: Barnes and Noble,
       1961.

1868   Tennyson, Charles. Alfred Tennyson. New York: Macmil-
       lan, 1949.

Periodicals

1869   Bandy, W. T. "A Misdated Swinburne Letter." Modern
       Language Notes, 64 (1949), 177-178.

Discusses a letter to John H. Ingram.
See also I. B. Cauthen, Jr., "Swinburne's Letter Concerning Poe," in Publications of the Bibliographical Society of America (entry 1883).

1870   Brooks, Philip. New York Times Book Review, July 3, 1949, p. 14.
Review of J. Carter and G. Pollard's The Firm of Charles Ottley (entry 1854).

1871   Cohen, J. M. "Swinburne Revalued." The Spectator, 183 (Nov. 18, 1949), 690-692.

1872   Dahl, C. "Swinburne's Loyalty to the House of Stuart." Studies in Philology, 46 (July 1949), 453-469.

1873   Hare, Humphrey. "'Within a Leyden Jar': Swinburne and Watts-Dunton (1879-1909)." Horizon, 1949.

1874   Lang, Cecil Y. "Swinburne on Keats: A Fragment of an Essay." Modern Language Notes, 64 (1949), 168-171.
Text of a manuscript fragment with notes.

1875   _____. "A Further Note on Swinburne and Whitman." Modern Language Notes, 64 (1949), 176-177.

1876   Quennell, Peter. New Statesman and Nation, 38 (Nov. 12, 1949), 552-553.

1950

Books

1877   Heath-Stubbs, John. The Darkling Plain. London: Eyre and Spottiswoode, 1950.

1878   Mayfield, John S. The Luck of an Autograph Hunter. Washington, D. C.: Fraternity, 1950.

1879   Saintsbury, George. "Reconsideration of Swinburne." Last Vintage: Essays and Papers. Ed. John W. Oliver, Arthur Melville Clark, and Augustus Muir. London: Methuen, 1950. pp. 72-76.

1880   Vines, Sherard. One Hundred Years of English Literature. London: Duckworth, 1950.

1881   Vivante, Leone. "Algernon Charles Swinburne." English
        Poetry and Its Contribution to the Knowledge of a Creative
        Principle. New York: Macmillan, 1950. pp. 262-306.

Dissertation

1882   Schroeder, Elver A. Swinburne as Thinker. University of
        Michigan, 1950.
        Microfilm Abstracts, 10 (1950), 118-119.

Periodicals

1883   Cauthen, I. B., Jr. "Swinburne's Letter Concerning Poe."
        Publications of the Bibliographical Society of America,
        44 (1950), 185-190.
        See also W. T. Bandy, "A Misdated Swinburne Letter,"
        in Modern Language Notes (entry 1869).

1884   Lang, Cecil Y. "Swinburne's Letters to Henry Arthur
        Bright." Yale University Library Gazette, 25 (1950),
        10-22.

1885   Souffrin, Eileen. "Swinburne et Banville." Revue de
        Littérature Comparée, 1950.

_____

                                  1951
_____

Books

1886   Browning, Robert. Dearest Isa: Robert Browning's Letters
        to Isabella Blagden. Ed. Edward C. McAleer. Austin:
        University of Texas Press, 1951.
        Swinburne mentioned several times.

1887   Buckley, Jerome Hamilton. The Victorian Temper: A Study
        in Literary Culture. Cambridge, Mass.: Harvard Univer-
        sity Press, 1951.
        This excellent book helps place Swinburne in the literary
        movements of his day. It is a standard reference work
        for students of Victorian literature.

1888   Firth, J. R. Firth. "Modes of Meaning." Essays and
        Studies, 1951.

1889   Pope-Hennesey, James. Monckton Milnes. London:
        Constable, 1951.

1890   Souffrin, Eileen.   "Swinburne et sa légende en France."
        Revue de Littérature Comparée, 1951.

1952

In 1952, Randolph Hughes's edition of Lesbia Brandon was published (London: Falcon). This extraordinarily well-annotated book
evoked much controversy, and it remains both interesting and controversial. Hughes was an experienced editor who had produced
editions of Swinburne's Lucretia Borgia (1942) and Pasiphaë &c
(1950) and who fearlessly expressed his opinions of Swinburne's
work.

Book

1891   Read, Herbert.   The Philosophy of Modern Art.   London:
        Faber and Faber, 1952.

Dissertation

1892   Connolly, Thomas E.   Swinburne as a Poetic Theorist.
        University of Chicago, 1952.

Periodicals

1893   Bryson, John.   New Statesman and Nation, 44 (Aug. 16,
        1952), 190.
        Review of Lesbia Brandon, ed. R. Hughes.

1894   Cassidy, J. A.   "Robert Buchanan and the Fleshly Contro-
        versy."   PMLA, 67 (March 1952).

1895   Connolly, Thomas E.   "Swinburne's Theory of the End of
        Art."   Journal of English Literary History, 19 (1952),
        277-290.
        Discusses Swinburne's political views and their effect on
        his poetic theories.

1896   Ferguson, DeLancey.   New York Herald Tribune Book Re-
        view, Oct. 12, 1952, 36.
        Review of Lesbia Brandon, ed. R. Hughes.

1897   Lang, Cecil.   "Lesbia Brandon."   Times Literary Supple-
        ment, Oct. 31, 1952, p. 716.
        Lang lists some of R. Hughes's errors in the 1952 edition
        of Lesbia Brandon.

1898   Maurer, Oscar.   "Swinburne vs. Furnivall: A Case Study in
       "Aesthetic' vs. 'Scientific' Criticism. "   Studies in English,
       31 (1952),   86-96.

1899   Super, R. H.   "A Grain of Truth about Wordsworth and
       Browning, Landor and Swinburne. "   Modern Language Notes,
       67 (1952),   419-421.
       Super disputes Edmund Gosse's veracity as a chronicler of
       Swinburne's life.

1900   Times Literary Supplement, July 4, 1952, 434.
       Review of Lesbia Brandon, ed. R. Hughes.

1901   Tomlinson, Philip.   The Spectator, 189 (July 18, 1952), 104.
       Review of Lesbia Brandon, ed. R. Hughes.

1902   West, H. F.   New York Times Book Review, Nov. 30, 1952,
       p. 4.
       Review of Lesbia Brandon, ed. R. Hughes.

1953

Books

1903   Grierson, H. J. C.   Algernon Charles Swinburne.   London:
       Longmans, Green, 1953.
       Handy short survey of Swinburne's work.
       Reprinted: "Algernon Charles Swinburne" in Dante Gabriel
       Rossetti: William Morris: Algernon Charles Swinburne
       (entry 2020).

1904   Mayfield, John S.   Swinburne's Boo.   Bethesda, Md.:   pri-
       vately printed, 1953.
       Reprinted: Washington, D. C.:   Goetz, 1954.
       Also: "Swinburne's Boo" in English Miscellany (Rome)
       (entry 1909).

1905   Quennell, Peter.   "Algernon Charles Swinburne. "   Singular
       Preference: Portraits and Essays.   New York: Viking,
       1953.   pp. 110-117.

1906   Temple, Ruth Z.   The Critic's Alchemy: A Study of the
       Introduction of French Symbolism into England.   New York:
       Twayne, 1953.

Periodicals

1907   Lang, C. Y.   "The First Chorus of Swinburne's Atalanta. "

Yale University Library Gazette, 27 (Jan. 1953), 119-122.
Reproduces a holograph.

1908 Marchand, L. A. "The Watts-Dunton Letter Books." Journal of the Rutgers University Library, 1953.

1909 Mayfield, John S. "Swinburne's Boo." English Miscellany
(Rome), 4 (1953), 161-178.
Also: Swinburne's Boo (entry 1904).

1910 Robinson, J. K. "A Neglected Phase of the Aesthetic Movement: English Parnassianism." PMLA, 68 (Sept. 1953).

1911 Wright, Brooks. "Swinburne's A Cameo." Explicator, 12
(1953), item 13.

1954

Books

1912 Angeli, Helen Rossetti. "Swinburne (i)" and "Swinburne (ii)."
Pre-Raphaelite Twilight: the Story of Charles Augustus
Howell. London: Richards, 1954. pp. 167-182.
Angeli defends Howell and blames Theodore Watts-Dunton
for most of Swinburne's problems.

1913 MacCarthy, Desmond. "Swinburne." Humanities. London:
Oxford University Press, 1954. pp. 172-175.

1914 Pound, Ezra. "Swinburne Versus His Biographers." Liter-
ary Essays of Ezra Pound. Ed. T. S. Eliot. London:
New Directions, 1954.
Reprinted from Poetry, March 1918 (entry 1334).

Dissertation

1915 Hess, Rudolf. Die Lyrik Algernon Charles Swinburnes in
deutschen Übertragungen. Mainz, 1954.

Periodical

1916 Lang, C. Y. "Some Swinburne Manuscripts." Journal of
Rutgers University Library, 18 (Dec. 1954), 1-12.

1955

Books

1917 Allen, Gay Wilson. The Solitary Singer: A Critical Biogra-
      phy of Walt Whitman. New York: Macmillan, 1955.
      Reprinted: New York: New York University Press, 1967.

1918 Groom, Bernard. "Rossetti, Morris, and Swinburne." The
      Diction of Poetry from Spenser to Bridges. Toronto:
      University of Toronto Press, 1955.

1919 Parrott, T. M., and R. B. Martin. "Algernon Charles
      Swinburne." Companion to Victorian Literature. New
      York: Scribner, 1955. pp. 248-253.

Dissertations

1920 Milstead, John. Swinburne's Elemental Imagery. University
      of Wisconsin, 1955.
      Dissertation Abstracts, 16 (1956), 748.

1921 Schmitz, Charlotte. Die schmückenden Beiwörter in den
      poetischen Werken von Algernon Charles Swinburne.
      Innsbruck, 1955.

Periodical

1922 Mayfield, John S. "Two Presentation Copies of Swinburne's
      'Atalanta in Calydon.'" Papers of the Bibliographical So-
      ciety of America, 49 (1955), 360-365.

1956

Books

1923 Graves, Robert. "'Mad Mr. Swinburne.'" Crowning Privi-
      lege: Collected Essays on Poetry. New York: Doubleday,
      1956.

1924 Hyder, Clyde K. "Algernon Charles Swinburne." The Vic-
      torian Poets: A Guide to Research. Ed. Frederic E.
      Faverty. Cambridge, Mass.: Harvard University Press,
      1956. pp. 140-160.
      This essay provides a good statement of the state of

Swinburne studies in 1956. Hyder not only discusses important primary and secondary materials but provides valuable insights of his own about the major difficulties pre-
sented by research into Swinburne.
See also 1968 essay: entry 2054.

1925 Nicolson, Harold George. "Swinburne and Baudelaire."
The English Sense of Humor: And Other Essays. London:
Constable, 1956. pp. 123-142.
Book reprinted: New York: Funk and Wagnalls, 1968.
Essay reprinted from Essays by Divers Hands, ed. G. K.
Chesterton (entry 1555).
See entry 1555 for other reprinting.

Dissertation

1926 Want, M. S. A New Approach to the Dramatic Works of
Swinburne. Leeds, 1956.

1957

Book

1927 Fairchild, H. N. "Swinburne." Religious Trends in English
Poetry. Volume IV: 1830-1880: Christianity and Romanticism in the Victorian Era. New York: Columbia University Press, 1957. pp. 432-455.

Periodicals

1928 Connolly, Thomas E. "Swinburne on 'The Music of Poetry.'"
PMLA, 72 (1957), 680-688.

1929 Lang, Cecil. "ALS: Swinburne to William Michael Rossetti."
Journal of Rutgers University Library, 14 (1957), 1-8.

1930 _____. "A Manuscript, a Mare's-Nest, and a Mystery."
Yale University Library Gazette, 31 (1957), 163-171.
About "A Leave-Taking."

1931 Marshall, Robert. "T. S. Eliot et le 'Baudelaire' de Swinburne." Le Bayou, No. 70 (1957), 432-438.

1932 Noyes, Alfred. "Dinner at The Pines: Reminiscences of
Swinburne." Listener, 57 (March 1957), 507-508.

1958

Dissertations

1933   Headings, Philip R.   The Tiresias Tradition in Western Lit-
          erature.   Indiana University, 1958.
          Discusses Matthew Arnold and Swinburne.

1934   Hively, Robert William.   Algernon Charles Swinburne as a
          Literary Critic.   University of Florida, 1958.

Periodicals

1935   Baum, Paull F.   "Swinburne's 'A Nympholept.'"   South At-
          lantic Quarterly, 57 (1958), 58-68.
          Good criticism.

1936   Henry, Anne W.   "A Reconstructed Swinburne Ballad."
          Harvard Library Bulletin, 12 (Autumn 1958), 354-362.

1959

In 1959, the first volume of The Swinburne Letters, edited by Cecil
Y. Lang, appeared.   Published over four years (through 1962) and
comprising six volumes, Lang's edition is a model of probity, intelligent editing, and thorough research.   It is the standard reference for Swinburne's letters, and is likely to remain such for many
more years.

Books

1937   Eckhoff, Lorentz.   The Aesthetic Movement in English Liter-
          ature.   Oslo: Oslo University Press, 1959.

1938   Pollard, Graham.   "The Case of The Devil's Due."   Thomas
          J. Wise: Centenary Studies.   Ed. William B. Todd.
          Austin: University of Texas Press, 1959.   pp. 38-44.
          Pollard identifies another of Wise's forgeries.

1939   Thompson, Francis.   "Mr. Swinburne" and "The Pity of It."
          The Real Robert Louis Stevenson: and Other Critical Es-
          says.   Ed. Terence L. Connolly.   New York: Boston Col-
          lege (by University Publishers), 1959.   pp. 155-161 and
          162-164, respectively.

1940 Todd, William B. "A Handlist of Thomas J. Wise." Thom-
      as J. Wise: Centenary Studies. Ed. William B. Todd.
      Austin: University of Texas Press, 1959. pp. 80-122.
      Todd states, "This list records 401 publications now at-
      tributed to Wise, 29 others in which he appears to be some-
      what involved, 23 suppressed or abortive issues, and some
      account of variants, proof-copies, and other miscellanea"
      (page 80). Todd updates the record of Wise's forgeries.

Periodicals

1941 Adams, Donald K. "Swinburne and Hazlitt." Notes and
      Queries, 6 (1959), 451-452.

1942 Baum, P. F. "The Fitzwilliam Manuscript of Swinburne's
      Atalanta, Verses 1038-1204." Modern Language Review,
      54 (1959), 161-178.

1943 Bissell, E. E. "Gosse, Wise and Swinburne." Book Col-
      lector, 8 (1959), 297-299.

1944 Bulletin from Virginia Kirkus' Service, 27 (Oct. 1, 1959),
      775.
      Review of Volumes I and II of The Swinburne Letters, ed.
      C. Y. Lang.

1945 Kerr, Lowell. "Swinburne and Correggio." Times Literary
      Supplement, July 31, 1959, p. 447.

1946 Lang, Cecil Y. "Swinburne's Lost Love." PMLA, 74
      (March 1959), 123-130.

1947 Maxwell, J. C. "Swinburne and 'The Cult of the Calamus.'"
      Notes and Queries, 6 (1959), 452.

1948 Paden, W. D. "Footnote to a Footnote." Times Literary
      Supplement, Oct. 23, 1959, p. 616.
      Discusses Swinburne's "A Word for the Navy."
      Commented on by A. R. Redway in Times Literary Supple-
      ment, Nov. 20, 1959 (entry 1950); and J. C. Troxell in
      Times Literary Supplement, Dec. 4, 1959 (entry 1953).

1949 Peters, Robert L. "Toward an 'Un-Definition' of Decadent
      as Applied to British Literature of the Nineteenth Century."
      Journal of Aesthetics and Art Criticism, 18 (1959), 258-264.

1950 Redway, A. R. Times Literary Supplement, Nov. 20, 1959,
      p. 677.
      Comments on W. D. Paden's "Footnote to a Footnote" in
      Times Literary Supplement, Oct. 23, 1959 (entry 1948).
      See entry 1953 for another comment on Paden's article.

1951 Tener, Robert H. "Swinburne as Reviewer." Times Liter-

ary Supplement, Dec. 25, 1959, p. 755.
Discusses the authenticity of attributions of Swinburne's
authorship.

1952   Todd, W. B.   "Swinburne Manuscripts of Texas." Texas
       Quarterly, 2 (Autumn 1959).
       Useful for researchers interested in manuscript sources.

1953   Troxell, Janet Camp.   Times Literary Supplement, Dec. 4,
       1959, p. 709.
       Comments on W. D. Paden's "Footnote to a Footnote" in
       Times Literary Supplement, Oct. 23, 1959 (entry 1948).
       See entry 1950 for another comment on Paden's article.

1954   Willingham, J. R.   Library Journal, 84 (Dec. 1, 1959), 3775.
       Review of Volumes I and II of The Swinburne Letters, ed.
       C. Y. Lang.

1960

Swinburne: A Selection, edited by Edith Sitwell (New York: Harcourt, Brace; and London: Weidenfeld and Nicolson), was published.
This interesting selection of Swinburne's work attracted more critical attention than most such editions.

Books

1955   Carroll, Lewis.   "The Little Man That Had a Little Gun."
       The Humorous Verse of Lewis Carroll.   New York:
       Dover, 1960.
       Printed in 1932 (entry 1723).

1956   Starkie, E.   "Swinburne and Pater."   From Gautier to Eliot:
       The Influence of France on English Literature, 1851-1939.
       New York: Humanities, 1960.   pp. 40-57.

Periodicals

1957   Altick, Richard D.   "Four Victorian Poets and an Exploding
       Island."   Victorian Studies, 3 (1960), 249-260.
       The reactions of Swinburne and others to the eruption of
       Krakatoa in August 1883.

1958   Bulletin from Virginia Kirkus' Service, 28 (Aug. 15, 1960),
       728.
       Review of Swinburne, ed. E. Sitwell.

1959   Chew, S. C.   New York Herald Tribune Book Review, Jan.
       10, 1960, p. 3.
       Review of Volumes I and II of The Swinburne Letters, ed.
       C. Y. Lang.   .

1960   Del Re, Raffaello.   "Il classicismo nella poesia di A. C.
       Swinburne. "   Convivium, 28 (1960), 20-44 and 165-179.

1961   Graaf, Daniel A. de.   "L'influence de Swinburne sur
       Verlaine et Rimbaud. "   Revue des Sciences Humaines,
       No. 97 (1960), 87-92.

1962   Gregory, Horace.   New York Times Book Review, Nov. 27,
       1960, p. 4.
       Review of Swinburne, ed. E. Sitwell.

1963   Klingopulos, G. D.   The Spectator, 205 (Oct. 21, 1960), 610.
       Review of Swinburne, ed. E. Sitwell.

1964   Maxwell, J. C.   "The Swinburne Letters and O. E. D. "   Notes
       and Queries, 7 (1960), 346-347.
       See also entry 1982.

1965   Partridge, Ralph.   New Statesman, 59 (May 14, 1960), 722.
       Review of Volumes I and II of The Swinburne Letters, ed.
       C. Y. Lang.

1966   Ray, G. N.   New York Times Book Review, Jan. 24, 1960,
       22.
       Review of Volumes I and II of The Swinburne Letters, ed.
       C. Y. Lang.

1967   _____.   New York Times Book Review, Dec. 25, 1960,
       p. 10.
       Review of Volumes III and IV of The Swinburne Letters,
       ed. C. Y. Lang.

1968   Robson, W. W.   The Spectator, 204 (June 3, 1960), 808.
       Review of Volumes I and II of The Swinburne Letters, ed.
       C. Y. Lang.

1969   Souffrin, Eileen.   "Swinburne et Les Misérables. "   Revue de
       Littérature Comparée, 34 (1960), 578-584.

1970   Times Literary Supplement, June 3, 1960, p. 352.
       Review of Volumes I and II of The Swinburne Letters, ed.
       C. Y. Lang.

1971   Times Literary Supplement, Oct. 14, 1960, p. 662.
       Review of Swinburne, ed. E. Sitwell.

1972   Tregenza, John.   "Victor Hugo and C. H. Pearson. "   Times
       Literary Supplement, March 18, 1960, p. 177.

1973   Willingham, J. R.   Library Journal, 85 (Sept. 1, 1960),
       2939.
       Review of Volumes III and IV of The Swinburne Letters,
       ed. C. Y. Lang.

1974   _____.   Library Journal, 85 (Dec. 15, 1960), 4477.
       Review of Swinburne, ed. E. Sitwell.

                              1961

Books

1975   Brown, E. K.   "Swinburne: A Centenary Estimate."   Vic-
       torian Literature: Modern Essays in Criticism.   Ed.
       Austin Wright.   New York: Oxford University Press, 1961.
       pp. 295-310.
       Reprinted from University of Toronto Quarterly, Jan. 1937
       (entry 1812).

1976   Turgenev, Ivan.   Complete Works: Letters.   Vol. I.   Mos-
       cow: 1960.   pp. ix and 125.

Dissertation

1977   Boswell, Grace Hadaway.   Swinburne's Mary, Queen of Scots,
       and the Historical Mary.   University of Georgia, 1961.
       Dissertation Abstracts, 21 (1961), 1937.

Periodicals

1978   Brown, T. J.   "English Literary Autographs XXXVII: Alger-
       non Charles Swinburne."   Book Collector, 10 (1961), 57.

1979   Christian Science Monitor, Jan. 12, 1961, p. 7.
       Review of Swinburne, ed. E. Sitwell.

1980   Ferguson, DeLancey.   New York Herald Tribune Lively Arts,
       Jan. 15, 1961, 34.
       Review of Swinburne, ed. E. Sitwell; and Volumes III and
       IV of The Swinburne Letters, ed. C. Y. Lang.

1981   Hargreaves, H. A.   "Swinburne's Greek Plays and God, 'The
       Supreme Evil.'"   Modern Language Notes, 76 (1961), 607-
       616.

1982   Maxwell, J. C.   "The Swinburne Letters and O. E. D."   Notes
       and Queries, 8 (1961), 345-346.
       See also entry 1964.

1983   New Yorker, 37 (Feb. 25, 1961), 135.
       Review of Swinburne, ed. E. Sitwell.

1984   Paden, W. D.   "A Few Annotations by Swinburne." Notes
       and Queries, 8 (1961), 469-470.
       Notes in an 1856 edition of the Oxford and Cambridge Maga-
       zine.

1985   Richart, Bette. Commonweal, 73 (Feb. 17, 1961), 538.
       Review of Swinburne, ed. E. Sitwell.

1986   Slater, Joseph. Saturday Review (New York), 44 (May 6,
       1961), 29.
       Review of Swinburne, ed. E. Sitwell.

1987   Times Literary Supplement, June 9, 1961, p. 358.
       Review of Volumes III and IV of The Swinburne Letters,
       ed. C. Y. Lang.

1962

The Novels of A. C. Swinburne: Love's Cross-Currents: Lesbia
Brandon, edited by Edmund Wilson, appeared in 1962.

Books

1988   Gosse, Edmund. "Swinburne: an Essay." The Swinburne
       Letters. Ed. C. Y. Lang. New Haven, Conn.: Yale
       University Press, 1962. Vol. VI. pp. 233-248.

1989   Paden, W. D.   "Swinburne, the Spectator in 1862, and Walter
       Bagehot." Six Studies in Nineteenth-Century English Liter-
       ature and Thought. Ed. Harold Orel and George Worth.
       Lawrence: University of Kansas, 1962. pp. 91-115.
       Supersedes S. C. Chew's "Swinburne's Contributions to
       The Spectator in 1862" in Modern Language Notes, Feb.
       1920 (entry 1419).

1990   Wilde, Oscar.   The Letters of Oscar Wilde.   Ed. Rupert
       Hart-Davis.   London: Hart-Davis, 1962.   New York:
       Harcourt, Brace and World, 1962.
       Swinburne mentioned many times.

Periodicals

1991   Buchen, I. R.   Saturday Review (New York), 45 (Dec. 29,
       1962), 36.
       Review of The Novels of A. C. Swinburne, ed. E. Wilson.

1992   Ferguson, DeLancey.   New York Herald Tribune Books, May
       13, 1962, p. 9.
       Review of The Swinburne Letters, ed. C. Y. Lang.

1993   Lang, C. Y.   "Atalanta in Manuscript."   Yale University Li-
       brary Gazette, 37 (July 1962), 19-24.

1994   Lucie-Smith, Edward.   "The Tortured Yearned as Well: An
       Enquiry into Themes of Cruelty in Current Verse."   Criti-
       cal Quarterly, 4 (1962), 34-43.

1995   Peters, Robert L.   "Algernon Charles Swinburne and the Use
       of Integral Detail."   Victorian Studies, 5 (June 1962), 289-
       302.
       Interesting study of a part of Swinburne's aesthetic views.

1996   Ray, G. N.   New York Times Book Review, May 13, 1962,
       p. 4.
       Review of The Swinburne Letters, ed. C. Y. Lang.

1997   Ricks, Christopher.   New Statesman, 64 (Aug. 10, 1962),
       176.
       Review of The Swinburne Letters, ed. C. Y. Lang.

1998   Times Literary Supplement, Aug. 10, 1962, p. 593.
       Review of The Swinburne Letters, ed. C. Y. Lang.

1999   Willingham, J. R.   Library Journal, 87 (June 15, 1962),
       2381.
       Review of The Swinburne Letters, ed. C. Y. Lang.

2000   Wilson, Edmund.   "Swinburne of Capheaton and Eton."   New
       Yorker, 38 (Oct. 6, 1962), 165-200.
       Review of The Swinburne Letters, ed. C. Y. Lang.
       Variant version of this essay appears in The Novels of A.
       C. Swinburne, ed. E. Wilson.

1963

2001   Adams, Phoebe.   Atlantic Monthly, 211 (March 1963), 164.
       Review of The Novels of A. C. Swinburne, ed. E. Wilson.

2002   Ehrenpreis, Anne Henry.   "Swinburne's Edition of Popular
       Ballads."   PMLA, 78 (1963), 559-571.
       About Ballads of the English Border.   Corrects errors
       made by T. J. Wise and William MacInnes.

2003   Grosskurth, P. M. "Swinburne and Symonds: An Uneasy
       Literary Relationship." Review of English Studies, 14
       (1963), 257-268.

2004   Igoe, W. J. Critic (Chicago), 21 (April 1963), 79.
       Review of The Novels of A. C. Swinburne, ed. E. Wilson.

2005   Johnson, Wendell Stacy. "Swinburne and Carlyle." English
       Language Notes, 1 (1963), 117-121.
       Johnson suggests a possible Thomas Carlyle influence on
       Swinburne's "Hertha."

2006   Leach, Elsie. "The Swinburne Letters and O. E. D." Notes
       and Queries, 10 (1963), 346-347.

2007   Packer, Lona Mosk. "Swinburne and Christina Rossetti:
       Atheist and Anglican." University of Toronto Quarterly,
       33 (1963), 30-42.

2008   Peters, Robert L. "Swinburne's Idea of Form." Criticism,
       5 (1963), 45-63.

2009   Time, 81 (Jan. 25, 1963), 84.
       Review of The Novels of A. C. Swinburne, ed. E. Wilson.

2010   Willingham, J. R. Library Journal, 88 (Jan. 15, 1963), 238.
       Review of The Novels of A. C. Swinburne, ed. E. Wilson.

2011   Wills, G. National Review, 14 (March 26, 1963), 238.
       Review of The Novels of A. C. Swinburne, ed. E. Wilson.

1964

New Writings by Swinburne, edited by C. Y. Lang, was published
in 1964.

Books

2012   Cassidy, John A. Algernon C. Swinburne. New York:
       Twayne, 1964.
       Twayne's English Author Series, No. 10.
       This book has been controversial from the time of its pub-
       lication. C. K. Hyder and others have complained about
       Cassidy's "errors and conjectures" (in Hyder's article the
       1968 edition of The Victorian Poets, page 236; entry 2054).
       The present bibliographer cannot agree with the stringency

of the remarks against Cassidy's book, although it might
confuse the beginning student of Swinburne.   Cassidy is an
intelligent critic whose ideas are iconoclastic enough to be
interesting.
Reviewed: R. A. Greenberg in Victorian Studies (entry
2039).

2013 Connolly, Thomas E.   Swinburne's Theory of Poetry.   New
York: State University of New York, 1964.
Study of the principles behind Swinburne's criticism.   Inter-
esting and of continuing value.
Reviewed: J. K. Robinson in Modern Philology (entry
2043); and Times Literary Supplement (entry 2031).

2014 Just, Klaus Günther.   "Die Rezeption Swinburnes in der
deutschen Literatur der Jahrhunderwende."   Festschrift für
Jost Trier zum 70. Geburtstag.   Ed. William Foerste and
Karl Heinz Borck.   Cologne: Böhlau, 1964.

Periodicals

2015 Kerr, Lowell.   "Swinburne and Correggio."   Manuscripts,
16 (1964), 24-27.

2016 Peters, Robert L.   "Swinburne and the Moral Design of Art."
Victorian Poetry, 2 (1964), 139-154.

2017 Poels, Bert.   "Gossaert, Baudelaire, Swinburne."   De
Nieuwe Taalgids, 57 (1964), 365-372.

2018 Rooney, Charles J. , Jr.   "A New Letter by Lowell."
American Literature, 36 (1964), 214-215.

1965

Books

2019 Fredeman, William E.   "Algernon Charles Swinburne: 1837-
1909."   Pre-Raphaelitism: A Bibliocritical Study.   Cambridge, Mass.: Harvard University Press, 1965.   pp. 216-
220.
Fredeman remarks, "Swinburne's intimacy with the Pre-
Raphaelite group at Oxford had a permanent influence on
his poetry" (page 217).   An excellent study.

2020 Grierson, H. J. C.   "Algernon Charles Swinburne."   Dante
Gabriel Rossetti: William Morris: Algernon Charles

Swinburne. Lincoln: University of Nebraska Press, 1965.
pp. 79-110.
British Writers and Their Work, No. 7.
This is an updated version of Algernon Charles Swinburne
(entry 1903).
A handy short reference work.

2021 Peters, Robert L. The Crowns of Apollo: Swinburne's
Principles of Literature and Art: A Study in Victorian
Criticism and Aesthetics. Detroit: Wayne State University
Press, 1965.
Probably the single best study of Swinburne's aesthetic
principles, this excellent work of criticism is a standard
reference for Swinburne scholars.
Reviewed: Hazard Adams in Journal of Aesthetics and Art
Criticism (entry 2035), J. K. Robinson in Modern Philology
(entry 2043), and Times Literary Supplement (entry 2031).

2022 Rossetti, Dante Gabriel. The Letters of Dante Gabriel Rossetti. 4 volumes. Ed. Oswald Doughty and J. R. Wahl.
London: Oxford University Press, 1965-1967.

2023 Wilson, Edmund. "Swinburne's Letters and Novels." The
Bit Between My Teeth: A Literary Chronicle of 1950-1965.
New York: Farrar, Straus, 1965.

Dissertations

2024 Cayer, Roger Leo. Algernon Charles Swinburne's Literary
Reputation: A Study of the Criticism of Swinburne's Works
in England from 1860 to 1960. New York University, 1964.
Useful outline of the history of critical responses to Swin-
burne's work.
Dissertation Abstracts, 25 (June 1965), 7240-7241.

2025 Raymond, Meredith Bragg. Swinburne's Poetics: Theory
and Practice. Boston University, 1965.
Dissertation Abstracts, 25 (1965), 4154-4155.
See entry 2090.

Periodicals

2026 Dahl, Curtis. "Swinburne's Mary Stuart: A Reading of
Ronsard." Papers on Language and Literature, 1 (1965),
39-49.

2027 _____. "Autobiographical Elements in Swinburne's Trilogy
on Mary Stuart." Victorian Poetry, 3 (1966), 91-99.

2028 Grigson, Geoffrey. New Statesman, 69 (Feb. 5, 1965), 201.
Review of New Writings by Swinburne, ed. C. Y. Lang.

2029 Mann, C. W. Library Journal, 90 (March 1, 1965), 1120.
Review of New Writings by Swinburne, ed. C. Y. Lang.

2030 Seronsy, Cecil C.   "An Autograph Letter by Swinburne on
      Daniel and Drummond of Hawthornden. " Notes and Queries,
      12 (1965), 303-304.

2031 "The Swinburne Case. " Times Literary Supplement, Nov. 4,
      1965, p. 980.
      Review of New Writings of Swinburne, ed. C. Y. Lang; R.
      L. Peters's Crowns of Apollo (entry 2021); and T. E. Con-
      nolly's Swinburne's Theory of Poetry (entry 2013).

1966

Books

2032 Buckley, Jerome H.   "Swinburne, Algernon Charles (1837-
      1909). " Victorian Poets and Prose Writers.   New York:
      Appleton-Century-Crofts, 1966.   pp. 45-47.
      Goldentree Bibliographies.
      Brief list of collections of Swinburne's works and of works
      about Swinburne.   This list should be useful to beginning
      students of Swinburne, although one is tempted to quibble
      over Buckley's selections and some works left out of his
      list.

2033 Just, Klaus G.   Übergange: Problems und Gestalten der
      Literatur.   Bern: Francke, 1966.

Dissertation

2034 Suiter, James E.   Swinburne and the Main Stream of Victori-
      an Poetic Theory.   New York University, 1966.
      Dissertation Abstracts, 27 (1966), 1348A.

Periodicals

2035 Adams, Hazard.   Journal of Aesthetics and Art Criticism,
      25 (Fall 1966), 107.
      Review of R. L. Peters's Crowns of Apollo (entry 2021).

2036 Bass, Eben.   "Swinburne, Greene, and 'The Triumph of
      Time. '" Victorian Poetry, 4 (1966), 56-61.
      Discusses similarities between the work of Swinburne and
      the work of Greene.

2037 Cassidy, John A.   Victorian Studies, 10 (1966), 203-208.
      Reply to R. A. Greenberg's review of Cassidy's Algernon
      C. Swinburne (entry 2039).   Cassidy asks about the errors

Greenberg mentions in his review.   Greenberg answers
Cassidy in entry 2040.

2038   Dahl, Curtis.   "Macaulay, Henry Taylor, and Swinburne's
        Trilogy. "   Papers on Language and Literature, 2 (1966),
        166-169.
        Dahl discusses possible influences of Macaulay and Taylor
        on Swinburne's verse dramas about Mary Queen of Scots.

2039   Greenberg, Robert A.   Victorian Studies, 9 (March 1966),
        285-287.
        Review of J. A. Cassidy's Algernon C. Swinburne (entry
        2012).
        Cassidy challenged Greenberg's comments in entry 2037.
        Greenberg answered Cassidy in entry 2040.

2040   _____.   "Answer to an Inquiry. "   Victorian Studies, 10
        (1966), 203-208.
        This is an answer to John A. Cassidy's reply (entry 2037)
        to Greenberg's review (entry 2039) of Cassidy's Algernon
        C. Swinburne (entry 2012).   Cassidy had asked about the
        errors Greenberg said were in the book.   In this reply,
        Greenberg cites many errors and conjectures he found in
        Cassidy's book.

2041   Powell, Everett G.   "The Manuscript of Swinburne's 'Off
        Shore. ' "   Library Chronicle of the University of Texas,
        8 (1966), 9-22.

2042   Reed, John R.   "Swinburne's Tristram of Lyonesse: The
        Poet-Lover's Song of Love. "   Victorian Poetry, 4 (1966),
        99-120.
        Interesting study.

2043   Robinson, J. K.   Modern Philology, 63 (May 1966), 371.
        Review of T. E. Connolly's Swinburne's Theory of Poetry
        (entry 2013) and R. L. Peters's Crowns of Apollo (entry
        2021).

1967

Books

2044   Croft-Cooke, Rupert.   Feasting with Panthers: A New Con-
        sideration of Some Late Victorian Writers.   London: W. H.
        Allen, 1967.   New York: Holt, Rinehart and Winston,
        1968.

Dissertation

2045   Lougy, Robert E.   Thematic Imagery and Symbolic Action in
       the Poetry of Algernon Charles Swinburne.   University of
       California at Davis, 1967.
       Dissertation Abstracts, 27 (1967), 2533A-2534A.

Periodicals

2046   Dahl, Curtis.   "The Composition of Swinburne's Trilogy on
       Mary Queen of Scots."   Tennessee Studies in Literature,
       12 (1967), 103-110.

2047   Gál, István.   "Arnold és Swinburne magyar tárgyu szonettjei."
       Filologicai Kozlony, 13 (1967), 84-101.

2048   Kinneavy, Gerald B.   "Character and Action in Swinburne's
       Chastelard."   Victorian Poetry, 5 (1967), 31-39.

2049   McGhee, Richard D.   "'Thalassius': Swinburne's Poetic
       Myth."   Victorian Poetry, 5 (1967), 127-136.

2050   Omans, Glen A.   "Some Biographical Light on Rossetti's
       Translations of Villon."   Victorian Newsletter, 31 (1967),
       52-54.

2051   "A Rare Find."   American Book Collector, 17 (March 6,
       1967).

2052   Rosenberg, John D.   "Swinburne."   Victorian Studies, 11
       (1967), 131-152.
       Reprinted: Swinburne: Selected Poetry and Prose, ed.
       J. D. Rosenberg (New York: Modern Library, 1968).

1968

Books

2053   Fuller, Jean Overton.   Swinburne: A Biography.   London:
       Chatto and Windus, 1968.   New York: Schocken, 1971.
       Fuller emphasizes Swinburne's relationship to Mary Leith,
       sometimes to the detriment of other aspects of his life.
       Her work with manuscripts makes this book useful to stu-
       dents of Swinburne.
       Reviewed: Choice (entry 2130); and Library Journal (entry
       2103).

2054   Hyder, C. K. "Algernon Charles Swinburne." The Victorian
        Poets: A Guide to Research.   Ed. Frederic E. Faverty.
        Cambridge, Mass.: Harvard University Press, 1968.
        pp. 227-250.
        Good survey of scholarship. Particularly useful for its
        discussion of French publications.
        See also 1956 essay: entry 1924.

Dissertations

2055   Betz, Dorothy K. M.   Baudelairian Imagery and Rhetoric in
        the Works of Several Later Nineteenth Century Poets.
        Cornell, 1968.
        Dissertation Abstracts, 28 (1968), 4163A.

2056   Paul, Felix L.   Swinburne the Moralist.   Columbia, 1968.
        Dissertation Abstracts, 29 (1968), 575A.

2057   Sypher, Francis J., Jr.   A Study of Swinburne's Poetry.
        Columbia, 1968.
        Dissertation Abstracts, 29 (1968), 1881A.

Periodicals

2058   Baylen, Joseph O.   "Swinburne and the Pall Mall Gazette."
        Research Studies, 36 (1968), 325-334.

2059   Goede, William J.   "Swinburne and the Whitmaniacs."
        Victorian Newsletter, 33 (1968), 16-21.

2060   Lougy, Robert E.   "Swinburne's Poetry and Twentieth-
        Century Criticism."   Dalhousie Review, 48 (Autumn 1968),
        358-365.

2061   McSweeney, Kerry.   "The Structure of Swinburne's Tristram
        of Lyonesse." Queen's Quarterly, 75 (Winter 1968), 690-
        702.

2062   Peters, Robert L.   "A. C. Swinburne's 'Hymn to Proser-
        pine': The Work Sheets." PMLA, 83 (Oct. 1968), 1400-
        1406.

2063   Raymond, Meredith B.   "Swinburne Among the Nightingales."
        Victorian Poetry, 6 (1968), 125-141.

2064   Wilson, F. A. C.   "Swinburne's Sicilian Blade: Three Bio-
        graphical Studies." North Dakota Quarterly, 36 (1968),
        5-18.

1969

Books

2065 Eliot, T. S. "Swinburne as Poet." British Victorian Liter-
      ature: Recent Evaluations. Ed. Shiv Kumar Kumar. New
      York: New York University Press, 1969. pp. 155-159.

2066 Enzensberger, Christian. "Algernon Charles Swinburne."
      Viktorianische Lyrik: Tennyson und Swinburne in der
      Geschichte der Entfremdung. Munich: Carl Hauser, 1969.
      pp. 133-199.
      Literatur als Kunst.
      Short, intelligent discussion of Swinburne's poetry. The
      early works are emphasized.

2067 Morley, J. M. "Morley: Attack on Swinburne." The Vic-
      torian Mind: An Anthology. Ed. Gerald B. Kauvar and
      Gerald C. Sorensen. New York: Putnam, 1969. pp. 328-
      335.
      See entry 48 for first printing and other reprintings.

2068 Rossetti, W. M. "Rossetti: Defense of Swinburne." The
      Victorian Mind: An Anthology. Ed. Gerald B. Kauver and
      Gerald C. Sorensen. New York: Putnam, 1969. pp. 336-
      343.
      Excerpt from W. M. Rossetti's Swinburne's Poems and
      Ballads (entry 23).
      See entry 23 for other reprinting.

Dissertations

2069 Jordan, John O. The Novels of Algernon Charles Swinburne.
      Stanford, 1968.
      Dissertation Abstracts, 29 (1969), 3975A.

2070 McSweeney, James K. A Study of the Themes of Nature,
      Death and Poetic Vocation in the Poetry of Swinburne.
      University of Toronto, 1969.
      Dissertation Abstracts, 29 (1969), 3149A.

2071 Thompson, Thelma R. P. Algernon Charles Swinburne: No
      Other God--A Vision of Life. University of Oklahoma,
      1969.
      Dissertation Abstracts, 29 (1969), 2231A.

Periodicals

2072 Burnett, T. A. "Swinburne's 'The Ballad of Bulgarie.'"
      Modern Language Review, 64 (1969), 276-282.
      Includes text.

2073 _____. Times Literary Supplement, Jan. 23, 1969.
      Letter about Swinburne and Mary Leith.
      See also entry 2079.

2074 Empson, William. "Swinburne and D. H. Lawrence."
      Times Literary Supplement, Feb. 20, 1969, p. 185.

2075 Greenberg, Robert A. "Swinburne's Heptalogia Improved."
      Studies in Bibliography, 22 (1969), 258-266.

2076 McGinnis, Robert M. "Swinburne's Chastelard and Wilde's
      Salome: Victorian Experiment in the Theatre of Cruelty."
      Komos, 2 (1969), 32-36.

2077 Miyoshi, Masao. "Narrative Sequence and the Moral System:
      Three Tristram Poems." Victorian Newsletter, 35 (1969),
      5-10.

2078 Wilson, F. A. C. "Swinburne's 'Dearest Cousin': The
      Character of Mary Gordon." Literature and Psychology,
      19 (1969), 89-99.

2079 _____. "Swinburne and Mary Gordon." Times Literary
      Supplement, Jan. 16, 1969.
      See also entry 2073.

1970

In 1970, Morse Peckham's unusual edition of Swinburne's Poems
and Ballads was published (New York: Bobbs-Merrill). Peckham
chose to leave out seventeen poems that, he asserts, Swinburne
wanted removed from the original edition. The edition may be
more valuable for Peckham's insightful, and often combative, commentary than for its texts of Swinburne's poems.

2080 Beckson, Karl, ed. Oscar Wilde: The Critical Heritage.
      New York: Barnes and Noble, 1970.
      Swinburne mentioned several times.

2081 Bratcher, James T., and Lyle H. Kendall, Jr. A Sup-
      pressed Critique of Wise's Swinburne Transactions: Ad-
      dendum to An Enquiry. Austin: Humanities Research
      Center, University of Texas, 1970.
      Bibliographical Monograph, No. 2.
      Reprinting of a 1914 pamphlet (entry 1190) accompanied by
      an introduction entitled "Wise's Swinburne Transactions"
      and notes explaining the history of the pamphlet.

2082   Cooper, Robert M. Lost on Both Sides: Dante Gabriel Ros-
       setti: Critic and Poet. Athens: Ohio University Press,
       1970.
       Swinburne mentioned frequently.

2083   Hyder, Clyde K., ed. Swinburne: The Critical Heritage.
       London: Routledge and Kegan Paul, 1970. New York:
       Barnes and Noble, 1970.
       Useful gathering of early views of Swinburne and his work.
       A fundamental research tool for students of Swinburne.
       Reviewed: Choice (entry 2094); and Times Literary Supple-
       ment (entry 2120).

2084   Peckham, Morse. Victorian Revolutionaries: Speculations on
       Some Heroes of a Cultural Crisis. New York: Braziller,
       1970.

Periodicals

2085   Coulling, Sydney M. B. "Swinburne and Arnold." Philologi-
       cal Quarterly, 49 (1970), 211-233.

2086   Wilson, F. A. C. "Swinburne's Victorian Huntress: Auto-
       biographical Traces in Atalanta in Calydon." Komos, 2
       (1970), 118-125.

2087   _____. "Swinburne in Love: Some Novels by Mary Gor-
       don." Texas Studies in Literature and Language, 11
       (1970), 1415-1426.

1971

This year was marked by a gathering of essays about Swinburne in
Victorian Poetry.

2088   Housman, A. E. The Letters of A. E. Housman.   Ed.
       Henry Maas. London: Hart-Davis, 1971.

2089   Panter-Downes, Mollie. At "The Pines": Swinburne and
       Watts-Dunton in Putney. London: Hamilton, 1971.
       The research background for this book sometimes seems
       inadequate, yet the book is often engaging.   It examines
       an interesting aspect of Swinburne's life.
       Reviewed: Book World (entry 2093); Economist (entry
       2097); Library Journal (entry 2102); New Statesman (entry
       2110); Saturday Review (entry 2115); and Times Literary
       Supplement (entry 2119).

2090 Raymond, Meredith B. Swinburne's Poetics: Theory and
      Practice. The Hague: Mouton, 1971.
      De Proprietatibus Litterarum, 17.
      See entry 2025.

Dissertation

2091 Ziemann, Gwendolyn T. Fate, Chance, and Free Will in
      Nineteenth Century Tristram and Iseult Legends. Arizona
      State, 1971.
      Dissertation Abstracts International, 32 (1971), 2659A.

Periodicals

2092 Baird, Julian. "Swinburne, Sade, and Blake: The Pleasure-
      Pain Paradox." Victorian Poetry, 9 (1971), 49-75.

2093 Book World, Aug. 8, 1971, p. 5.
      Review of M. Panter-Downes's At "The Pines" (entry 2089).

2094 Choice, 8 (March 1971), 66.
      Review of Swinburne: The Critical Heritage, ed. C. K.
      Hyder (entry 2083).

2095 Choice, 8 (Oct. 1971), 1022.
      Review of Poems and Ballads, ed. M. Peckham.

2096 Cook, David A. "The Content and Meaning of Swinburne's
      'Anactoria.'" Victorian Poetry, 9 (1971), 77-93.

2097 Economist, 239 (April 17, 1971), 59.
      Review of M. Panter-Downes's At "The Pines" (entry 2089).

2098 Findlay, Leonard M. "Swinburne and Tennyson." Victorian
      Poetry, 9 (1971), 217-236.

2099 Greenberg, Robert A. "Gosse's Swinburne, 'The Triumph of
      Time,' and the Context of 'Les Noyades.'" Victorian Po-
      etry, 9 (1971), 95-110.

2100 Kribbs, Jayne K. "Swinburne: A New Approach to 'The
      Triumph of Time.'" Arlington Quarterly, 3 (1971), 114-
      125.

2101 Library Journal, 96 (March 15, 1971), 965.
      Review of Poems and Ballads, ed. M. Peckham.

2102 Library Journal, 96 (Sept. 15, 1971), 2775.
      Review of M. Panter-Downes's At "The Pines" (entry 2089).

2103 Library Journal, 96 (Dec. 1, 1971), 4003.
      Review of J. O. Fuller's Swinburne (entry 2053).

2104 Lougy, Robert E. "Thematic Imagery and Meaning in Atalanta in Calydon." Victorian Poetry, 9 (1971), 17-34.

2105 McGann, Jerome J. "'Ave Atque Vale': An Introduction to Swinburne." Victorian Poetry, 9 (1971), 145-163.

2106 McSweeney, Kerry. "Swinburne's 'Thalassius.'" Humanities Association Bulletin, 22 (1971), 50-55.

2107 _____. "Swinburne's Poems and Ballads (1866)." Studies in English Literature, 1500-1900, 11 (1971), 671-685.

2108 _____. "Swinburne's 'A Nympholept' and 'The Lake of Gaube.'" Victorian Poetry, 9 (1971), 201-216.

2109 Mathews, Richard. "Heart's Love and Heart's Division: The Quest for Unity in Atalanta in Calydon." Victorian Poetry, 9 (1971), 35-48.

2110 New Statesman, 81 (April 16, 1971), 534.
      Review of M. Panter-Downes's At "The Pines" (entry 2089).

2111 Paul, Karen, and William H. McClain. "Stefan George's Swinburne Translations." Modern Language Notes, 86 (1971), 706-714.

2112 Peattie, Roger W. "William Michael Rossetti and the Defense of Swinburne's Poems and Ballads." Harvard Library Bulletin, 19 (1971), 356-365.

2113 Raymond, Meredith B. "'The Lake of Gaube': Swinburne's Dive in the Dark and the 'Indeterminate Moment.'" Victorian Poetry, 9 (1971), 185-199.

2114 Ridenour, George M. "Swinburne on 'The Problem to Solve in Expression.'" Victorian Poetry, 9 (1971), 129-144.

2115 Saturday Review (New York), 54 (Aug. 21, 1971), 23.
      Review of M. Panter-Downes's At "The Pines" (entry 2089).

2116 Shmiefsky, Marvel. "Swinburne's Anti-Establishment Poetics." Victorian Poetry, 9 (1971), 261-276.

2117 Stuart, Donald C. "Swinburne: The Composition of a Self-Portrait." Victorian Poetry, 9 (1971), 111-128.

2118 Sypher, Francis Jacques, Jr. "Swinburne and Wagner." Victorian Poetry, 9 (1971), 165-183.

2119 Times Literary Supplement, April 23, 1971, p. 470.
      Review of M. Panter-Downes's At "The Pines" (entry 2089).

2120 Times Literary Supplement, July 16, 1971, 836.

Review of Swinburne: The Critical Heritage, ed. C. K.
Hyder (entry 2083).

2121   Wilson, F. A. C. "Fabrication and Fact in Swinburne's
The Sisters." Victorian Poetry, 9 (1971), 237-248.

2122   _____. "Swinburne's Prose Heroines and Mary's Femmes
Fatales." Victorian Poetry, 9 (1971), 249-256.

2123   Wymer, Thomas L. "Swinburne's Tragic Vision in Atalanta
in Calydon." Victorian Poetry, 9 (1971), 1-16.

1972

In 1972, a collection of Swinburne's criticism, Swinburne as Critic,
edited by Clyde K. Hyder, was published (London: Routledge and
Kegan Paul).

Books

2124   McGann, Jerome J. Swinburne: An Experiment in Criticism.
Chicago: University of Chicago Press, 1972.
Reviewed: Choice (entry 2149); Journal of Aesthetics and
Art Criticism (entry 2155); Library Journal (entry 2136);
Times Literary Supplement (entry 2161); and Virginia
Quarterly Review (entry 2196).

2124a Stevenson, Lionel. "Algernon Charles Swinburne." The
Pre-Raphaelite Poets. Chapel Hill: University of North
Carolina Press, 1972. pp. 184-252.
Interesting discussion of Swinburne's ideas.

Dissertations

2125   Brenneisen, Lee E. K. Plot, Character, and Setting in the
Novels of Algernon Charles Swinburne. Stanford, 1972.
Dissertation Abstracts International, 33 (1972), 268A-269A.

2126   Crawford, Donald A. Imagistic-Structural Design in Swinburne's Poetry. New York University, 1972.
Dissertation Abstracts International, 32 (1972), 5177A.

2127   Fricke, Douglas C. A Critical Study of Swinburne's Poems
and Ballads (1866). Pennsylvania State University, 1972.
Dissertation Abstracts International, 33 (1972), 310A.

Periodicals

2128 Bell, Alan. "Gladstone Looks for a Poet Laureate." Times
      Literary Supplement, July 21, 1972, p. 847.
      Partly about Swinburne's unsuitability for the position of
      Poet Laureate.

2129 Chakravarti, Sudesha. "The Influence of French Literature
      on Swinburne." Essays Presented to Prof. Amalendu Bose:
      Bulletin of the Department of English (Calcutta University),
      8 (1972-1973), 44-60.

2130 Choice, 9 (March 1972), 58.
      Review of J. O. Fuller's Swinburne (entry 2053).

2131 Fisher, Benjamin F., IV. "Some Swinburne Letters." Li-
      brary Chronicle, 38 (1972), 140-146.

2132 _____. "Swinburne's Tristram of Lyonesse in Process."
      Texas Studies in Literature and Language, 14 (1972), 509-
      528.

2133 Jenkins, William D. "Swinburne, Robert Buchanan, and W.
      S. Gilbert: The Pain that Was All but a Pleasure."
      Studies in Philology, 69 (1972), 369-387.
      Gilbert and Sullivan's Patience related to Swinburne and
      others.

2134 LeBourgeois, John Y. "Some Unpublished Letters of Swin-
      burne." Notes and Queries, 19 (1972), 255-263.
      Twenty-five letters.

2135 _____. "Swinburne, Lord Lytton, and John Forster."
      Notes and Queries, 19 (1972), 417-419.

2136 Library Journal, 97 (Oct. 15, 1972), 3315.
      Review of J. J. McGann's Swinburne (entry 2124).

2137 Mayfield, John S. "Swinburne's Atalanta in Calydon: The
      Oxford 'Facsimile.'" Book Collector, 21 (1972), 532-537.

2138 Meyers, Terry L. "Swinburne's Later Opinion of Arnold."
      English Language Notes, 10 (1972), 118-122.

2139 Peattie, Roger W. "Swinburne and His Publishers."
      Huntington Library Quarterly, 36 (1972), 45-54.

2140 Times Literary Supplement, Dec. 15, 1972, p. 1537.
      Review of Swinburne as Critic, ed. C. K. Hyder.

2141 Wilson, F. A. C. "Indian and Mithraic Influences on Swin-
      burne's Pantheism: 'Hertha' and 'A Nympholept.'" Papers
      on Language and Literature, 8 (supplement, 1972), 57-66.

1973

Books

2142   Fletcher, Ian.   Swinburne.   Harlow, Essex: Longman Group,
       1973.
       Writers and Their Work.
       This short book includes a discussion of Swinburne and a
       bibliography.   Some bibliographic entries are incomplete;
       the titles of some works are silently abbreviated.

2143   Skinner, B. F.   "Reflections on Meaning and Structure."
       I. A. Richards: Essays in His Honor.   Ed. Reuben
       Brower, Helen Vendler, and John Hollander.   New York:
       Oxford University Press, 1973.   pp. 199-209.

Dissertations

2144   Bishop, Nadean H.   The Mother Archetype in Arnold's
       Merope and Swinburne's Atalanta in Calydon.   University
       of Wisconsin at Madison, 1973.
       Dissertation Abstracts International, 33 (1973), 6862A-
       6863A.

2145   Gotwalt, John M.   Organicism in Swinburne's Songs Before
       Sunrise.   Pennsylvania State University, 1973.
       Dissertation Abstracts International, 33 (1973), 5723A-
       5724A.

2146   Hill, John E.   Dialectical Aestheticism: Essays on the
       Criticism of Swinburne, Pater, Wilde, James, Shaw and
       Yeats.   University of Virginia, 1973.
       Dissertation Abstracts International, 33 (1973), 3648A-
       3649A.

2147   Williams, Edwin W.   Algernon C. Swinburne as Poet-Prophet.
       University of North Carolina at Chapel Hill, 1973.
       Dissertation Abstracts International, 34 (1973), 291A-292A.

Periodicals

2148   Byars, Julie A.   "Eight Unpublished Letters from A. C.
       Swinburne."   Notes and Queries, 20 (1973), 95-97.
       About Swinburne and the Fortnightly Review.

2149   Choice, 10 (June 1973), 620.
       Review of J. J. McGann's Swinburne (entry 2124).

2150   Choice, 10 (June 1973), 624.
       Review of Swinburne as Critic, ed. C. K. Hyder.

2151   Fisher, Benjamin Franklin, IV. "Rossetti and Swinburne in
       Tandem: 'The Laird of Waristoun.'" Victorian Poetry, 11
       (1973), 229-239.

2152   _____. "Some Swinburne Letters." Library Chronicle,
       38 (1973), 140-146.
       Seven letters.

2153   Garner, Stanton. "Harold Frederic and Swinburne's Locrine:
       A Matter of Clubs, Copyrights, and Character." American
       Literature, 45 (1973), 285-292.

2154   Jordan, John O. "The Sweet Face of Mothers: Psychological
       Patterns in Atalanta in Calydon." Victorian Poetry, 11
       (1973), 101-114.

2155   Journal of Aesthetics and Art Criticism, 32 (Winter 1973),
       307.
       Review of J. J. McGann's Swinburne (entry 2124).

2156   Landow, George P. "Swinburne to W. J. Linton and J. W.
       Inchbold: Two New Letters." Modern Language Review,
       68 (1973), 264-267.

2157   LeBourgeois, John Y. "Swinburne and Simeon Solomon."
       Notes and Queries, 20 (1973), 91-95.
       About the relationship of the two men.

2158   Library Journal, 98 (Feb. 1, 1973), 411.
       Review of Swinburne as Critic, ed. C. K. Hyder.

2159   Peattie, Roger W. "Swinburne and His Publishers." Hunting-
       ton Library Quarterly, 36 (1973), 45-54.
       About William Michael Rossetti, J. C. Hotten (the publish-
       er), and Swinburne.

2160   Sypher, Francis Jacques. "Victoria's Lapse from Virtue: A
       Lost Leaf from Swinburne's La Soeur de la Reine." Har-
       vard Library Bulletin, 21 (1973), 349-355.

2161   Times Literary Supplement, Nov. 23, 1973, p. 1434.
       Review of J. J. McGann's Swinburne (entry 2124).

2162   Wilson, F. A. C. "Swinburne, Racine, and the Permissive
       Morality." English Language Notes, 10 (1973), 212-216.

2163   _____. "Swinburne and Kali: The Confessional Element
       in Atalanta in Calydon." Victorian Poetry, 11 (1973), 215-
       228.

2164   Workman, Gillian. "La Soeur de la Reine and Related 'Vic-
       torian Romances' by Swinburne." Harvard Library Bulle-
       tin, 21 (1973), 356-364.

1974

In 1974, Swinburne's A Year's Letters (also known as Love's Cross-Currents), edited by Francis Jacques Sypher, was published (New York: New York University Press). Its text was taken from manuscript, thus making the edition of special interest to scholars.

Books

2165   Grigson, Geoffrey. "Four Ways of Making Fudge." The
       Contrary View: Glimpses of Fudge and Gold. Totowa,
       N. J.: Rowman and Littlefield, 1974. pp. 166-176.

2166   Henderson, Philip. Swinburne: The Portrait of a Poet.
       London: Routledge and Kegan Paul, 1974.
       This excellent biography is well researched and carefully
       written. Henderson is an experienced biographer who
       brings much skill and acumen to his work. If there is a
       work that supplants Georges Lafourcade's biography of
       Swinburne (entry 1728), this is the one. This should be a
       standard reference for students of Swinburne.
       Reviewed: Phoebe Adams in The Atlantic (entry 2173);
       Noel Annan in New York Review of Books (entry 2174);
       Economist (entry 2176); R. S. Fraser in Library Journal
       (entry 2177); Terry L. Meyers in Journal of English and
       Germanic Philology (entry 2218); New Statesman (entry
       2187); New Yorker (entry 2188); and B. Duffy in Southern
       Review (entry 2214).

2167   Irvine, William, and Park Honan. The Book, the Ring, and
       the Poet: A Biography of Robert Browning. New York:
       McGraw-Hill, 1974.
       Swinburne mentioned several times.

2168   Mayfield, John S. Swinburneiana: A Gallimaufry of Bits and
       Pieces About Algernon Charles Swinburne. Gaithersburg,
       Md.: Waring, 1974. London: Fuller d'Arch Smith, 1974.

2169   Peters, Robert L. "Algernon Charles Swinburne and the Use
       of Integral Detail." Pre-Raphaelitism: A Collection of
       Critical Essays. Ed. James Sambrook. Chicago: University of Chicago Press, 1974. pp. 206-219.
       Patterns of Literary Criticism.

Dissertations

2170   Lindsey, Edith D. Medievalism in the Poetry of Swinburne.
       University of Alabama, 1974.
       Dissertation Abstracts International, 34 (1974), 6595A.

2171   Powell, James K. Theatre of the Mind in Late Victorian

Literature: Swinburne, Pater, Wilde, Beardsley and
Symons. University of Kentucky, 1974.
Dissertation Abstracts International, 35 (1974), 2238A.

2172 Roetzel, Priscilla A. Pre-Raphaelite Style in Painting and
Poetry. University of North Carolina at Chapel Hill, 1974.
Dissertation Abstracts International, 34 (1974), 5835A.

Periodicals

2173 Adams, Phoebe. The Atlantic, 234 (Oct. 1974), 120.
Notice of P. Henderson's Swinburne (entry 2166).

2174 Annan, Noel. New York Review of Books, 21 (Nov. 28,
1974), 19.
Review of P. Henderson's Swinburne (entry 2166).

2175 Breen, Jennifer. "Wilfred Owen: 'Greater Love' and Late
Romanticism." English Literature in Transition (1880-
1920), 17 (1974), 173-183.

2176 Economist (London), 251 (April 13, 1974), 76.
Review of P. Henderson's Swinburne (entry 2166).

2177 Fraser, R. S. Library Journal, 99 (Oct. 1, 1974), 2471.
Review of P. Henderson's Swinburne (entry 2166).

2178 Greenberg, Robert A. "Swinburne." Victorian Poetry, 12
(Autumn 1974), 276-277.
Survey of works on Swinburne that appeared in 1973, with
short comments.

2179 Koloski, Bernard J. "The Swinburne Lines in The Awakening." American Literature, 45 (1974), 608-610.
Discusses two lines from Swinburne's "A Cameo" that ap-
pear in Kate Chopin's The Awakening.

2180 Levin, Gerald. "Swinburne's 'End of the World' Fantasy."
Literature and Psychology, 24 (1974), 109-114.

2181 Maxwell, J. C. "Swinburne and Thackeray." Notes and
Queries, 21 (1974), 15.
Discusses "Dolores."

2182 Mayfield, John S. "Swinburne in Miniature." Courier
(Syracuse University Library), 11 (1974), 38-39.

2183 Meyers, Terry L. "Swinburne Footnote." Literary Sketches,
(Midsummer 1974), 7-9.
About Swinburne's will.

2184 _____. "Swinburne: Four More Letters." Notes and
Queries, 21 (1974), 216-217.

2185   Monteiro, George.   "The First Printing of Swinburne's 'Two
       Brothers.'"   Notes and Queries, 21 (1974), 466.

2186   Murfin, Ross C.   "Athens Unbound: A Study of Swinburne's
       Erectheus."   Victorian Poetry, 12 (1974), 205-217.

2187   New Statesman, 87 (March 22, 1974), 406.
       Review of P. Henderson's Swinburne (entry 2166).

2188   New Yorker, 50 (Sept. 16, 1974), 148.
       Review of P. Henderson's Swinburne (entry 2166).

2189   Paley, Morton D.   "The Critical Reception of A Critical Es-
       say."   Blake Newsletter: An Illustrated Quarterly, 8
       (1974), 32-37.
       Discusses Swinburne's William Blake.

2190   Peattie, Roger W.   "Swinburne's Funeral."   Notes and
       Queries, 21 (1974), 466-469.

2191   Pfeiffer, Karl L.   "Interpretation und Marxismus: Über-
       legungen zur marxistischen Methode aus Anlass von
       Christian Enzensbergers Viktorianische Lyrik."   Anglia,
       92 (1974), 349-379.

2192   Reeves, William J.   "'Triton of the Minnows'--Swinburne on
       Arnold."   American Notes and Queries, 12 (1974), 169-170.

2193   Secor, Robert.   "Swinburne at His Lyre: A New Epigram by
       Browning."   Studies in Browning and His Circle, 2 (1974),
       58-60.

2194   Sypher, Francis J., Jr.   "'My Dear Ulrica ...': Swinburne's
       Earliest Letter."   Quarterly Journal of the Library of Con-
       gress, 31 (1974), 92-96.
       A letter dated December 5, 1848, to Ulrica Fenwick, the
       daughter of Swinburne's tutor. Accompanied by notes and
       pictures.

2195   _____.   "Swinburne's Debt to Campbell in 'A Forsaken
       Garden.'"   Victorian Poetry, 12 (1974), 74-78.

2196   Virginia Quarterly Review, 50 (Winter 1974), xx.
       Review of J. J. McGann's Swinburne (entry 2124).

2197   Weitzel, Roy L.   "Toward a 'Bright White Light': London's
       Use of Swinburne in Martin Eden."   Jack London Newslet-
       ter, 7 (1974), 1-8.

1975

Dissertations

2198   Bizzaro, Patrick Anthony. The Aesthetic of Beauty in
        Nineteenth-Century England: Shelley, Rossetti, and Swin-
        burne. Miami University (Ohio), 1975.
        Dissertation Abstracts International, 36 (1975), 2212A.

2199   Crow, John Harrison. Dying Generations: Shifting Arche-
        typal Patterns in Romantic and Victorian Poetry. Emory
        University, 1975.
        Dissertation Abstracts International, 36 (1975), 2841A.

2200   Fallis, Jean Thomson. The Sacred and the Profane: Trans-
        valuation of Religious Symbol in Hopkins, Rossetti, and Swin-
        burne. Princeton, 1974.
        Dissertation Abstracts International, 36 (1975), 1524A.

2201   Wexler, Eric Joseph. Mythological Strategy in the Poetry of
        Swinburne and Meredith. Yale, 1974.
        Dissertation Abstracts International, 36 (1975), 333A.

Periodicals

2202   Baker, William. "A. C. Swinburne to Herbert Spencer, 12
        March 1881: An Unpublished Letter." Notes and Queries,
        22 (1975), 445-447.

2203   Choice, 12 (Sept. 1975), 847.
        Review of A Year's Letters, ed. J. Sypher.

2204   Coleman, Viralean. "Althaea's Speeches on Remembrance in
        Atalanta in Calydon." Publications of the Arkansas Philo-
        logical Association, 1 (1975), 14-20.

2205   Forbes, Jill. "Two Flagellation Poems by Swinburne."
        Notes and Queries, 22 (1975), 443-445.

2206   Goodwin, K. L. "An Unpublished Tale from The Earthly
        Paradise." Victorian Poetry, 13 (1975), 91-102.

1976

Books

2207 Fricke, Douglas C. "The Proserpine Figure in Swinburne's
      Poems and Ballads I. " Aeolian Harps: Essays in Litera-
      ture in Honor of Maurice Browning Cramer. Ed. Donna G.
      Fricke and Douglas C. Fricke. Bowling Green, Ohio:
      Bowling Green University Press, 1976. pp. 191-205.

2208 Marmaras, Apostolos, and Lilika Marmaras. "An English
      Translation of the Ancient Greek Dedicatory Verses to
      Atalanta in Calydon. " Aeolian Harps: Essays in Litera-
      ture in Honor of Maurice Browning Cramer. Ed. Donna G.
      Fricke and Douglas C. Fricke. Bowling Green, Ohio:
      Bowling Green University Press, 1976. pp. 179-189.

2209 Walder, Anne. Swinburne's Flowers of Evil: Baudelaire's
      Influence on Poems and Ballads, First Series. Stockholm:
      Almqvist and Wiksell, 1976.
      Acta Universitatis Upsaliensis, Studia Anglistica
      Upsaliensia, 25.

Dissertations

2210 Riede, David George. Swinburne: A Study of Romantic
      Mythmaking. University of Virginia, 1976.
      Dissertation Abstracts International, 37 (1976), 2204A.
      See also entry 2246.

2211 Snider, Clifton Mark. The Struggle for the Self: A Jungian
      Interpretation of Swinburne's Tristram of Lyonesse. Uni-
      versity of New Mexico, 1974.
      Dissertation Abstracts International, 36 (1976), 6716A.

Periodicals

2212 Davis, Mary Byrd. "Swinburne's Use of His Sources in
      Tristram of Lyonesse. " Philological Quarterly, 55 (1976),
      96-112.

2213 Duffy, Betty. Southern Review, 12 (1976), 434-437.
      Review of P. Henderson's Swinburne (entry 2166).

2214 Encounter (London), 47 (July 1976), 71.
      Review of A Year's Letters, ed. J. Sypher.

2215 Fricke, Douglas C. "The Idea of Love in Swinburne's 'The
      Sundew. ' " English Language Notes, 13 (1976), 194-201.

2216 Greenberg, Robert A. "Swinburne and the Redefinition of
      Classical Myth. " Victorian Poetry, 14 (1976), 175-195.

2217 Harrison, Antony H. "Swinburne's Tristram of Lyonesse:
      Visionary and Courtly Epic." Modern Language Quarterly,
      37 (1976), 370-389.

2218 Meyers, Terry L. Journal of English and Germanic Philol-
      ogy, 75 (1976), 456-458.
      Review of P. Henderson's Swinburne (entry 2166).

2219 _____. "Two Swinburne Letters." Notes and Queries,
      23 (1976), 63-66.

2220 _____. "Shelley's Influence on Atalanta in Calydon." Vic-
      torian Poetry, 14 (1976), 150-154.

2221 Paley, Morton D. "John Camden Hotten, A. C. Swinburne,
      and the Blake Facsimiles of 1868." Bulletin of the New
      York Public Library, 79 (1976), 259-296.

2222 Schmidt, A. V. C. "Eliot, Swinburne and Dante: A Note on
      The Waste Land, Lines 215-248." Notes and Queries, 23
      (1976), 17-18.

2223 Schuldt, Edward P. "Three Unpublished Balliol Essays of
      A. C. Swinburne." Review of English Studies, 27 (1976),
      422-430.

2224 Sypher, Francis Jacques. "New Letters by Swinburne."
      Harvard Library Bulletin, 24 (1976), 55-59.

2225 Times Literary Supplement, March 12, 1976, p. 283.
      Review of A Year's Letters, ed. J. Sypher.

2226 Wilson, Stephen Clifford. "Swinburne, Tennyson and The
      Sisters." Notes and Queries, 23 (1976), 407-408.

1977

Books

2227 Cockshut, Anthony Oliver John. Man and Woman: A Study
      of Love and the Novel, 1740-1940. London and New York:
      Oxford University Press, 1977.

2228 Eichler, Rolf. Die Entdeckung des Dialog bei Byron, Shelley,
      Swinburne und Tennyson. Heidelberg: Winter, 1977.

2229 Williamson, Audrey. "Swinburne: Poet and Enfant Terrible."

Artists and Writers in Revolt: the Pre-Raphaelites.   Cranbury, N.J.:   Art Alliance, 1977.   pp. 161-181.

Dissertations

2230   Frisch, Adam J.   Toward an Imaginative Drama: Dramatic
       Techniques in Coleridge, Browning, Swinburne, and Hardy.
       University of Texas at Austin, 1977.
       Dissertation Abstracts International, 38 (1977), 2805A.

2231   Young, Robert Stephen.   Tennyson and Swinburne and the
       Metaphor of Love: The Quest for Spiritual Values in
       Nineteenth Century England.   University of Arizona, 1977.
       Dissertation Abstracts International, 38 (1977), 2820A.

Periodicals

2232   Bala, Kum Adarsh.   "The Poetry of Algernon Charles Swin-
       burne."   Triveni, 45 (1977), 43-48.

2233   Brisman, Leslie.   "Swinburne's Semiotics."   Georgia Review,
       31 (1977), 578-597.

2234   Ditman, Stevan C.   "The Muse and the Lexicon: A Note on
       Swinburne's 'Herse.'"   Pre-Raphaelite Review, 1 (1977),
       76-80.

2235   Fricke, Douglas C.   "Swinburne and the Plastic Arts in
       Poems and Ballads I (1866)."   Pre-Raphaelite Review,
       1 (1977), 57-79.

2236   Greenberg, Robert A.   "Swinburne."   Victorian Poetry, 15
       (Autumn 1977), 278-279.
       Brief survey of works on Swinburne that appeared in 1976,
       with comments.

2237   Grenander, M. E.   "Ambrose Bierce Describes Swinburne."
       The Courier (Syracuse University Library), 14 (Fall 1977),
       23-24.
       Discusses and includes an 1872 description of Swinburne by
       Ambrose Bierce.
       See also entry 2242.

2238   Haas, Adrienne E.   "Swinburne and the Elizabethan Drama-
       tists: The Romance of a Life-Time."   Wascana Review,
       12 (1977), 65-83.

2239   Harrison, Antony H.   "Swinburne's Craft of Pure Expres-
       sion."   Victorian Newsletter, 51 (1977), 16-20.

2240   Hyder, Clyde K.   "Swinburne and Plautus: A Man of Three."
       Victorian Poetry, 15 (1977), 377.

2241   Mayfield, John S.   "A. C. Swinburne's Atalanta in Calydon,
       1865." Notes and Queries, 24 (1977), 416.

2242   _____.   "Postscriptum." The Courier (Syracuse Univer-
       sity Library), 14 (Fall 1977), 25-26.
       A Note about M. E. Grenander's article (entry 2237).

1978

Books

2243   Bradley, Ian.   William Morris: and His World.   New York:
       Scribner, 1978.
       Swinburne mentioned several times.

2244   Levey, Michael.   The Case of Walter Pater.   New York:
       Thames and Hudson, 1978.
       Swinburne mentioned many times.

2245   Murfin, Ross C.   Swinburne, Hardy, Lawrence and the Bur-
       den of Relief.   Chicago: University of Chicago Press, 1978.
       Reviewed: K. Cushman in Library Journal (entry 2250); A.
       Heuser in Victorian Studies (entry 2283); I. B. Nadel in
       Concerning Poetry (entry 2270); and R. C. Schweik in Mod-
       ern Fiction Studies (entry 2273).

2246   Riede, David G.   Swinburne: A Study of Romantic Mythmak-
       ing.   Charlottesville: University Press of Virginia, 1978.
       This is a good, original critical study.   Riede presents
       powerful arguments for the literary excellence of Swin-
       burne's later poetry.
       Reviewed: A. Heuser in Victorian Studies (entry 2283).
       See also R. A. Greenberg for comments on Riede's book
       (entry 2280).
       See also entry 2210.

2247   Trevelyan, Raleigh.   A Pre-Raphaelite Circle.   London:
       Chatto and Windus, 1978.   Totowa, N.J.: Rowman and
       Littlefield, 1978.

Dissertations

2248   Dologite, Dorothy Geraldine.   The Evolution of Swinburne's
       Femme Fatale Mythology.   St. John's University, 1978.
       Dissertation Abstracts International, 39 (1978), 4267A-
       4268A.

2249 Lutzweit, Timothy Walter. The Mind in the Wilderness:
      Nature, Literary Imagination and Art Nouveau. University
      of Notre Dame, 1978.
      Dissertation Abstracts International, 39 (1978), 1593A-
      1594A.

Periodicals

2250 Cushman, Keith. Library Journal, 103 (1978), 2522.
      Review of R. C. Murfin's Swinburne, Hardy, Lawrence
      (entry 2245).

2251 Harrison, Antony H. "The Aesthetics of Androgyny in Swin-
      burne's Early Poetry." Tennessee Studies in Literature,
      23 (1978), 87-99.

2252 Kohl, Norbert. "L'Art pour l'art in der Asthetik des 19.
      Jahrhunderts." Zeitschrift für Literaturwissenschaft und
      Linguistik, 8 (1978), 159-174.

2253 McSweeney, Kerry. "Swinburne's Tennyson." Victorian
      Studies, 22 (1978), 5-28.

2254 Meyers, Terry L. "Shelley and Swinburne's Aesthetic of
      Melody." Papers in Language and Literature, 14 (1978),
      284-295.

2255 Redford, Bruce B. "'A God With the World Inwound': Swin-
      burne's 'A Nympholept' and Classical Stoicism." Victorians
      Institute Journal, 7 (1978), 35-55.

2256 Ridenour, George M. "Time and Eternity in Swinburne:
      Minute Particulars in Five Poems." ELH, 45 (1978),
      107-130.

2257 Riede, David G. "Swinburne's 'On the Cliffs': The Evolution
      of a Romantic Myth." Victorian Poetry, 16 (1978), 189-
      203.

2258 Staines, David. "Swinburne's Arthurian World: Swinburne's
      Arthurian Poetry and Its Medieval Sources." Studia Neo-
      philologia, 50 (1978), 53-70.

1979

Books

2259 Ober, William B. "Swinburne's Masochism: Neuropathology

and Psychopathology." Boswell's Clap and Other Essays:
Medical Analyses of Literary Men's Afflictions. Carbon-
dale: Southern Illinois University Press, 1979. London:
Pfeffer Simons, 1979.
Ober suggests that Swinburne was brain-damaged at birth.

2260 Sessa, Anne Dzamba. Richard Wagner and the English.
Cranbury, N.J.: Fairleigh Dickinson University Press,
1979.

2261 Thomas, Donald. Swinburne: The Poet in His World. London: Weidenfeld and Nicolson, 1979. New York: Oxford
University Press, 1979.
Good biography.
Reviewed: R. A. Greenberg in Victorian Studies (entry
2280); P. Keating in Times Literary Supplement (entry
2267); and C. McIntosh in Country Life (entry 2268).

2262 Wilde, Oscar. Selected Letters of Oscar Wilde. Ed.
Rupert Hart-Davis. London: Oxford University Press,
1979.
Swinburne discussed several times.
For complete edition of Wilde's letters, see entry 1990.

Dissertation

2263 Esrig, Mark. Swinburne as Intrinsic Critic: The Development and Influence of His Criticism. Ohio University,
1979.
Dissertation Abstracts International, 40 (1979), 2071A.

Periodicals

2264 Fletcher, Pauline. "Romantic and Anti-Romantic Gardens in
Tennyson and Swinburne." Studies in Romanticism, 18
(1979), 81-97.

2265 Greenberg, Robert A. "Swinburne." Victorian Poetry, 17
(1979), 249-251.

2266 Harrison, Antony H. "The Swinburnian Woman." Philological Quarterly, 58 (1979), 90-102.

2267 Keating, P. Times Literary Supplement, Dec. 7, 1979,
p. 90-91.
Review of D. Thomas's Swinburne (entry 2261).

2268 McIntosh, C. Country Life, 166 (1979), 49.
Review of D. Thomas's Swinburne (entry 2261).

2269 Meyers, Terry L. "Further Swinburne Letters." Notes and
Queries, 26 (1979), 313-320.
Fourteen letters.

2270   Nadel, I. B. Concerning Poetry, 12 (1979), 90-93.
       Review of R. C. Murfin's Swinburne, Hardy, Lawrence
       (entry 2245).

2271   Peters, Robert. "The Tannhauser Theme: Swinburne's
       'Laus Veneris.'" Pre-Raphaelite Review, 3 (1979), 12-28.

2272   Rosenbaum, Jean Watson. "Of Hunts and Hunters: Atalanta
       in Calydon." Pre-Raphaelite Review, 3 (1979), 41-53.

2273   Schweik, Robert C. Modern Fiction Studies, 25 (1979), 305-
       306.
       Review of R. C. Murfin's Swinburne, Hardy, Lawrence
       (entry 2245).

2274   _____. "Swinburne, Hopkins, and the Roots of Modern-
       ism." University of Hartford Studies in Literature, 11
       (1979), 157-172.

1980

The listings for 1980 and 1981 are partial.

Books

2275   Palmer, Jerry. "Fierce Midnights: Algolagniac Fantasy and
       the Literature of the Decadence." Decadence and the 1890s.
       Ed. Ian Fletcher. New York: Holmes and Meier, 1980.
       pp. 88-106.

2276   Snodgrass, Chris. "Swinburne's Circle of Desire: A Deca-
       dent Theme." Decadence and the 1890s. Ed. Ian Fletcher.
       New York: Holmes and Meier, 1980.   pp. 60-87.

Dissertations

2277   Anderson, Mary Rita. Art in a Desacralized World: Nine-
       teenth Century France and England. University of California,
       Berkeley, 1979.
       Dissertation Abstracts International, 41 (1980), 764A.
       Discusses l'art pour l'art.

2278   Jacobs, Joanne Ciske. The Tristram Myth in Arnold, Tenny-
       son and Swinburne: Sources and Moral Vision. University
       of Notre Dame, 1979.
       Dissertation Abstracts International, 40 (1980), 4013A.

2279   Wilson, William Arthur.   <u>Swinburne: The Poetry of Consola-</u>
       <u>tion and the Aesthetics of Absence.</u>   University of Virginia,
       1979.
       <u>Dissertation Abstracts International,</u> 41 (1980), 266A.

Periodicals

2280   Atkinson, F. G.   "Some Unpublished Swinburne Letters."
       <u>Notes and Queries,</u> 27 (1980), 219-221.

2281   Birchfield, James D.   "New Light on the Swinburne-Leith
       Correspondence."   <u>Kentucky Review,</u> 1 (1980), 52-63.

2282   Gitter, Elizabeth G.   "Arnold and Rossetti: Two Voices in
       Swinburne's 'The Triumph of Time.'"   <u>Pre-Raphaelite Re-</u>
       <u>view,</u> 3 (1980), 48-57.

2283   Greenberg, Robert A.   <u>Victorian Studies,</u> 24 (Autumn 1980),
       125-126.
       Review of D. Thomas's <u>Swinburne</u> (entry 2261).

2284   _____.   "Swinburne."   <u>Victorian Poetry,</u> 18 (1980), 280-
       282.

2285   Harrison, Antony H.   "'Love Strong as Death and Valour
       Strong as Love':   Swinburne and Courtly Love."   <u>Victorian</u>
       <u>Poetry,</u> 18 (1980), 61-73.

2286   Heuser, Alan.   <u>Victorian Studies,</u> 23 (Winter 1980), 277-278.
       Review of R. C. Murfin's <u>Swinburne, Hardy, Lawrence</u>
       (entry 2245) and D. G. Riede's <u>Swinburne</u> (entry 2246).

2287   Lorsch, Susan E.   "Algernon Charles Swinburne's 'Evening of
       the Broads':   Unmeaning Landscape and the Language of
       Negation."   <u>Victorian Poetry,</u> 18 (1980), 91-96.

2288   Mayfield, John S.   "A Swinburne Collector in Calydon."   <u>Li-</u>
       <u>brary of Congress Quarterly,</u> 37 (Winter 1980), 25-34.

2289   Meyers, Terry L.   "Further Swinburne Letters--II."   <u>Notes</u>
       <u>and Queries,</u> 27 (1980), 221-226.

2290   _____.   "Swinburne's Conception of Shelley."   <u>Pre-</u>
       <u>Raphaelite Review,</u> 3 (1980), 36-47.

2291   Murfin, Ross C.   "'Hymn to Priapus':   Lawrence's Poetry
       of Difference."   <u>Criticism,</u> 22 (1980), 214-229.

2292   Northey, Margot.   "Control and Freedom: Swinburne's
       Novels."   <u>English Studies in Canada,</u> 6 (1980), 292-306.

2293   Siegchrist, Mark.   "Artimis's Revenge: A Reading of Swin-
       burne's <u>Atalanta in Calydon.</u>"   <u>Studies in English Litera-</u>
       <u>ture,</u> 20 (1980), 695-712.

1981

Partial list.

2294   Sillars, S. J.   "Tristan and Tristram: Resemblance or
       Influence?"   Victorian Poetry, 19 (Spring 1981), 81-86.
       Richard Wagner and Swinburne.

2295   Stevenson, Catherine Barnes.   "Swinburne and Tennyson's
       Tristram."   Victorian Poetry, 19 (Summer 1981), 185-189.

2296   Wilson, William.   "Algernon Agonistes: 'Thalassius,'
       Visionary Strength, and Swinburne's Critique of Arnold's
       'Sweetness and Light.'"   Victorian Poetry, 19 (Winter
       1981), 381-395.

[Entry numbers for book-length studies, including dissertations, are under-lined.]